# The
# WILDLIFE
# GARDENER

# *The* WILDLIFE GARDENER

## John V. Dennis

Drawings by Matthew Kalmenoff

ALFRED A. KNOPF   NEW YORK   *1985*

THIS IS A BORZOI BOOK
PUBLISHED BY ALFRED A. KNOPF, INC.

Library of Congress Cataloging in Publication Data

Dennis, John V.
The wildlife gardener.

Bibliography: p.
Includes index.
1. Wildlife attracting.   2. Gardening.   I. Title.
QL59.D46   1985   639.9'2   84-48653
ISBN 0-394-53582-0

Manufactured in the United States of America
FIRST EDITION

# Contents

# *Acknowledgments*

More than to anyone else, I am indebted to my wife, Mary Alice, for her encouragement and her participation in our many ventures into wildlife gardening. Once again I am indebted to my editor, Barbara Bristol, for her help and her painstaking care in getting my manuscript ready for publication. I want to thank the Long Point Bird Observatory in Ontario for sending me reports and the editors of *Nature Society News* and *The Birdwatcher's Digest* for publishing questionnaires that led to information on hummingbirds and how to attract them. For information on plants used by birds for nesting purposes, I am grateful to Donald A. McCrimmon, Jr., for allowing me access to the North American Nest Record Cards at the Cornell Laboratory of Ornithology. It is difficult to single out the many other persons who have provided assistance, but to all of them, and especially to Richard Ussher, Cedric M. Smith, Robert W. Sampson, Gary M. Williamson, Helen Bates, Jean Bancroft, Pat Murphy, Hal H. Harrison, and Roger A. Morse, I owe a debt of gratitude.

# The
# WILDLIFE
# GARDENER

# *Introduction*

It can safely be said that the compelling reason that turns so many of us into wildlife gardeners is the pleasure of having living animals in the yard. To be able to look out of the window and see them takes us away from our cares and transfers us into another realm. On the bleakest of days in early spring our spirits revive when we see birds thronging to the feeders and small mammals moving about once again after their winter's somnolence. Squirrels and chipmunks are eating food that has fallen to the ground from the bird feeders. Our curiosity is aroused by a largish mammal with reddish-brown fur that has disappeared into the shrubbery. We watch closely over the next few days to see if it reappears. Early one morning we see a raccoon pawing the ground, sniffing, and then moving on to another spot. We know that this was the visitor of a few days ago. But what is it doing in our yard?

When warmer weather arrives, the scene changes. Winter birds have gone north and their place is taken by newcomers that have spent the winter in lands to the south of us. Many of the new arrivals are brightly colored, especially the male of the species, whose purpose is now to establish a territory and attract a mate. Both ends are served by keeping to a high perch and pouring out a song that continues with little letup throughout the day.

Newly opened flowers are beginning to attract swarms of honeybees whose winter stores may now be exhausted. Early butterflies, such as the spring azure, are also visiting flowers. Not until later will we see hummingbird moths or a variety of butterflies coming to our flower garden. If we are lucky our spring flowers may attract hummingbirds. This will be a reminder to put out hummingbird feeders. The stage is now set for a whole new act in the drama of life. Scarcity has given way to abundance. Courtship, mating, nesting, and territorial squabbles are now the order of the day in the bird world. Much the same kind of activity is taking place among other groups of animals. Everything seems to be happening at once and we are privileged spectators. We can expect our guests to provide us with entertainment throughout a large part of the year, but we must do our part by supplying food, water, and shelter.

But what about the animals we do not see? Much of the animal community remains hidden and is rarely or never visible. Some species are nocturnal, others live underground, and still others stay hidden under debris or in dense tangles. What about these invisible forms? Do the night-flying moths, small reptiles, toads, salamanders, shrews, and moles add anything to our enjoyment?

I can only say that many people, myself included, obtain satisfaction in playing host to as large a share of the wildlife community as the resources of our yards will permit. We do not necessarily have to see all of our visitors to enjoy them. There can be a sense of satisfaction in simply knowing that some happen to be around. We learn of the unseen presence of animals by the tracks they leave and the sounds they make. It is always a surprise to me to see how many tracks have been made in the fresh snow after a fall during the night. Birds and small mammals leave their marks long before we are abroad.

Every time I hear the quavering notes of a screech owl at night or the hoot of a larger owl, I get a thrill that stays with me for as long as I am awake. One night in early summer in Nantucket, I heard a chuck-will's-widow outside my window calling its name over and over in the manner of all members of the goatsucker family. Far north of its normal range limits, which extend to southern New Jersey, this bird had flown much too far on its way north that spring. If anything, the mystery of a voice in the night is a reward as great as clearly viewing an animal in broad daylight.

How deeply should we become involved in learning about the animal life that responds to our overtures? Should we remain casual observers or take a more scientific approach? While not all of us have the dedication of an Olive Goin, Helen Hoover, Frank Lutz, or John Terres, we can derive a great deal of satisfaction from keeping records and watching our lists grow from year to year—compiling nesting records, migration schedules, or notes on feeding and behavior. But before we can become fully involved, we will need to improve our skills in one very important area—*identification*. This will take time and practice. Yet thanks to ever better field guides and manuals, there is hardly a group in the animal or plant kingdom that cannot be studied with pleasure. My advice is to learn as much about the animal life near where you live as your time and interests permit. While learning, keep notes and up-to-date lists; later on you may regret not having done so. At the same time, I would not suggest taking an overly scientific approach. We may simply want to enjoy whatever comes our way. Our main objective should be to help wildlife during a time when so many forms are losing their natural habitat and are being exposed to the hazards of pesticides and other kinds of pollution.

In cities and suburbs, of course, there may not be room for hedgerows, extensive wildlife plantings, and ponds; whatever we do in small yards has to be done on a relatively small scale. Yet whatever overtures we make in the way of food, water, and shelter usually bring an immediate response. The gratifying part of providing for wildlife in the city or suburb is that you know that there is an appreciative clientele waiting and ready to take advantage of whatever you have to offer. In the country, animals are shier and there may already be adequate food and shelter. Here the response to one's overtures is much slower and sometimes scarcely apparent at all.

Although this book has primarily been directed to people who have yards of their own, I should point out that ownership of land is not necessarily a prerequisite to being a wildlife gardener. I recall being shown a delightful wildlife garden outside a school classroom window. The second-grade students, who, with the help of their teacher, had done the planting and erected the bird feeders, were among the keenest young naturalists I have ever encountered. They knew the names of most of the birds shown in my slide presentation and had a good grasp of the needs and habits of wild animals. It shouldn't take much searching in our neighborhood to find opportunities to put our skills in wildlife gardening to work. Help from the wildlife gardener will be welcomed by schools, libraries, hospitals, nursing homes, park authorities, or neighbors living nearby.

One way to get others involved is to give talks to groups in your neighborhood or wherever lecture opportunities exist. In my experience people always listen eagerly to advice on what to plant and the best ways to feed birds. Most people get their start in natural history through birds and only later branch out into other fields of study. Many begin by feeding birds and then discover that not all of the birds that visit their yards respond to artificial feeding. Some, like kingbirds, crested flycatchers, and waxwings, never or almost never visit feeders. To help these birds and at the same time provide additional sources of food for birds that do visit feeders, the beginner discovers that he should plant for birds as well as feed them. This is the beginning of a whole new interest. Not only birds but other forms of wildlife will be drawn to the plantings. Some will be attracted primarily by the flowers and others by the fruit. Knowing what to plant and the forms of animal life that will respond is the first step in becoming a wildlife gardener.

If we have a yard of our own, we can experiment with plants and extend our interest to as many groups in the animal kingdom as we have time for. From birds we may go on to small mammals, bees, and butterflies. As our horizons widen, we become wildlife gardeners involved with the whole spectrum of nature.

As our broader interest develops, we will begin adding still more plants to our yard and weeding out older ones that have less to offer. During this stage it is easy to make mistakes. Every yard is different, and finding the right plant or plants for the right locations takes time and often involves a certain amount of trial and error. Sometimes it is better to start off with a poorly planted yard. This brings me to a yard in Massachusetts and the solutions my wife and I arrived at in restoring it to a condition where it would be a haven for wildlife.

The house we bought in 1972 was on the outskirts of town on the island of Nantucket. Surrounded by about an acre of land, the house, like many others on the island, not only looked old but was old. Built in 1799, it had changed hands many times and weathered many a violent North Atlantic gale. Lying some twenty-five miles off the southeastern coast of Massachusetts, the island of Nantucket is so exposed to winds and salt spray that some plants fare poorly. At the same time, the climate is mild enough so that a number of southern plants, such as southern magnolia, do well if planted in sheltered places. There was such a dearth of plantings in the front half of our yard that we felt very much exposed to the elements. Even if wildlife hadn't been a consideration, we would have had to do something about this part of the yard.

This is not to say that there were no plantings at all. A sizable American elm dominated a spot between the house and the street. Directly behind the elm and affording some shade and protection to the south side of the house were two large sycamore maple trees. A red cedar by the kitchen door looked so scraggly and moribund that we wondered if we would have to remove it. Years ago someone had tied a wire around the trunk and it had become embedded in the wood. In spite of this injury, the tree continued to live and, if anything, is more vigorous today than it ever was. Another red cedar, this one young and healthy, grew in the middle of a particularly sterile piece of ground where a tennis court had once been. A hydrangea bush, several lilac bushes, and rambler roses growing over the front of the house completed the list of plantings in the front part of the yard. The rest of the space was given over to lawn.

Making up to some extent for the openness of the front yard was a privet hedge that began at the street and circled about half the property. Unlike many privet hedges, which are closely clipped and have neither flowers nor fruit, this one grew to about twenty feet and offered a number of advantages to wildlife. Butterflies visited the powerfully fragrant blossoms in summer and birds would begin seeking the fruit in late fall and winter.

We decided to leave the hedge very much as it was, and we applied the same philosophy to an overgrown tract at the rear half of our yard. In sharp contrast to the front with its open lawn and several trees, this patch of wilderness contained a dense growth made up of the island's scrub flora. Here could be found a mixture of native and introduced plants, their branches interlaced and providing nesting cover for birds and food in the form of fruits and berries. Within a radius of fifteen feet, one could find wild cherry, bayberry, arrowwood viburnum, beach plum, wild rose, bush honeysuckle, and flowering crab apple. Sometimes engulfing other plants and pushing its way everywhere were blackberry bushes. One did not enter this wild domain without carrying clippers and wearing gloves and protective clothing. Eventually we did clear a "nature trail" through this part of our property; otherwise we left everything very much the way it was.

The "nature area," as we called this part of the yard, was adjacent to the former tennis court. Around the cedar tree, the hard-packed soil of the court had become seeded with grasses and clovers and also a variety of weeds, including yarrow, plantain, sorrel, and cat's-ear. The weeds seemed to be winning the battle for dominance. During summer dry spells, the hard soil held so little moisture that the grass soon turned brown and even the weeds would begin to wither. How could we restore this part of the yard and return it to a state where robins would begin searching for worms and we could take pleasure walking on the grass?

An even more difficult problem was presented by the grassy slopes on two sides of the old tennis court. So steep that they were difficult to cut with a lawn mower, the slopes would be ideal sites, we decided, for wildlife plantings. But first the tough sod had to be removed and something planted that would hold the soil. I knew just the plant for such a situation—coralberry. The roots would hold the soil and, moreover, this was a plant with good ornamental and wildlife values. Fortunately we had friends on the island with too much coralberry in their yard. We took all they had to offer for the slopes and also to surround a heating-oil tank next to the house. I filled in parts of the slope not covered by coralberry with a number of other shrubs, including elderberry, rugosa rose, autumn olive, bayberry, arrowwood, and Scottish broom. The latter is a moorland plant on Nantucket, having been brought to the island by the early settlers. I grow this plant partly for sentiment and partly for its early summer display of bright yellow blossoms.

In a few years the slopes of the old tennis court were as thickly grown with shrubs as the nature area. Ring-necked pheasants visiting our feeders in winter could now cross the yard by keeping to overgrown slopes instead of having to dash across a wide-open space. Also the slope plantings were close enough to the feeders to provide cover for such visitors as catbirds, house finches, towhees, cardinals, goldfinches, and mourning doves. Still closer to the feeders was a multiflora rose bush that was only a cutting when I planted it. Now it covers an area ten feet wide and reaches a maximum height of eight feet. I keep the edges of this large shrub well clipped so that it will not spread any farther. It is a perfect haven for birds seeking cover, and the small hips provide food for pheasants and mockingbirds in winter.

Using trial-and-error methods, we began planting flower beds that we had created along a picket fence facing the street and elsewhere about the yard. Nearly everything we planted did well except hollyhocks, zinnias, pyrethrum, and nasturtium. If a plant didn't live up to our expectations, we saw no use in growing it. All too often the spindly, unhappy plant is a magnet for insect attack and is the first plant to die when there is a dry spell. Generally you can tell what does well by looking into neighbors' yards, but this does not always hold true.

The key to success, whether it is the flower garden, vegetable garden, or lawn, we decided, was plenty of compost and manure. One of the first things we did was start a compost heap. Using grass clippings, fallen leaves, leftover vegetables from the kitchen, and liberal amounts of horse manure from a nearby stable, we soon had enough rotted compost to start enriching flower beds and parts of the lawn. Without waiting for more compost, I applied lime and horse manure to large sections of the yard. Soon earthworms were responding to this treatment, and it is to their increased numbers that we are largely indebted for the restoration of our lawn. The soil is now porous and can absorb moisture. Even though most of the weeds are still present, they are overshadowed and even crowded out by grasses and clovers that grow so luxuriantly that the grass has to be cut much more often.

I make a practice of not cutting parts of the lawn where bees are visiting the blossoms of white and red clover. I let these gatherers take their harvest before resuming my cutting. The clover blossoms also attract butterflies. I am pleased to say that one of our neighbors has a similar philosophy and does not cut portions of his lawn where there are stands of chicory. The blue flowers of this plant are more pleasing, to his way of thinking, than green grass. As the seeds of the chicory begin to ripen, goldfinches and house finches find their way to the blossoms and feed at length upon what must be a delicacy for them. The same thing happens when the seeds of our cosmos begin to ripen.

Once we had completed our original objectives, which were to rejuvenate the lawn and put in plantings, we began to notice that we were playing host to a surprising number of butterflies. Some were attracted by our flowers and some by larval food plants growing in the yard. The black swallowtail laid its eggs on Queen Anne's lace growing in our nature area. Milkweed and tall grasses furnished food for other species. Couldn't we do still more to encourage butterflies? Few groups have suffered more from pesticides.

It wasn't long before we discovered that butterfly bush (buddleia) did well on Nantucket and the fragrant flowers attracted a host of butterflies throughout the blossom period. Both white- and purple-flowered butterfly bushes can be found growing in a surprisingly large number of yards on Nantucket. From late July until mid-September, which is the flowering season, the bushes attract butterflies, hummingbird moths, honeybees, and bumblebees. Not only did we plant a number of these bushes in our yard but I began taking a yearly count of the Lepidoptera at my bushes and a number of others scattered through the town. Of some dozen species of butterflies that visit butterfly bush on Nantucket, the most common were painted lady, cabbage butterfly, red admiral, monarch, and red-spotted purple. Hummingbird moths are especially common visitors, with sometimes three or four at a single bush. We have good seasons and bad ones for butterflies on Nantucket, but I would say that most species seem to be holding their own.

Another group that has been hard hit by pesticides is the amphibians. Aerial spraying of the island with DDT and other chemicals prior to 1970 decimated the amphibian population and, according to some accounts, resulted in the complete extermination of Fowler's toad. More recently there have been sightings of live toads (presumably Fowler's toad), so there is reason to believe that this species may not have been completely exterminated after all. Whatever the case, we are hoping to lure toads to our yard. Our next project is to build a small pond that could serve as a breeding place for toads and frogs.

Aside from special projects, such as the ones I have mentioned, wildlife gardening is very much like any other gardening. Most of one's efforts go into routine gardening activities, such as cultivating, planting, mowing, and pruning. There is just as much emphasis upon good landscaping and keeping the yard tidy. If there is a difference, it is in the somewhat less manicured look of the wildlife garden. But beauty is always a prime objective. Although no two people have quite the same concept of what is beautiful, I have noticed that passersby often stop and look approvingly at a garden that has been landscaped for wildlife. We have had this kind of attention paid to our yard in Nantucket.

If for no other reason than good publicity, the wildlife gardener wants his yard to be admired and copied. The more gardens like his that there are in the neighborhood, the better it is for the wildlife he wants to help. Even a very small yard with its plantings and bird feeders helps make up for the loss of natural habitat. When we stop to think of the millions of yards that do offer benefits of this kind, we can take a more optimistic view regarding the future of America's wildlife. Much depends upon saving natural habitats of all kinds and solving problems related to pollution and toxic chemicals. But when one adds suburban yards to the land that has been set aside as wildlife refuges, nature preserves, and parks, the picture becomes brighter. In doing what we can to help, we have the pleasure of a better-planted yard and the animal life that goes with it.

# I / Planting for Wildlife

Development on the outskirts of towns and cities
has forced wildlife to find new homes.
Also, in many parts of the
country, large-scale farming operations have replaced
the small farms of the past. With
farms becoming ever larger and
more mechanized, wildlife
habitats have disappeared.
Large fields have replaced
small ones. Stone walls,
overgrown fencerows,
hedges, old orchards,
and woodlots, so impor-
tant to wildlife, have
been removed. Wet-
lands have been
drained.

But as wildlife
habitats disappeared,
new and sometimes better
ones have taken their places.
The one that is of special interest

*White-throated sparrow visiting pyracantha*

to us is the immediate surroundings of our own home. As an environment, the yard can surpass natural habitats in its capacity to hold and
maintain wildlife populations. In England, for example, the mature

suburb has been reported to have slightly more birds than deciduous woodland and many more than open grassland. Even more striking differences have been recorded on this side of the Atlantic. For example, the changes in the bird population that have taken place in suburban sections of St. Petersburg, Florida, have been carefully documented. With the complete destruction of wild habitat prior to development, the bird population was temporarily eliminated. When houses were built and yards planted, birds appeared and reached approximately the population density that had existed previously, but the species composition was very different. As plantings matured, the bird population doubled and several new breeding species arrived. The mature suburb in St. Petersburg, therefore, had a bird population with a density twice as great as that of the natural habitat that it replaced. Although house sparrows accounted for a sizable proportion of the new population, more popular species, such as the mourning dove, mockingbird, cardinal, red-bellied woodpecker, and purple martin, were well represented.

An even more striking difference between natural habitat and mature suburb was recorded by J. T. Emlen in a 1974 issue of *The Condor*. He compared the bird population of a residential section of Tucson, Arizona, with that of outlying desert scrubland. The suburb had once been desert scrub very much like the desert census area used for comparison. Thanks to the availability of water, feeding stations, and plantings, the bird population of the residential area had a density twenty-six times as great as that of the desert scrub! The urban birds were predominantly seed-eaters. They obtained about half their food at feeding stations and the other half from seeds of weeds and lawn grasses. Hummingbirds in the residential area were assisted by the presence of hummingbird feeders. Water, nearly absent in the desert, was plentiful in the well-irrigated residential area.

But not every suburban yard is a haven for wildlife. There must be *diversity*. This is achieved through having a variety of habitats in one's yard and in other yards throughout the neighborhood. Even if our neighbors' yards are too open or bare, we can make up for this shortcoming by having a well-planted yard ourselves. Within a relatively small space, we should find room enough for a lawn, flower beds, low shrubs and a hedge, taller shrubs, and trees. George Reiger, in *Gardening with Wildlife*, tells of a study conducted in Fort Collins, Colorado.

In neighborhoods with a high floral diversity, sources of water, and open space in the form of a park or undeveloped land, residents reported seeing between 30 and 183 species of birds. On the other hand, residents living in neighborhoods with the lowest habitat diversity never saw more than 20 species.

Like birds, mammals are successful immigrants to the urban habitat and they, too, thrive wherever there is adequate diversity. But since early times their presence has been regarded with suspicion because of the havoc wreaked by small rodents. The vessels of the early colonists brought the brown rat, black rat, and house mouse to our shores. Also, the settler soon found his clearings invaded by native mammals having a taste for corn and other crops. Invading towns and cities, some of these mammals entered his home. Today, with most of our food coming from shelves in grocery stores and with our houses tight enough to keep out unwanted guests, we can be more accepting of small mammals. As a source of entertainment, squirrels, chipmunks, and raccoons are about on a par with birds. But many of the mammals are so secretive and so seldom seen that most people are not aware that they exist.

The measures that benefit birds are of about equal value to mammals. Birdhouses may be occupied by white-footed mice, flying squirrels, and squirrels of other kinds. Fruit- and berry-bearing shrubs are patronized by mammals. Brush piles, hollow trees, and dense hedges are used as cover by both mammals and birds. Many small mammals, including squirrels, opossums, raccoons, and skunks, come to birdbaths to get a drink. The last three come after dark and therefore are seldom seen. And to the despair of some and the joy of others, food at bird-feeding stations is as popular with those mammals as it is with the birds it was meant for.

Central Park in the heart of crowded Manhattan offers a good example of how readily mammals adapt to life in city parks. The *New York Times* reported in 1983 that no fewer than 13 native species of mammals make their residence in the park or are visitors. Also found in Central Park were nine species of fish, a freshwater jellyfish, eight species of reptiles and amphibians, and, as confirmed by sightings made over a period of many years, 269 species of birds. While most of the birds by far were seen while passing through on spring or fall migration, 42 species have nested.

Insects comprise another and much larger segment of the wildlife community that has adapted to yards, gardens, and parks in cities and suburbs. The well-known entomologist Frank E. Lutz once boasted to his colleagues at the American Museum of Natural History in New York City that he could find 500 species of insects in his small suburban yard in New Jersey across the Hudson River. His 75-by-200-foot lot near the center of Ramsey contained a few trees, shrubs, flowers, some lawn, and a small vegetable garden. Not only did he greatly exceed his goal but he found a number of unexpected insects, including a bee that had never before been recorded north of Mexico and the West Indies. After several years of collecting and observing, Dr. Lutz was able to announce that he had recorded no fewer than 1,402 insect species in his small yard. His count included 477 species of moths and butterflies, 259 beetles, 258 flies (Diptera), 167 ants, bees, and wasps (Hymenoptera), and lesser numbers of grasshoppers, crickets, dragonflies, caddis flies, true bugs, and others.

Finally, there are the reptiles and amphibians. Without strong ties to particular plants, the herps, as they are collectively called, are often burrowers or residents of damp places, living under stones and logs or, in many cases, spending all or part of their lives in water. Since it is difficult to duplicate the conditions that suit most herps, we rely largely upon happenstance in getting our share of these interesting but poorly understood animals. Some, we would rather not have, but the trill of treefrogs and the croaking of frogs give us a respite from the many mechanical noises that assail our ears. There is also much to be said for the control that herps exert upon burgeoning insect populations.

In contrast to the city park, which is landscaped primarily for use by people, a suburban yard, although much smaller, can for its size become a richer wildlife habitat. We can prevent disturbance and cater to the needs of wildlife in the many ways that I suggest in the chapters that follow. Our first consideration should be the kind of landscaping needed to achieve the all-important diversity mentioned earlier. Such factors as the size of our yard and how much of it is already planted will enter into our planning, but a few basic principles can be applied to almost any yard regardless of its size.

The steps that will make our yard more attractive to wildlife are neither difficult to follow nor at odds with good landscaping. First, we should have a good balance between lawn and taller vegetation. Most yards have relatively extensive lawns and not enough space devoted to

*Wildlife garden*

trees, shrubs, hedges, and flower beds. Only half our acreage or less should be in lawn if we are to offer maximum advantages to wildlife. At the same time, open space is important in letting in sunlight and providing the "edge effect" that is essential for good nesting habitat for birds. Also, it is along the edge where most flowers are seen in bloom and where fruits and berries ripen most luxuriantly. This is where the largest numbers of bees, butterflies, and day-flying moths are to be found. We will have more than enough edge space if our yard contains openings in the form of lawns, flower and vegetable beds, walks, and driveways. Our aim will be to border these openings with an appropriate assortment of plants. I do not necessarily mean tall plants. Even a border between well-cut lawn and a lawn that is allowed to grow several inches tall is an edge. Such an edge may offer a haven to numerous insects, including butterflies, and to toads, grass-inhabiting snakes, like the garter snake, and the many birds that find food among the taller grasses. Still another kind of edge is that between lawn and a ground cover such as English ivy, periwinkle (*Vinca minor*), or pachysandra. Although many of the smaller forms of wildlife will use the ground cover as a place of refuge, it is along the edge that the greatest amount of activity will be found. When cutting the lawn, note how quickly the crickets, grasshoppers, "hop" toads, and other small amphibians or reptiles disappear into the slightly taller growth at the edge.

In creating edge, we should have low plants in front, facing lawn or other open space, and progressively taller plants behind them. This is both pleasing to the eye and helpful to wildlife. Lower growth will act as a canopy to give shelter to animals that use the interior for escape purposes or living quarters. Annuals in front, perennials looming somewhat taller behind them, and then shrubs backed by small trees make an especially effective combination.

Departing from more conventional landscaping practices, we may want to reduce lawn space by planting one or more small islands in the middle of the lawn. This would be a good place to use some of our largely neglected native small trees and shrubs. We have good ornamentals and wildlife plants among the sumacs, viburnums, dogwoods, and bayberries. Our native hollies offer bright red berries and many are evergreens, providing a touch of green through the long winter months. For something out of the ordinary but with fall fruiting for wildlife and spiny trunk and foliage, I would recommend our native devil's-walking-stick (*Aralia spinosa*). Mountain ash is excellent for more northern yards and I wouldn't overlook the birches with their papery bark and seed-filled catkins that attract the attention of goldfinches and other seed-eaters.

The island may contain only one kind of woody plant or a combination of several. But for added effectiveness in supplying food and cover for wildlife, the ground below should be allowed to grow up into tall grasses, asters, goldenrod, and other forbs. The wildlife gardener may also want to circle the outside perimeter with spring bulbs. The end result may be a small oasis in the lawn that sparkles with beauty and holds an unusually large quota of wildlife species.

Having filled some of the lawn space with plants and perhaps lined walkways and the driveway, where else can we place new plantings? If our property border is open on one or more sides, we may want to plant hedges or evergreen windbreaks opposite adjacent properties. Instead of the pine or hemlock hedge, which, when clipped, offers little food value to wildlife, I would suggest glossy abelia (*Abelia grandiflora*) for more southern yards. The flowers appear all summer and invite nectar-

feeders of all kinds. The privets, suitable for both northern and southern yards, offer food and nest sites for birds but shouldn't be severely
clipped. The barberries are good hedge plants and their dense twig
structure and thorns protect the yard from prowling dogs and cats.
Some of the hollies are among the best of the impenetrable hedge plants.
I particularly like Japanese holly (*Ilex crenata*) and its variety *convexa*.
This holly can be made into a tight hedge or allowed more freedom to
grow as it likes. If not clipped too severely, it will provide winter food
for birds.

Flowering dogwood and the flowering crab apples, both beautiful
when in bloom and later in fruit, should be given places of honor near
the house. I prefer to use these small trees alone or in groups and not
mixed in with other plants. The same goes for redbud (*Cercis canadensis*). Its beauty and contribution to wildlife occur in early spring when
the flowers appear. Out of gratitude for its spring display, we can forgive it for its mediocre performance the rest of the year. Like the redbud, the hawthorns are not always pleasing to the eye, but their spring
blossoms, fall fruit, and the thorny haven they provide for nesting birds
make them one of the few small trees I would consider if I had only a
small amount of space left in my yard.

If we lack adequate foundation plantings around the house, I
would advise a mixture of evergreens, using any of the following: hollies, arborvitae, Chinese juniper, red cedar, and yew. I would not recommend large rhododendrons, however. These much-used ornamentals
take up too much room and offer few advantages to wildlife. Much the
same can be said of andromeda (*Pieris* spp.), relatives of rhododendron
belonging to the heath family.

Plants that have outstanding displays of bright-colored fruits
should be at exposed sites where they can be admired. I would reserve
the corners of the house or outbuildings for pyracantha with its gorgeous red fruits that last well into winter. Nandina deserves much the
same treatment. Flowering quince looks good by itself, perhaps near
the driveway or the street. The low-growing or dwarf cotoneasters can
be used as ground cover or as part of the planting scheme in a rock
garden. Bare walls and sides of buildings afford good opportunities to
use some of the plants already mentioned and others as well. We may
want to install trellises for climbing roses or have pyracantha, cotoneaster, or yew espaliered against a wall. With little assistance on our part,

Boston ivy, English ivy, or Virginia creeper will cover sides of walls and buildings. Finally, pick a sunny location for butterfly bush (*Buddleia* spp.) and chaste tree (*Vitex agnus-castus*), both highly attractive to bees and butterflies.

For winter and early spring, the most difficult times of the year for wildlife, we need plants that hold their fruits or seed crops well and also plants for shelter. Pine, hemlock, spruce, and fir are important for the shelter they give wildlife from strong winds and frigid cold. Particularly in more northern sections, the yard should have a good balance between evergreens and deciduous species.

The advantages of having suitable wildlife plantings will be partially lost if we over-clip or under-clip our hedges, shrubs, and small trees. Severe clipping removes blossoms and fruit buds, thereby ruining the plant's value as a source of food for wildlife. Moreover, the severely clipped hedge can become so impenetrable that birds will not use it for nesting purposes. If allowed to bloom and bear fruit, hedge plants, such as privet, holly, yew, and barberry, provide valuable sustenance for wildlife. On the other hand, small trees, shrubs, and vines that are not clipped or pruned may become ungainly. Judicious pruning not only improves the appearance of the plant but makes it a more compact and better site for shelter and for nesting by birds.

To be treasured and not cut down are the one or two old trees in

*Goldfinch coming to alder catkin*

the yard that have outlasted lightning, storms, and cleanup operations. So long as these trees are not too blighted, we should leave them where they are. Tall trees act as a magnet to migrant birds. The birds first settle in the treetops and then, if there are adequate inducements below, they may fly down into the yard. The taller trees provide their share of insects for hungry birds. The orioles, in particular, confine their nesting to the higher branches of trees. Woodpeckers use the dead stubs and branches of old trees as places to excavate roosting and nesting cavities. One of the choicest sites used by woodpeckers and other hole-nesting birds is the old apple tree with its hollow trunk and dead branches. A dead tree can be pruned until it is of a safe and suitable size. Vines can be allowed to grow over the dead tree, thereby giving it a more presentable appearance.

So far in our venture into gardening for wildlife, we haven't departed significantly from standard landscaping practices. We have reduced lawn space but preserved open areas for their edge effect. We have used many of the same plants grown by our neighbors but have added a few, including more native species than are found in most yards. If there is a noticeable difference, it is in the greater species diversity in our yard and special attention we have given to plants used by wildlife. While we have trimmed, pruned, and cut, it was not so much for neatness as to improve the usefulness of our plants to wildlife. Our yard is reasonably neat but not manicured. We have let tall grasses and other forbs grow along edges. Dead limbs on trees haven't been ruthlessly pruned. We have left the old apple tree, gnarled and twisted as it is, to produce a few more crops. The same solicitude is applied to a nearly dead tree, partially shorn of its limbs but heavily overgrown with vines. Our yard has more curved borders than straight lines. There is a natural look to our yard reminding one of verdant countryside.

Like most yards in the neighborhood, ours will contain a full quota of bird feeders. Instead of using old-fashioned bird tables or throwing a large share of the food on the ground, we have probably progressed to the extent of putting most of the food we offer in tubular hanging feeders. Here it will be protected from the weather and not be within easy reach of troublesome guests. The hanging feeders are ideal for offering sunflower seeds and there are special models for holding

*Old tree is a wildlife haven*

thistle (niger). If the hanging feeder seems too exclusive, we can fasten on the bottom the seed tray designed for that particular model. Seeds dislodged by birds feeding higher up will fall into the tray and be taken by cardinals and other birds that normally will not feed by clinging to small perches.

We should not altogether eliminate ground feeding. Many birds are adapted to feeding on the ground and only reluctantly, if at all, will come to elevated feeders. I cater to ground feeders, like the mourning dove, brown thrasher, rufous-sided towhee, and white-throated sparrow, by sprinkling some millet and cracked corn on the ground each day. Ground feeders also receive food that has fallen from hanging feeders. But in wet weather, I offer very little food this way. Under damp conditions, seeds, and especially cracked corn, spoil very quickly. The mold that then forms sometimes constitutes a health risk to birds.

Sometimes undesirable bird species will become fixtures at our feeders. I don't mind a few starlings, grackles, cowbirds, or red-winged blackbirds at my feeders, but when they come in flocks and appear day after day, I find it necessary to take measures to discourage them. Indeed, the sooner we begin to discourage them, the better our chances of success. No longer offer as much food on the ground, remove seed trays, and use only the few feeders that these visitors cannot handily exploit. After experimenting with a large number of feeders, I can recommend the following as nearly blackbird-proof but not so exclusive as to discourage the birds we wish to cater to: Hyde's Six Side Silo, Gemini Feeder by Aspects, Garden Pole Feeder and BJ-Jr by Droll Yankee. After a period of violent fluttering before feed ports, the undesirable birds usually give up and we can return to our normal feeding routine.

I use black oil sunflower seeds in my feeders the year round. They offer more kernel per weight than the larger striped sunflower and are easier for smaller birds to open. Thistle seeds are highly popular with goldfinches and other small finches and have the advantage of *not* being

*An avid ground feeder*

taken by larger, more aggressive birds. If starlings are a problem, refrain from offering suet, suet mixtures, bakery products, raisins, fruit,
and mixed bird seed. Once they have departed, we can go back to the
softer foods that are popular with wrens, mockingbirds, kinglets, warblers, and orioles. By manipulating the way we use foods and feeders,
we can to a large degree regulate the number and kinds of birds we
have at our feeders. In Chapter 6, I suggest ways to outwit squirrels.

Bird feeding should be initiated as soon as the weather begins to
turn cool in the fall. Unless we have neighbors who feed birds through
the winter, we should continue our feeding program without interrup-
tion until all danger of late snowstorms is behind us. Bird feeding can
be conducted throughout the year with benefits to birds and pleasure to
ourselves, but the most important period from the standpoint of providing birds with the extra food they need is winter and early spring.

We will supply water for birds and other wildlife as well as birdhouses and possibly nest boxes for squirrels and raccoons. Our inducements to wildlife will blend in with the surroundings. If there is
anything unsightly, it will be carefully hidden from view behind the
house or garage. Brush piles, rotting logs, stone piles, and compost will
all have their designated spots and uses. Refuse of this kind will provide
much-needed habitat for small reptiles and amphibians.

This will also be the part of the yard where we will try to find
space for a wild garden. It can be either a section allowed to grow up
into plants that have seeded themselves, or an area where we exert some
control through extra planting, pruning, and thinning. Natural habitat
of this kind will provide some of the food plants needed by butterflies
and moths during their larval stage. Field mice will establish nests in
underground burrows, and bumblebees will discover the empty nests
and use them for their own. A whole new web of life will reveal itself
in this little-disturbed part of the yard. All this we can have with almost
no effort on our part.

There is one management activity, however, that I would recommend for both tended and untended parts of the yard. This is rooting
out undesirable plants. One of the most insidious of these is Japanese
honeysuckle. In spite of being one of our best wildlife plants, it is so
rampant and invasive that we have to destroy it before it gets too good
a start. Much the same can be said of poison ivy, which is also a valuable
wildlife food plant. The best rule to follow in respect to any plant that

is going to run riot at the expense of our other plants is to eradicate it before it gains too firm a foothold.

Finally, what about city dwellers who have only a tiny yard, a balcony, or a roof garden? Can they attract a share of the birdlife to be found in cities? After looking into plants best suited for city conditions, I have been pleasantly surprised to learn that there are a number that rate highly both as ornamentals and as bird attractors. For those who live in warmer sections, I would recommend nandina for its attractive qualities and the ease with which it can be grown almost anywhere. There are dwarf forms ranging in height from one to four feet that are ideal for planting in tubs. Even if birds do not discover the red fruits, we can enjoy the bright autumn foliage and the fruit that may cling to plants all winter.

What has been said about nandina applies equally well to pyracantha. Somewhat hardier, pyracantha has red or orange fruits that are better liked by birds. Used as espaliers on walls or sides of buildings, pyracantha need take up scarcely any space at all. Some varieties, such as Tiny Tim, grow no taller than three feet and are well suited for planting in tubs.

Several of the hollies can be used in much the same way as nandina or pyracantha and have about the same bird appeal. We should look for dwarf forms if space is at a premium. The following can easily be grown in tubs: Heller Japanese holly (*Ilex crenata* var. 'Helleri'), compact inkberry (*I. glabra compacta*), and Maryland dwarf American holly (*I. opaca* var. 'Maryland Dwarf'). When growing hollies, make sure there is at least one male or staminate plant present to furnish pollen for female plants.

If there is a vine made for city conditions, it is Boston ivy. It will cover a bare wall and offer some of the brightest fall foliage we can expect to see anywhere. Less appreciated is the fact that the blue fruits of Boston ivy are eagerly consumed by birds in the fall. I could also mention the suitability of the cotoneasters, barberries, and some others for city planting. But I am of the opinion that the plants I have mentioned are among the very best for bird use and for the limited space that is normally available.

# 2 / Water—Key to More Wildlife

No other ingredient we can offer is more important in bringing wildlife to the yard than water. Most of us are already familiar with the way birds respond to a birdbath, spray from a garden sprinkler, or a rain puddle. They drink long and earnestly and then begin a series of visits for bathing and splashing. I can always count on having more bird species over a period of time at my birdbath than at my bird feeders. I am also aware that quite a number of other animals besides birds use my birdbaths. They may not come as openly or as freely as birds but, like birds, they are drawn to water for a variety of purposes. Thirsty mammals come almost as eagerly to the birdbath as do birds. Raccoons come not only to drink but often to wash their food.

*Raccoon catching tadpoles*

Mrs. Herbert Clay of Louisville, Kentucky, has both gray foxes and striped skunks coming to a birdbath at a summer house in the country. She strongly recommends that the birdbath be brought down from its pedestal and placed on the ground. This makes the water more accessible to mammals, and birds, too, prefer the lower level for their use. I agree completely with her recommendation, as long as cats are not a problem, and also her advice not to overfill the birdbath. The bath should slope gradually toward the middle, have a rough surface, and nowhere be over three inches deep. The average depth should be about one and one-half inches. Most important of all, the bath should not be allowed to go dry. Daily care, including a change of water, is almost essential when a birdbath is being heavily used.

Both Mrs. Clay and I find that a slow water drip is effective in bringing birds to the bath. The sight and sound of dripping water act as stimuli to bring birds from all parts of the yard to the place where the birdbath is located. For those who do not want to go to the trouble of rigging up their own drip, there are fountain drips on the market that can be attached by way of tubing to an outdoor faucet. The Beverly Company of New Harbor, Maine, markets a drip of this kind and so does Audubon Workshop of Northbrook, Illinois.

There is also the challenge of a three-tier birdbath equipped with a pump that recycles the water. Mr. Fintel of Lewes, Delaware, has a bath of this kind in which the water flows steadily from the uppermost basin to a second basin one inch lower and down another six inches to a basin at ground level. After passing through a filter, the water is pumped up to repeat the cycle. Mr. Fintel states that the ripple effect of flowing water is a powerful attractant in drawing birds. His most surprising guest was a screech owl. As the owl went through its ablutions, splashing water in the same way as other birds, more and more small birds gathered around at a safe distance to watch and scream abuse at their archenemy.

## INSECT VISITORS

Almost any source of water, from rainwater in a tin can to a swimming pool, will draw insects, ranging from ones that are in disrepute to ones that are better liked. The mosquitoes can safely be said to rate lowest in our esteem. There are several ways we can deal with them. Most mosquitoes favor a stagnant body of water or a temporary pool where there will be few predators to prey upon their larvae. The early stages in the mosquito's life cycle are spent in the water. The female lays her eggs there and these usually hatch after two or three days. Next we see a highly active stage in which the larvae, known as wigglers, swim about in the water feeding upon plant debris and at frequent intervals come to the surface to obtain air. In from one to two weeks, as a rule, the wigglers are transformed into a less active stage, known as the pupal stage. This lasts only a few days and is followed by transformation into the winged adults. The adult male mosquito feeds upon nectar and plant juices; only the female enters our bedroom to cause us sleepless nights. Many species of mosquitoes do not attack humans but confine their blood-taking to birds, mammals, and other forms. One of the most worrisome aspects of the presence of mosquitoes is that some species carry diseases that affect us, our pets, and domestic livestock.

Keeping in mind that it takes about two weeks for the larvae of most species of mosquitoes to develop into adults, we can effectively prevent reproduction from taking place by frequently emptying and changing water in likely breeding places. We do this anyway with the well-maintained birdbath, but we sometimes overlook small sources such as water in outdoor saucers under flower pots or water that may have accumulated in cans or other rubbish. But what about garden ponds and other bodies of water that are not so easy to drain at frequent intervals?

One of the best solutions to a mosquito problem in larger bodies of water, and sometimes small ones as well, is mosquito-larvae-eating fish. The species most often used is the mosquito fish or gambusia (*Gambusia affinis*). Only one to two inches long, this little fish has such an insatiable appetite for mosquito larvae and is so effective in cleaning them out that it has been introduced all over the world for use in mosquito control. A single pair of mosquito fish was reported to have consumed over five thousand mosquito larvae in ten weeks. Mosquito fish liberated into ornamental pools soon eliminate any mosquito larvae. Since this fish also feeds upon small aquatic animals and vegetable matter, it can thrive in the absence of mosquitoes. The female gives birth to living young. A native of the southeastern United States, this tiny fish can be introduced successfully to almost any body of water.

Killifish or topminnows (*Fundulus* spp.) are wide-ranging close relatives of the mosquito fish and are also highly useful in keeping mosquitoes under control. From three to six inches long and, in some species, with dark vertical stripes on the sides, killifish inhabit fresh, brackish, and salt water. After unsuccessfully introducing goldfish to his birdbath to control mosquitoes, Mr. Fintel turned to a killifish known as a mummichog as a better solution. He had discovered that the brightly colored goldfish attracted the attention of raccoons and were quickly caught and eaten. But the drably colored mummichogs were overlooked by night-prowling raccoons and lived to perform the services for which they were intended.

Although mostly found on quiet waters of lakes, ponds, and streams, water bugs also find their way to water we have in our yard. They comprise a large group that includes the water striders, giant water bugs, water scorpions, backswimmers, and water boatmen. With the exception of the water boatmen, which are largely herbivorous, the

*Small pond*

water bugs are ferocious predators that attack any aquatic animals small enough for them to handle. The birdbath will occasionally be visited by backswimmers and water boatmen. The water bugs do not inconvenience our bird guests and are of interest to those of us whose goal is a well-rounded wildlife community.

If well established at swimming pools, backswimmers and a giant water bug known as the electric light bug can be a nuisance to bathers. They are capable of giving a painful jab to anyone who comes in contact with them. On the other hand, water bugs eat the larvae of mosquitoes and biting midges.

We do not necessarily have to have water in our yard to be visited by water bugs and other insects closely associated with water. Many are attracted to outdoor lights and lights in our windows. Among our nocturnal visitors from wetland habitats are mosquitoes, mayflies, midges, crane flies, predaceous diving beetles, electric light bugs, and water boatmen. If there is water in our yard, some stay and become more or less permanent residents.

We may already have honeybees living nearby. They require water at times and may become a nuisance by descending in large numbers upon such sources as the birdbath or swimming pool. Whether water is clean or dirty seems to make no difference to them. So long as we do not disturb them, they are not likely to inflict their stings on us.

No one should have any complaints about dragonflies or damselflies. Readily drawn to water, these colorful insects have an insatiable appetite for other insects, including many of the most bothersome kinds. We seldom give them proper credit for the inroads they make upon the fly, mosquito, and midge populations.

## REPTILES AND AMPHIBIANS

One of the more pleasing sights on a warm day in summer is to see a toad or frog toward dusk in the birdbath absorbing moisture through its skin. This is how toads and frogs "drink." To be generous welcomers of these valuable amphibians to our yard, we should provide them with a breeding place. The birdbath is not large enough and a swimming pool is too heavily chlorinated as a rule. Also, the sides of a swimming pool are so steep that the larvae, as they become air-breathing and ready to leave, cannot climb out. Under these conditions they are doomed to die. Needed is a shallow pool having one or more sides that slope gradually to the water. In Chapter 12, I'll mention the success that Mrs. Olive Goin in Florida had with a water-filled cement basin, four feet long, three feet wide, and four inches deep. This small body of water proved to be a popular breeding place for toads and frogs, helping her to achieve a total of fourteen species in this group for her yard.

A cement basin of this size is not hard to construct and will take up comparatively little yard space. The basin should be in semi-shade and in an out-of-the-way place where it won't become a major attraction for dogs and small children. It should be remembered that cement is highly alkaline and that a long curing period is needed before a cement pool is ready for safe use by aquatic animals. A good plan is to build a pool in the fall; by spring it should be ready for use by toads, frogs, and small fish.

Aquatic animals, including frogs, toads, and turtles, are often so hard-pressed for water that they select unlikely or unsafe places for living quarters. This is seen in the considerable mortality that takes place in swimming pools. The aquatic animal has no trouble entering a pool but because of the steep sides is unable to escape. Among the most common victims at swimming pools are toads. They tire and drown after a number of hours of paddling about. Turtles also have trouble making a departure. I once found a small painted turtle in a swimming pool and know of a case where a snapping turtle was an unwelcome guest at a swimming pool in Virginia. When swimming pools are not in use, they should be tightly covered over with canvas tops. This will prevent animals from falling in and will keep out leaves and other debris.

As an interesting sidelight, I have heard of a number of cases where canvas tops of swimming pools, on becoming partially filled with rainwater, became breeding places for toads and frogs and habitat for water bugs. Sometimes hundreds of tadpoles appear in these water-filled depressions. If allowed to mature, the tadpoles develop into small toads or frogs, thereby adding to the local population. Whether swimming pools turn into a menace or a boon to aquatic wildlife depends very much upon the way they are managed. They can provide positive benefits.

*Green frog eating worm*

## MUD FOR NEST BUILDING

I recall running a dairy farm in Virginia where part of the cattle yard could not be drained. Water from nearby roofs and a cattle drinking trough kept this part of the barnyard perpetually in a state of wetness. The hoofs of the cattle would churn up the wet soil and keep it soft and muddy to a depth of eight inches or more. But what was the despair of the farmer was a boon to wildlife.

Pipe organ and black-and-yellow mud daubers used the mud to build well-designed nests. These they plastered to the walls of farm buildings. The tubular columns of the pipe organ mud dauber are truly a work of art. Parallel rows of these columns look like miniature pipe organs. An equally spectacular work is produced by the potter wasp. Also using clayey mud, the potter wasp builds a small urnlike nest, which it attaches to twigs and stems of plants. Our muddy barnyard furnished not only building material for wasps but the food with which they provisioned their larvae. Spiders were abundant in and around the barnyard. In typical wasp or hornet fashion, a mud dauber will sting and paralyze a spider and take it to its mud nest, where it will eventually become fresh food for newly developing young.

The special scents and aromas of the barnyard attracted a number of butterfly species. Red-spotted purples, tiger swallowtails, and pearl crescents were among those that sometimes appeared in numbers to siphon up moisture from the manure-impregnated soil. I'll have more to say about the special feeding habits of butterflies in Chapter 8.

During the nesting season, a number of bird species depend in part or entirely upon mud for nest construction. A layer of mud is a part of every robin and wood thrush nest. The black phoebe in the West plasters mud against the sides of buildings, bridges, and bare faces of cliffs to form a cup-shaped nest. The cliff swallow, which nests in colonies, does the black phoebe one better by building a globular nest of mud, which it attaches to similar surfaces. The entrance is at the side. Another colonial nester, the barn swallow, builds a mud nest reinforced with straw, which it often places on tops of beams and rafters in barns. Mud is used to varying degrees in nest construction by rusty and Brewer's blackbirds, grackles, and eastern phoebes.

While most of us would not want to duplicate the conditions of the barnyard, we can easily supply a source of mud for builders such as those I have mentioned. One way is to allow water from an outdoor faucet to trickle down to nearby soil. In order to make the wet soil more suitable for building purposes, we should thoroughly work it until it has reached the consistency of the mud pies children take delight in.

If a wet place of this kind is undesirable near the house, a hose can be used to conduct water to a more distant part of the yard. The edge of a flower or vegetable bed and the soil next to a compost heap are appropriate sites for an experiment of this kind. Try to find soil that is somewhat clayey in consistency. The presence of humus is not a drawback. In fact, birds can build a stronger nest if the mud contains plant fibers. We need supply mud only during the two or three months of late spring and summer when nest building is underway.

## THE FARM POND

From the standpoint of space, the farm is a far more suitable place to build ponds than residential suburbs. Many farmers build one or more ponds on their property and sometimes place a high priority on the use of pond waters by wildlife. If the pond is partially or completely fenced off from cattle, it will support far more wildlife than a pond with heavily trodden banks that support little in the way of vegetative cover. The protected pond is a home for fish, turtles, frogs, and dragonflies. Ducks and geese—both domestic and wild—find a haven on its waters. Herons and egrets will come to search for living food in the shallows. Kingfishers, attracted by small fish, will poise overhead on fluttering wings before suddenly making a dive. Red-winged blackbirds will nest in low growth that surrounds the pond, singling out willows and cattails. Swallows, drawn by emerging insect life, will swoop low over the water catching their prey. Other insect-eating birds, such as the eastern kingbird, will also be present. Muskrats will make their home at the pond's edge and even during the day will be seen swimming about the pond, head above the water and leaving a small wake behind them.

In *From Laurel Hill to Siler's Bog,* John K. Terres told of the arrival of plant and animal life at a newly constructed pond near Chapel Hill, North Carolina. Wind and water brought seeds that soon sprouted and revegetated the raw earth at the edge of the pond. Animal life made its appearance with equal swiftness. Muskrats were the first of the small mammals to claim a place at the pond's edge. They were followed by mink, raccoons, and an occasional fox. Around the time that the mammals were showing themselves, wild ducks, herons, and kingfishers were discovering the advantages of a newly created body of water. Food, in the form of small fish, insect larvae, and tadpoles, was now plentiful.

On a warm night, only ten months after the pond had been created, Terres said, there was such a loud chorus of frogs and toads that he couldn't hear the usual familiar hooting of owls or barking of foxes. He estimated that there were now as many as one hundred thousand tadpoles living in the shallows. Whirligig beetles were also present in the thousands. Traveling in compact masses on the surface of the pond, the formations would quickly break up and scatter at the least sign of danger. They were the only beetles making their home on the surface film of the water. These beetles have a unique adaptation that permits them to scan the air above and at the same time look downward into the watery depths below them. Their eyes are divided into two separate pairs—one for downward vision and one for upward vision. When diving below to search for insect food, each beetle carries a bubble of air with it. The whirligigs shared their realm with giant water bugs, water scorpions, and predaceous diving beetles. There was no such thing as peaceful coexistence among these predators. Eat or be eaten was the law of this strife-torn community. If anything, the struggle for existence is harsher and more deadly in the water than it is on land. Waiting at the edge of the pond were bullfrogs—the most rapacious of freshwater predators. Their prey included other frogs and their tadpoles and even tadpoles of their own kind. Terres reported that once in a while a bullfrog could be seen leaping into the air in an attempt to capture a low-flying bird or bat.

*Green heron stalking fish*

# THE BOG GARDEN

If there is a boggy area in our yard, this small wetland will be an ideal place to grow moisture-loving plants that are of value to wildlife. But all of them need not be wildlife plants. As in all our gardening for wildlife, we are parties to whatever is being done and should receive a full share of the benefits. If our plantings add beauty to the yard and at the same time assist wildlife, we will have accomplished our goal. Nowhere will it be easier to carry out this objective than at our small wetland and neighboring pond or small pool. Some of our most beautiful flowering plants are perfectly suited for the landscaping that needs to be done here and many will be useful to wildlife.

With so many plants to choose from, we may have difficulty in deciding which ones to grow in our bog garden. There are bog primulas, native orchids, insectivorous plants, and gunneras with their giant leaves. These plants would make an interesting combination, to say the least. But with our emphasis on wildlife, I would rather grow plants that offered our guests a little more in the way of food and shelter. As we shall see in chapters that follow, among our biggest drawing cards are flowers rich in nectar. A succession of such flowers from early spring through early fall will be the best invitation we can give to hummingbirds, sphinx moths, butterflies, and bees. It so happens that a number of choice nectar-producing plants grow in moist to very wet habitats. My list of candidates for the bog garden includes buttonbush, jewelweed, cardinal flower, turtlehead, joe-pye weed, forget-me-not, iris, and swamp milkweed. Somewhat more a plant of shallow water than a bog, pickerel weed also should be considered. Its long stalked leaves and blue flowers provide the right kind of contrast if water lilies are the other dominant form of plantlife. The flowers of pickerel weed are well patronized by butterflies.

Once having established a flower garden for nectar-feeders, we might consider adding a few other plants solely for their charm and beauty. Water-loving buttercups, including tall buttercup (*Ranunculus acris*) and swamp buttercup (*R. septentrionalis*), are worth growing for their bright yellow blossoms. Like the buttercups, marsh marigold is a member of the crowfoot family and bears yellow flowers. A wildflower of more northern sections, the marsh marigold will brighten our bog with its flowers in April. Taking up less room than any of the others, violets with their small white or blue flowers will also do their part to add color in the spring. Except for furnishing food for several butterflies during their larval stage, violets, like the previous plants, are not much used by wildlife. Two that grow well in wet situations are marsh blue violet (*Viola cucullata*) and lance-leaved violet (*V. lanceolata*) with white flowers. One last suggestion for the bog garden is a plant for warm climates—elephant's-ear. Its large, aptly named leaves give the corner of the garden where the plant is grown an exotic look.

## THE HOME LILY POND

On a much smaller scale and containing far fewer plant and animal species than most ponds in wilder habitats is the small lily pond that we may have on our terrace or at the edge of a rock garden. Perhaps no more than five feet in diameter, a foot and a half deep, and lined with cemented rocks, this small pool will have been designed primarily to lend beauty to the yard. Regardless of design, the pond will contain some of the same plants and animals as the much larger farm pond. It is a microcosm, as it were, having a similar ecology but without the abundance and dramatic changes that take place in larger bodies of water.

The centerpiece of this small aquatic garden is the water lily. Few can resist the beauty of these ancient plants with their broad leaves and perpetual blooms through the summer months. The leaves and stems provide a substrate or lodging place for a host of aquatic organisms ranging from water beetles and freshwater snails to tiny, invisible worms known as rotifers. The floating or slightly raised leaves of water lilies, which prevent the water from becoming too warm in hot weather, provide shade for fish, resting places for frogs and dragonflies, breeding places for water beetles and snails, and attachment sites for rotifers, midge larvae, and freshwater hydra. Like other aquatic plants, water lilies aerate the water, performing the essential service of supplying oxygen to aquatic organisms and at the same time removing carbon dioxide.

Although there are any number of tropical water lilies suitable for use in home lily ponds, I find our native species as satisfactory as any. Yellow pond lily or spatterdock (*Nuphar advena*) will grow almost anywhere in shallow water. It produces small globular flowers which are yellow and on stems well above the water. This is not a showy plant but it is easy to grow. We are likely to have equally good luck with fragrant water lily (*Nymphaea odorata*). With its nearly heart-shaped leaves that float on the water and fragrant floating white flowers, it is one of our more beautiful water lilies. The blossoms are open only during the morning. The American lotus (*Nelumbo lutea*) is much too large for small lily ponds. But its showy, parasollike leaves and yellow flowers on raised petioles provide such an exotic look that we may be tempted to build a larger pond just to accommodate this plant.

At the opposite end of the scale from the American lotus is a native lily, Carolina fanwort (*Cabomba caroliniana*), whose one-inch-wide white flowers barely protrude above the water. The equally small leaves are threadlike and borne on submerged stems. The plants also have a few floating leaves which are less than an inch long and not threadlike. Although we cannot regard this plant as very ornamental, it is much used in ponds and aquariums as food and shelter for freshwater organisms and for its good oxygenating properties. It can be propagated by cuttings or seeds.

The standard procedure in growing water lilies is to place a six-inch piece of the rootstock or rhizome in rich earth at the bottom of the pond. Normally planting is done at a depth of a foot and a half and in a container which is lowered into the pond. One authority recommends that planting be done in a wicker basket so that later on the plant will not become pot-bound. Even without a pond, we can obtain good results by planting water lilies in metal or wooden tubs. These take up less room but cannot be expected to support as large an aquatic community as the more conventional lily pond. If we have only a limited amount of space, the tub idea is a good one to try. It is a means of bringing a portion of the water garden to almost any site, including a tiny yard in a city.

If our pond is to hold fish, we will need to consider still other plants. In terms of food and aeration of the water, we can't go wrong in using standard aquarium plants. Rooted in the soil at the bottom of a pond or fish bowl, these plants have finely dissected leaves and grow below the surface. The submerged stems and leaves aerate the water and provide food for vegetarian members of our small pond community. One of the easiest of all plants to use is coontail or hornwort (*Ceratophyllum demersum*). This plant thrives without root attachment to the bottom. All one needs to do is drop a few sprigs of the plant into the water and it will grow without further attention. A little more care must be taken with such other aquarium plants as variable-leaf milfoil (*Myriophyllum heterophyllum*), waterweed (*Elodea canadensis*), and anacharis (*Egeria densa*). All are good plants for our purpose and their tender foliage will provide food and shelter for fish. It should be remembered that, with some exceptions, it is only the young fish or fry, as they are called, that eat plant food. Older fish are likely to be carnivorous.

Care should be taken *not* to let our aquarium plants reach natural bodies of water. All too many of our waterways are clogged with either native or exotic aquarium plants that were unintentionally introduced by owners of fish ponds or aquariums. Plants removed from the aquarium should be placed in the compost heap, not the nearest stream or pond. To be avoided altogether, in my opinion, for use in lily or fish ponds are small floating plants like the duckweeds (*Lemna* spp.) or those pervasive one-celled plants—the algae. Although plants of this kind may arrive on their own, particularly algae, I would not encourage them. They proliferate at a rapid rate and can soon cover the surface, blocking out sunlight and smothering organisms living in the water below. Certain of the algae can turn the water a soupy green and, moreover, cause the water to have an unpleasant odor. We can get rid of unwelcome growth of this kind by frequently changing the water and also by introducing aquatic animals that feed upon green vegetable matter. Help can be had from goldfish, small pond-dwelling turtles, tadpoles, freshwater snails, freshwater mussels, and waterfowl.

If we are to have ducks in the pond, as well as fish, lilies, and some of the other plants mentioned, we will have to change our thinking somewhat. First of all, our pond will have to be large enough to accommodate these extra guests; secondly, ducks are far more vegetarian in their habits than fish. While fish will nibble at plants, ducks, along with coots, moorhens (gallinules), and geese, will eat leaves, stems, seeds, and tubers of aquatic plants and sometimes devour an entire plant. Services of this kind are needed if aquatic vegetation is getting the upper hand. But too much browsing can destroy the well-balanced plant community that we have gone to so much trouble to establish. It is better, therefore, to encourage waterfowl in city park ponds, farm ponds, lakes, and streams. But if we should have the opportunity to grow plants for waterfowl, we will need to offer a somewhat different selection than we would grow in our lily pond.

In addition to the undesirable duckweed, another floating plant, with even smaller leaves, watermeal (*Wolffia* spp.), is also eagerly taken by waterfowl. Pondweeds (*Potamogeton* spp.), arrowheads (*Sagittaria* spp.), wild rice (*Zizania aquatica*), naiads (*Naias* spp.), and wild celery (*Vallisneria spiralis*) are other plants or groups of plants that can be grown at the pond for waterfowl. But even if we offer a rich harvest of natural food, we cannot meet the needs of a sizable wintering population of waterfowl unless we supply food artificially. It is important to offer waterfowl wholesome grain, such as wheat, corn, and barley, when cold weather sets in. With nearly everyone else offering bakery products, we do the birds a favor by supplying them with more nutritious food.


## VERNAL POOLS

In contrast to more permanent bodies of water, vernal pools are formed by rain and melting snow during the spring and may have a life expectancy ranging from a few days to many months. During a wet year, with new supplies of water entering the pool, the life expectancy can be quite long. Temporary pools of this kind are common during the spring in fields and woodlands and sometimes we find them in poorly drained parts of our yard. In a race against time, many animals use vernal pools as breeding places. Among the amphibians, toads are likely to have the greatest success. It takes only one to two months for most toads to complete the aquatic stages of their existence. In contrast, the time it takes from egg laying to completion of early aquatic stages is much longer in other amphibians—about three to four months in most frogs and even longer in salamanders. One of the longest immature stages is seen in the bullfrog. The tadpoles take two years to develop—good reason for bullfrogs not to depend upon vernal pools.

Although there is the risk that the pool will dry up before the organisms using it have had time to hatch, there is one big advantage in carrying out reproduction in waters of this kind. They are safer from the standpoint of predation. Absent or nearly so will be such ferocious hunters as bullfrogs, predatory fish, and predaceous insects of many kinds. To be sure, almost every meat-eater of field and forest has a taste for small, easy-to-catch tadpoles. However, some thinning of numbers is necessary, for a single female toad may lay anywhere from 5,000 to 15,000 eggs.

Some organisms are so perfectly adapted to life in vernal pools that premature drying will not seriously interfere with their survival. One of the best adapted of such organisms is the fairy shrimp, which has a wide distribution over North America. Only about an inch long and nearly transparent, these relatives of the crayfish swim on their backs and propel themselves about with eleven pairs of feathery legs. The best time to find them is in late winter and early spring. By the time warm weather arrives, they will have disappeared. Eggs that can withstand dry conditions and are adapted to long periods of dormancy ensure the presence of future generations.

The scuds are another group that has successfully adapted to vernal pools. Like fairy shrimps, they are small crustaceans that live on decaying vegetable matter and animal remains. One author describes them as having the appearance of miniature armadillos. They are predominantly mud dwellers and can be found in a wide range of freshwater habitats.

Almost any woodland pool or stream, including vernal pools, will have a population of water striders. Running about on the surface of the water and sometimes jumping into the air to seize a passing insect, the water bugs belonging to this group seem never to get wet. They are perfectly adapted to life on the thin surface film which is their home and hunting grounds. If a pool begins to dry up, this does not inconvenience them in the slightest. They take wing and fly to another body of water.

In terms of our own yard, the vernal pool is likely to be the source of some of the aquatic insects and amphibians that visit us, particularly if vernal pools form in the spring in areas near where we live. But we do not necessarily have to rely on chance visits to obtain species we need for the pond in our yard. With a small net and a container or two in hand, we can search out vernal pools and capture tadpoles and other forms that we might want to bring home with us. Sometimes expeditions of this kind take on the aspect of a rescue mission. If we reach a vernal pool in the final stages of drying up, we may save the lives of hundreds of tadpoles. Those we do not take home with us can be liberated in more permanent bodies of water. If we are keeping tadpoles in an aquarium, we should provide them with proper food and make sure that they are able to leave the water on becoming air-breathing sub-adults. Young tadpoles eat minute plant and animal matter. When about half grown, they require meat. It will now be time to supply them with dead earthworms or small scraps of meat.

Water brings us into contact with far more forms of life than we ever dreamed were at our doorsteps. Nearly every phyllum of the animal kingdom is represented. If some of these animals seem too lowly and small to be of interest to us, we should remember that no matter what they are, they will be a part of a food chain that helps support higher forms of life, including ourselves. This is as true of mosquitoes and biting flies as it is of better-liked animal life. However, we do not

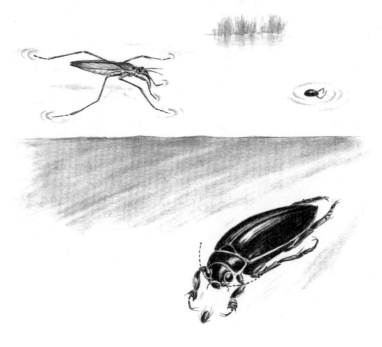

*Water strider and predaceous diving beetle*

necessarily have to endure the presence of the ones that cause us discomfort. We have allies ranging from mosquito fish and dragonflies to toads and purple martins that will keep our premises clear if we will only let them do the job and not try to do it ourselves with insecticides. This is a theme that I will pursue further in the pages that follow.

# 3 / Food Plants for Birds

## IN WINTER

Winter bird feeding should
be supplemented by bird
food plantings. Usually
these take the form of
berry-bearing shrubs
that hold their
fruit well into
winter. The fact
that fruits of
some plants re-
main attached
to twigs or
branches
all winter is
a happy cir-
cumstance. We
enjoy the display

*Cedar waxwing perched in red cedar*

and birds have something to
fall back on during times of scarcity.

Why birds pass up some fruits during the fall fruiting season and
eat others is something of a mystery. In some cases, fruits are left because a determined bird defends the supply, thereby preventing other
birds from getting a share. A lone mockingbird never tires of chasing
other birds from its chosen food sources. This is sometimes the reason

a bush is still loaded with fruit in midwinter. But generally the factor that saves a particular fruit from being eaten is something more subtle. Such qualities as hardness, pithiness, and astringency keep birds from eating fruit for long periods after it ripens. The same kind of selectiveness is seen at bird-feeding stations. Some seeds and grains are promptly eaten while others are reserved until later or never used.

Long exposure to the weather softens fruit and, as a rule, reduces astringency. This would seem to be a good reason why birds wait instead of consuming food as quickly as they can. We also wait until some fruits are more palatable. For example, the persimmon, with its high tannin content, is unacceptable to us in early fall. Later, after the fruit has aged on the tree for a while, the flavor improves and we accept it gladly.

Birds respond well to sweetness but often seem much more tolerant of bitter or astringent foods than we are. Something that is too bitter, however, is rejected. Often when two berry-bearing shrubs of the same species are growing side by side in a yard, birds will strip one of its fruit and leave the fruit of the other intact. Doubtless some slight difference in the chemical makeup of the fruits causes birds to react in this way. In the end, the fruit of the unpopular shrub may finally be eaten. This is one way that food is conserved until birds need it most.

In selecting shrubs to plant for birds in winter, we should be guided not only by bird-attracting qualities but also by how well the plants please us. The person who has his heart set on pyracantha should by all means stick to this colorful shrub if it suits his yard and serves the needs of his bird guests. At the same time, there should be a willingness to experiment. Other shrubs may be equally well suited to the yard and as good or better from the standpoint of food for birds. If there isn't space for additions, we can often make it by clearing land of plants that are less desirable for food. Special emphasis should be placed upon plants that hold their fruits well into winter. At the same time, we should think of the rest of the year and the birds that will visit us if we have the proper plantings. But the goal of a continuous supply of natural plant food is impossible if the yard is small and difficult even with a large yard. When faced with a difficult choice, it is better to have food for birds in winter, when they need it most, than to use up space on plants that yield their fruit at other seasons.

In selecting winter bird food plants for my yard, I keep in mind the needs of only about ten bird species. In the part of Maryland where I spend my winters, birds begin to exhaust natural supplies of fruits and berries by about mid-February. With the loss of natural supplies, birds must either go hungry, move on to seek new sources of food, or settle for feeding stations and ornamental plantings near houses. Not all wintering birds are adapted to moving on, and many, in spite of all the enticements we offer them, have yet to catch on to feeding stations. This leaves our ornamental plantings as a major source of food for a number of birds in late winter. In Maryland, I find that I need to cater especially to wintering robins and cedar waxwings. Also coming to my bird food plantings will be the inevitable mockingbird that tries to chase away every other bird. Yellow-rumped warblers, cardinals, house finches, and white-throated sparrows supplement their feeding station diet by feasting upon late fruits still clinging to bushes in my yard. Other visitors to my plantings may include flickers and the one or two catbirds and brown thrashers that have remained behind. I have yet to be visited by wintering bluebirds—a species that is not at all uncommon in winter on the Eastern Shore of Maryland. If I were living in the Far West, I would need to think of plantings for Bohemian waxwings as well as cedar waxwings and also such unfamiliar birds to Easterners as the varied thrush and Townsend's solitaire.

Among the best shrubs for winter bird use are the fire thorns or pyracanthas. I always find space for several bushes in my yard. Widely grown where winters are not too cold in the West and Midwest, pyracantha is hardy in the East from Massachusetts southward. The most widely grown of the several species is scarlet fire thorn (*Pyracantha coccinea*). The variety 'Lalandei,' with orange-red fruit, is particularly recommended for beauty and hardiness. A companion plant, and one that also bears striking clusters of bright red fruits, is nandina. Bamboolike with its feathery foliage, nandina normally attains a height of about five feet and is best suited for the South and Southwest. Birds are usually slow to harvest the fruits. Nandina thrives in sun or shade and withstands dry weather.

The photinias are another group of red-fruited shrubs best suited for warmer sections. Chinese photinia (*Photinia serrulata*), a shrub or small tree, flourishes in the South and the south-central states. Some years birds harvest the fruits of the photinias and some years they do not. Christmasberry or toyon (*Heteromeles arbutifolia*) is sometimes mistaken for photinia. Very popular in California, this red-fruited evergreen is an excellent winter bird food plant.

The hollies, which loom importantly as winter bird food plants, present the difficult question of which one or ones to use. Few are able to withstand the winters of the central plains states, but English holly, American holly, and Japanese holly do well as far north as New England. Winterberry (*Ilex verticillata*) and inkberry (*I. glabra*) are still hardier and can be grown from Canada's Maritime Provinces southward. Both are natives with good ornamental properties and should be planted more widely. Several other natives, yaupon, dahoon, and possum haw, are at home in the Southeast.

Our choice depends upon our tastes and where we live. All of the hollies offer winter food for birds. If red is to our taste, we have the red-fruited American holly, English holly, Chinese holly, winterberry, possum haw (*I. decidua*), and yaupon (*I. vomitoria*) to choose from. We should make sure, however, that the holly we select is adapted to our hardiness zone. The same holds true for black-fruited species. We may want to try the black-fruited inkberry (*I. glabra*) or the very popular Japanese holly (*I. crenata*), which with its small evergreen leaves makes a good hedge plant. Birds seem to favor the black fruits of holly as much as they do the red ones. Regardless of which holly we have planted, birds always seem to wait for a while before eating the fruit. They may wait only a short time or a very long time, as in one instance when it took cedar waxwings until May to discover the fruits of an American holly in my yard. In North Carolina, I noticed that robins and mockingbirds had just begun to sample the oversized red berries of Chinese holly (*I. cornuta*) in mid-February. But in Nantucket in early November, after the first hard freeze of the season, I observed robins and flickers swarming to the fruits of winterberry holly.

The hollies, along with pyracantha and nandina, are such good ornamentals that we would plant them anyway even if we were not catering to winter birds. But it is well to remember that hollies require acid soil and that most species will not bear fruit unless the male or staminate plant is present.

The barberries, like the hollies, are apt to hold their fruit well into winter. The commonly planted Japanese barberry (*Berberis thunbergii*), with its spiny stems and red fruit, is sometimes completely ignored by

birds. Nevertheless, this
barberry is useful as a source
of cover and nesting sites for birds.
If the fruit, as sometimes is the case,
helps returning migrants, this is another
plus. The very similar European barberry
(*B. vulgaris*), a handsome shrub growing to
about seven feet and with bright red fruit, has
greater bird appeal, and the same is true of the Darwin barberry
(*B. darwinii*). As alternate hosts for a wheat rust, most barberries
should not be grown in wheat-raising districts.

If we are looking for thorny shrubs that offer many of the same
advantages as the barberries but have more showy flowers, I would
suggest roses. I do not mean the highly cultivated ones. We may grow
the horticultural varieties if we wish, but they will offer few advantages
to birds and other wildlife. It is far better for wildlife to have a tangle
of rugosa roses (*Rosa rugosa*) with their large red hips. The hips, rich
in vitamin C, are well within the capacity of the cardinal and other
strong-beaked birds. Better yet, if we are looking for a rose ideal for
nesting cover which also produces a rich harvest of small hips that furnish birds with food through the winter, there is the Japanese or multiflora rose. Although there are complaints about the aggressiveness of
this rose and its habit of spreading into areas where it is not wanted, I
have had no trouble with the ones I've planted. Donald Wyman in his

*Gardening Encyclopedia* recommends planting only an occasional single shrub and not a whole hedgerow. In this way it is much easier to prevent plants from getting out of control. I agree that this is the best policy.

Of the many viburnums, only the American and European high-bush cranberries can be counted on to keep their fruit through the winter. In the North, where these two viburnums thrive, no amount of ice or snow can dim the bright translucent beauty of the red fruit. Indeed, against a background of snow, the clusters of bright red fruit are more decorative than ever. Birds generally wait until spring before sampling the fruit of either of the highbush cranberries. If discovered by a flock of waxwings or pine grosbeaks, the fruit disappears rather quickly. But why do birds wait so long and why are there only a few species that take the fruit?

I sampled the fruit of a highbush cranberry growing on Nantucket on the early date of October 27 and did not find it particularly tart. The fruit was soft, slightly shriveled, and had a somewhat cranberrylike taste. Why birds leave the highbush cranberry fruit and take so many others that seem less palatable to us is one of those small mysteries that remains to be solved.

Among the plants with far less showy fruit, the privets are still very much in evidence, although in many areas they are being replaced by yews and junipers. As sources of winter bird food, the privets deserve far more attention than is usually given them. The plants, however, must not be so heavily clipped that they are left without flowers and the fruit that follows. On Nantucket, where winter gales laden with salt spray sweep across the island from time to time, tall privet hedges are a familiar sight. The hedges protect yards and houses from the damaging effects of the storms. The privet most commonly used is California privet (*Ligustrum ovalifolium*). The fruit doesn't ripen until late fall. Some bird use can be expected by early winter.

Other good privets for use in the North include border privet (*L. obtusifolium*), common privet (*L. vulgare*), and ibota privet (*L. ibota*). Although none of these plants are prized ornamentals, they grow well in poor soils and can withstand unfavorable city conditions.

In the South and Southwest, the privets turn up in somewhat different guise than they do in the North. Japanese privet (*L. japonicum*) is a beautiful evergreen with lustrous, glossy leaves and clusters of blue-black fruit. Like most privets it is used as a hedge plant. Glossy privet (*L. lucidum*), also common in the South, has handsome foliage but is more treelike and often grown as a small tree.

The black or blue-black fruits of the privets are generally ignored by birds during early winter. Whether it takes time for the fruits to become more palatable or birds are more hungry in late winter, I cannot say, but by February there is a rush to take them. From February until mid-April, I see much use of privets at my Maryland home by catbirds, mockingbirds, robins, cedar waxwings, house finches, purple finches, and white-throated sparrows. Surprisingly, even as late as May and June, some bushes remain untouched, leaving the impression that birds are not overly fond of privet fruits. But it must be remembered that birds, as a rule, are not thorough harvesters. They tend to leave some of the crop untouched regardless of how tempting it may be.

Not to be excluded from the winter bird food plants are several small thicket-forming shrubs that are planted mainly for ornament and soil erosion control. Among these, coralberry (*Symphoricarpos orbiculatus*) is especially well suited for planting on steep slopes and other difficult sites. Its purplish-red corallike berries cling to twigs through the winter. The fruit is seldom taken by songbirds but is sometimes eaten with relish by ruffed grouse, ring-necked pheasants, and other game birds. Much the same can be said of snowberry (*S. albus*), another small shrub with persistent fruit. The fruits are white, quite showy, but perhaps of little food value. Birds seldom eat them unless hard-pressed.

The same uses and drawbacks apply almost equally well to the chokeberries (*Aronia* spp.). The red or black fruits, depending upon the species, are apt to hang on through the winter until they become almost raisinlike. Yet it is plants like coralberry, snowberry, and chokeberry that so often come to the rescue of birds caught by late spring snowstorms. During times of dire emergency birds are not finicky about what they eat. I have been told of robins stuffing themselves on chokeberries during a March snowstorm.

The junipers are evergreen shrubs whose symmetry and tidy appearance make them ideal for foundation planting. Nurserymen have given us so many forms and varieties that it is difficult to know which ones to choose. We can have anything from low prostrate forms to tall columnar treelike types. In most cases the parent stock can be traced either to our native red cedar (*Juniperus virginiana*) or to Chinese juniper (*J. chinensis*). Other stock can be traced to common juniper (*J. communis*) as well as several others. All the junipers provide excellent cover and good nesting sites for birds. It is more difficult to recommend ones best suited as bird food plants. The fruits cling to plants all winter and our native red cedar is sometimes with ripe fruit the year round. Ordinarily birds clean out the supply well before the end of winter. Users include flickers, sapsuckers, crows, bluebirds, mockingbirds, robins, waxwings, starlings, yellow-rumped warblers, red-winged blackbirds, cardinals, purple finches, and white-throated sparrows. The red cedar is one of the most popular of all winter bird food plants. There is less use by birds of the many ornamental varieties, but Pfitzer juniper, a commonly planted variety of Chinese juniper, is well patronized by mockingbirds, robins, and cedar waxwings.

In *Beyond the Bird Feeder*, I suggested that we make more use of fencerow plants. I described them as more drought- and disease-resistant than most plants we buy and added that they are adapted to our local soil and climate conditions. These benefits most certainly apply to our native red cedar and also equally well to the sumacs. Somehow the sumacs (*Rhus* spp.), with their picturesque habit and brilliant fall coloring, have caught on better as ornamental plants in Britain, where they are not native, than with us. Although not everyone agrees that sumacs are highly rated bird food plants, I have noticed good usage by birds from about November onward. A correspondent in Ontario reported no fewer than fourteen species feeding on sumac fruits from October 25 until May 25. The fuzzy reddish fruits, which grow in candelabra-like clusters, however, seem to be in greatest demand when snow lies deep on the ground. Toward the end of winter, when few other foods are available, the sumacs are often the most important lifesavers of all.

What has been said of the sumacs applies almost equally well to the bayberries or wax myrtles (*Myrica* spp.). For the most part seashore or lakeshore plants, the bayberries are beginning to gain popularity for use in landscaping. Their waxy evergreen or nearly evergreen leaves and clusters of even more waxy small gray fruits make these shrubs desirable for home planting. As with the sumacs, bird use extends over a long period. Along the coast, bayberry is one of the most important winter bird food plants. Users include tree swallows, flickers, bluebirds, and yellow-rumped warblers. As in the hollies and many sumacs, there are male and female plants.

Among the small trees, the crab apples and hawthorns are generally thought of as extending their harvests no later than the fall months. While this is generally true, fruits on some trees, especially those of certain species, do cling to branches well into winter. Among the crab apples, two of the best for winter birds are Zumi crab (*Malus zumi calocarpa*) and the 'Bob White' variety of Siberian crab (*M. baccata*). The fruits of the crab apples are in reality miniature apples, small enough to be easily consumed by robins, waxwings, and many other birds. We use the fruit for making jellies.

Birds take to the fruits of the hawthorns with about the same eagerness as they do to the crab apples. One of the most commonly planted hawthorns is Washington thorn (*Crataegus phaenopyrum*), which also happens to be the best for winter ornament and bird food. I've seen cedar waxwings and house finches taking the fruit of this haw as early as late October. Nevertheless, if the crop is large enough, there is likely to be some left over for birds during the winter. This is particularly true where Washington thorn is planted in large numbers as a street tree. Two other haws that sometimes can be counted on for winter bird food are glossy hawthorn (*C. nitida*) and cockspur thorn (*C. crus-galli*).

*Catbird perched on bayberry branch*

If space is left for larger trees or we already have some in our yard, it is well to remember that there are a number that are good suppliers of winter bird food. But if we have just begun to plant, it is debatable whether to devote space to smaller plants or a tree that will overshadow everything. To be sure, trees have many values, including shade and a certain grandeur not to be found in lesser plants. But looking at the question only from a bird-attracting standpoint, we should ask ourselves if the tree provides food, shelter, and nesting sites. If it does, our tree may be a better investment than the shrubs which would occupy the same space. This is likely to be true of trees that produce cones, catkins, or seed pods. The seed-bearers will attract a somewhat different group of birds than plants with fruits or berries. Chickadees, nuthatches, and most finches, for example, respond more readily to winged seeds than they do to fruits. By having both trees and shrubs, we attract a greater variety of birds than we would with only one or the other.

Keeping their seeds safely hidden in cones or catkins through the fall and part of the winter, pines, spruces, larches, hemlocks, white cedars (arborvitaes), alders, and birches shed their seeds slowly and thereby sustain wildlife over a long period of time. Squirrels by gnawing and crossbills by prying out seeds with their scissorlike bills are among the first to sample the harvest. As they mature, cones and catkins open wider, and woodpeckers, nuthatches, and small finches come to the trees to claim their share. Other birds will be waiting for the seeds that fall to the ground. This woodland cafeteria scene can be duplicated to some extent in our yards by having trees of the kinds mentioned. The fact that many of these trees have ornamental as well as wildlife value makes their presence all the more worthwhile.

In mentioning red cedar, as I have earlier, and arborvitae (*Thuja* spp.), I should point out that since there are so many small or dwarf forms, it is not always easy to distinguish between what is a tree and what is a shrub. If a tree, our arborvitae may grow to sixty feet and our red cedar to ninety feet. Obviously, if our yard is small, we may not be able to accommodate plants of this size. Always consider the eventual size a plant may reach; if we don't, we may find that everything else has been shaded out or dwarfed by large trees.

# SPRING

This is the time of the year when we look forward to the return of migrants that flew south in the fall and to the renewal of birdsong and the beginning of the nesting season. However, this is not the time to stop offering food. Winter has a way of suddenly returning in the form of a heavy snowfall accompanied by strong winds and freezing temperatures. Such returns of winter are normally expected in more northern states. The food that had been so plentiful in the form of emerging insects and other small invertebrates has disappeared. The dried fruits and berries still hanging from trees and shrubs are not likely to appease the appetites of hungry resident birds or to be enticing enough to attract migrants.

Fortunately, finches and some other birds have found a new source of food even before the first sunny days of spring. In spite of cold and snow, the early buds and blossoms of forsythia, lilac, and fragrant honeysuckle are available to birds from about February onward. Sometimes bushes are so heavily pruned by house finches that we are deprived of the full glory of their floral display. Even though we do not ordinarily plant these shrubs for the food they offer birds, it is nice to know that they come in handy during times of emergency. The same can be said of fruit trees, including peach, pear, apple, crab apple, cherry, and plum. All produce early buds well liked by birds. Modest pruning by birds is said to improve the harvest. Seldom is there a problem with over-pruning.

Sap is another food that birds can usually count on during a return of winter weather. Wherever sap begins to flow as a result of broken twigs and branches or the work of woodpeckers, birds of many kinds soon make their appearance. Nutritious and often pleasant-tasting, sap is an important food in early spring for hummingbirds and many other birds. Sap also attracts insects and this is sometimes of benefit to insectivorous birds. Early one spring, birds leaving my feeding station invariably went to a nearby sugar maple to sip the sweetish sap dripping from holes bored by a sapsucker. The holes that sapsuckers drill in nearly all trees, including maples, birches, and apple trees, may mar the appearance of the trees and sometimes seriously weaken them, but there is some compensation in the help given to birds during a difficult time of the year.

In addition to the dried fruits that may have outlasted the winter, there are a few fruits and berries that begin to ripen in the spring. In the South, thorny elaeagnus (*Elaeagnus pungens*) is a fall bloomer whose fruit appears in May. As with other members of the genus, the fruit is highly attractive to birds. Although not early enough to help birds during late snowstorms, February daphne (*Daphne mezereum*), true to its name, blooms in February. Bright red fruits, well liked by birds, begin to ripen in May. Buds, blossoms, and the early winged seeds of several elms, including American elm, invite the attention of birds during the spring months. Finally, rounding out the not overly sumptuous vegetable diet of birds in spring are the luscious fruits of the white mulberry (*Morus alba*). In the South, the fruits begin to ripen in April; in more northern states, in early June. Unlike red mulberry, whose fruits ripen in summer, white mulberry has only a short fruiting season.

*Mountain ash*

## SUMMER

By early June most of us have slowed or halted our bird-feeding operation and we no longer watch anxiously for a sudden change in the weather. As we can see from the behavior of birds, the nesting season is in full swing. A few uncertain youngsters are already out of the nest and begging food from their hard-pressed parents. The demand for food to fill gaping mouths is so great that we are likely to forgive parent birds for the raids they make upon our strawberry patch or early-fruiting cherry trees. If we have gone out of our way to please, we may have planted berry-bearing shrubs to assist birds at this time of the year.

Higan cherry (*Prunus subhirtella*), with small black cherries ripening in June, is a good plant to grow for early-nesting birds. Equally

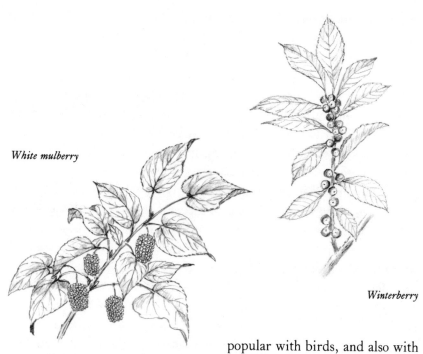

*White mulberry*

*Winterberry*

popular with birds, and also with squirrels and chipmunks, are our native serviceberries. Shadbush or downy serviceberry (*Amelanchier canadensis*) is the most common species. Even before the fruits ripen in late June, birds and small mammals begin their harvesting. Overshadowed by American elderberry, a late summer and fall producer of black fruits well liked by birds, is the early-blooming and early-fruiting scarlet elderberry (*Sambucus pubens*). Well suited to cooler, more northern sections, this elderberry is quite decorative and should be planted much more than it is.

At the risk of red stains from bird droppings on pavements and clothes drying on lines, we may be willing to have one of the best summer bird-attracting plants of all—the red mulberry (*Morus rubra*). With a long fruiting season from June into August, this small tree is a bird cafeteria par excellence. I have seen as many as twenty bird species in one of these trees when the fruit is ripe. Mammal feeders include raccoons, possums, squirrels, and chipmunks.

The buckthorns are a more recent addition to the gardener's list of good summer bird food plants. Alder buckthorn (*Rhamnus frangula*) and its variety *columnaris* are now commonly offered by nurseries. The plants have dark green foliage and a steady succession of small white flowers and fruits through the summer. The small fruits, as they ripen, turn from green to red and finally to black. Not only are the fruits decorative but they are almost as popular with birds as the mulberries. Other buckthorns, including coffeeberry (*R. californica*) in the West and common buckthorn (*R. cathartica*) in the East, have about the same ornamental and bird-attracting qualities as the alder and can be considered an addition to the garden. It must be admitted, however, that in some places the buckthorns are being spread far and wide by birds and are coming to be regarded as weeds.

Although the dogwoods are commonly thought of as fall-fruiting, two species, suitable for planting in the yard, have fruits that ripen in summer. Gray dogwood (*Cornus racemosa*) and red osier dogwood (*C. sericea*), both natives, are shrubby, thicket-forming species that are well suited for streamside planting or for providing escape cover for wildlife. Both produce white fruits that are well liked by birds.

The honeysuckle genus *Lonicera* provides us with both vines and large shrubs with attractive flowers and fruits. Called bush honeysuckles, the large shrubs supply birds with excellent cover, nesting sites, and food in the form of bright red berries. The summer-fruiting Tatarian honeysuckle (*L. tatarica*) and the very similar Morrow honeysuckle (*L. morrowii*) not only are widely used as hedges and garden plants but have been spread by birds into wild habitats. The bush honeysuckles fruit so prolifically in late summer that birds scarcely dent the harvest.

Before moving on to late-season food plants for birds, I should point out that in late summer and early fall vacant lots, roadsides, railroad embankments, overgrown fields, and woodlots offer birds such a profusion of ripe fruits that our yards are sometimes deserted. Visit these wild areas and it will soon be obvious that birds have made their own choices in regard to what they prefer to eat at this time of the year. If it is not wild grapes, blackberries, elderberries, wild cherries, or our native viburnums, it may be exotic plants, such as bush honeysuckles, that have escaped into the wild. This is a season of plenty when birds seem slowest to respond to the food we have to offer.

# FALL

By early fall, if not sooner, birds of many species will have gathered into flocks. Whether in closely knit flocks, like those of red-winged blackbirds, grackles, starlings, or cedar waxwings, or in loose flocks, like those of robins, birds will sooner or later invade our yard. In early fall, flocks are not apt to overrun feeding stations, for artificial foods normally do not have this much appeal until the arrival of cold weather and snow. As long as natural foods are plentiful, the flocks will be visiting woodland borders, open fields, barnyards, and other places where grain, weed seeds, oak mast, and wild fruits and berries are easily obtained.

If we live in a well-wooded suburb, small town, or somewhere in the country, we will sooner or later be visited by gregarious birds of the kinds mentioned. One fall a clatter on my rooftop that sounded like falling hailstones told me that a large flock of grackles was harvesting acorns in nearby oak trees. The noise came from the empty husks and partially eaten meats raining down from the trees. On another occasion, the hard seed pits of fruits of a large flowering dogwood in our yard caused a similar clatter. This time the harvesters were robins and starlings.

Our concern when large flocks of birds discover food sources in our yard is that they will quickly exhaust the supply and leave nothing for later use. Although birds do sometimes exhaust a supply, as I have mentioned earlier, a certain shrub or tree may be completely stripped while nearby a plant of exactly the same species is left untouched until much later. I recall that one fall a large red cedar at the edge of a cemetery near where we live in Maryland was patronized for several days by robins and other flocking species. Working from the top of the tree downward, the birds methodically stripped the entire tree of a heavy crop of berries. Yet other red cedars nearby were scarcely touched at all, their fruit left for later in the season when the need would be greater.

My feeling about plants for fall bird food is that I am not going to use up valuable space on trees or shrubs unless they are outstanding from an ornamental standpoint. Otherwise I will reserve the space for winter bird food plants as well as some for spring and summer. My rationale is based upon planting for times of the year when birds most need the food. Certainly winter and early spring, with so much severe weather coupled with a scarcity of natural foods, is a time when birds are hard-pressed. Again, when young are in the nest or being fledged, substantial sources of food are vital if it is to be a successful nesting season. In late summer and fall, there is no such pressing need and natural plant foods are at the peak of their abundance. At this time of the year I supply birds with food primarily because of the pleasure they give me.

Of the plants that meet my difficult standards in the fall, flowering dogwood (*Cornus florida*) is one that easily makes the grade. This small tree has such gorgeous blossoms in spring and bright red fruits in early fall that I wouldn't want to omit it. Almost equally handsome are such other dogwoods as the Japanese dogwood (*C. kousa*) with its strange raspberrylike fruits and another imitator, the cornelian cherry (*C. mas*)

*Cardinal and autumn olive*

with largish cherrylike fruits. Two other species to consider are Siberian dogwood (*C. alba*) with white or bluish-white berries and alternate-leaved dogwood (*C. alternifolia*) with dark blue berries.

The viburnums are such good bird food plants and so decorative that I can always find space for one or two more. I've already mentioned the highbush cranberries, whose fruits cling to the bushes all winter. I would place our native arrowwood (*Viburnum dentatum*) with its blue fruits at the top of the list. The plants do well in our yard in Nantucket. But I haven't the space for Siebold viburnum (*V. sieboldii*), a large shrub with handsome fruits that first turn red and then black. Birds eagerly consume the harvest as soon as it ripens. Whichever viburnum does well in the region where you live is probably the one to plant if you have the space for it. There is a long list to choose from.

Large size does not deter me from growing the autumn olive (*Elaeagnus umbellata*). Reaching a height of about twelve feet, autumn olive is somewhat sprawling but has handsome green leaves with a silvery sheen and small reddish fruits in the fall. Birds begin taking them as soon as they are ripe. I have four bushes in our yard in Nantucket. Not to be confused with autumn olive is a larger member of the genus, Russian olive (*E. angustifolia*). Once acclaimed as a splendid plant for bird food, Russian olive, in spite of handsome silvery willowlike leaves, is too ungainly and therefore has been superseded by the smaller, more shapely autumn olive.

Still limiting my search to handsome ornamentals, I cannot refrain from mentioning the mountain ashes. Small trees adapted to cool climates, the mountain ashes have such showy clusters of red or orange (white in a few species) fruits that they serve to dress up any yard. If the fruits are not consumed in the fall by cedar waxwings and flocking species, they will hang on the trees for a long time and provide a touch of color around Christmastime. The most commonly planted of these trees is European mountain ash (*Sorbus aucuparia*).

The flowering crab apples look their best when they are covered with blossoms in the spring. Depending upon the species, the flowers may be white, pink, or red. The fruits also vary in color from species to species. The red-fruited Sargent crab apple (*Malus sargentii*) is a shrub reaching a height of only six to eight feet and therefore is suitable for small yards. The Japanese flowering crab apple (*M. floribunda*) with pink to reddish flowers and red fruits is a favorite of mockingbirds, cedar waxwings, and various northern finches. Several of the crab apples, as I have mentioned, hold their fruit well into winter. I should not overlook our common apple tree, which is a member of the same genus. Although not regarded as a handsome ornamental, the apple tree is so picturesque-looking and so well liked by birds that even aging specimens should be preserved. The fruit, buds, and blossoms are utilized by ruffed grouse, cedar waxwings, and a number of finches.

The cotoneasters are handsome plants well suited to rock gardens and can be used to line walks or, in the case of rock spray (*Cotoneaster horizontalis*), to espalier against a house or stone wall. In Britain, where cotoneasters are very popular, they rank as one of the more important fall bird food plants. The same would probably apply with us as well if cotoneasters were planted more often. With so many other ornamentals with equally colorful fruits, we tend to do without them. In a way this is unfortunate. With their many uses and bright red fruits in most species, they add a splash of color and receive a modest amount of attention from birds.

No summary of fall bird food plants would be complete without mention of the greatest food producers of all—the mast-bearers. In this group are the oaks, hickories, walnuts, pecans, beeches, hornbeams, and several others. Since most birds cannot break through the hard shells or seed cases of anything as tough as hickories or walnuts, the harvest is largely left to squirrels and other rodents. But many woodpeckers, nuthatches, and jays are able to break open the seed cases of softer-shelled varieties. Sometimes motor vehicles crush nuts that have fallen from trees and in this way, and other ways as well, a large portion of the wildlife community is able to join the feast when there is a good mast crop. But the mast-bearing trees are notably unreliable. Some years the crop is excellent, other years there may be none at all. Therefore, in terms of a steady harvest for birds, we should not place too much confidence in the oaks and other mast producers. This is why I have put much more emphasis upon plants that annually produce a crop of fruits or berries.

It would be convenient, after listing these many plants that provide food for birds at various times of the year, if I could name five or ten that were tops and could be recommended without qualification. Unfortunately, few plants are suited to all types of soil and all the moisture, temperature, and other climatic conditions that exist throughout North

America. Therefore, to a large extent, our choice is limited to plants that do well locally. Out of the many possible choices I have provided, probably only half would do well, say, in southern California or Maine.

Birds are not difficult to please. All of the plants I have listed have a sizable number of bird patrons. Some of them, like the mockingbird, robin, and cedar waxwing, are found from coast to coast; others, like the Bohemian waxwing and Townsend's solitaire, are limited in their distribution to the West. Still others, like the evening grosbeak and purple finch, breed in the North from coast to coast and move quite far south some winters and not so far in others.

We never know which of the migrants or nomadic wanderers will visit our yards or when. That is part of the fun. We can be sure, however, that with suitable plantings birds will visit our yards and that some will stay on and on. It takes time and a certain amount of experimentation to find out which plants bear well and serve the needs of our guests. We learn as we go and there is always room for improvement.

# 4 / Nesting Sites for Birds

One of the surest and best ways to increase the bird population is to offer suitable nesting sites. This can be done on even the smallest properties. By providing birdhouses and the right assortment of plants, we can significantly increase the nesting population. Moreover, we can play a decisive role in determining which species we will have nesting with us. There is nothing wrong with showing favoritism. After all, it is partly through man's mistakes and thoughtlessness that some birds have become too numerous

*Flicker at nest hole*

for their own good and ours, while others have decreased. If we can help birds that are losing out in the struggle, I see no reason why we shouldn't so long as we use non-lethal methods. We have already seen how we can manipulate our bird-feeding program so as to favor less aggressive birds and native species over introduced ones. We can do much the same in providing nesting sites.

Birds can be divided into three groups on the basis of their choice of nesting sites: (1) ground nesting, (2) cavity and ledge nesting, and (3) plant nesting.

Chances are that the ground-nesters will be the most poorly represented in our yard. Birds in this group either need more cover than most of us have if they are to nest or require wide-open expanses of lawn, fields, or meadow. Certain of the waterfowl, gallinaceous birds, towhees, and song sparrow need cover in the form of tall grass, weedy tangles, brush piles, or ground beneath low overhanging limbs. On the other hand, the more open the yard is, the better for nesting killdeer, horned lark, meadowlark, and bobolink.

If we live near a lake or pond, there is always the chance of nesting mallards or other waterfowl. Ducks greatly prefer nesting on a small island rather than on the mainland. Here they will be safer from romping dogs and predators. By making provision for a small island in a pond, we should have good luck in attracting nesting ducks. It helps to start out with a few domestic ducks. These will act as decoys to bring in the wild ones. Habitat conditions for waterfowl of all kinds will be improved if the island and borders of the pond are allowed to grow up in reeds and other wetland vegetation.

The gallinaceous birds, including quail, pheasants, and grouse, make up one of the largest groups of ground-nesters. Several have adapted to man and his habitats and use hedgerows, overgrown fence-rows, and even garden shrubbery as nesting cover. The bobwhite, whose cheery call notes are heard throughout much of the East, sometimes surprises us by nesting close to our house. Arthur C. Bent, in his "life histories," tells of spending several days weeding and mowing without being aware of the presence nearby of a bobwhite nesting at the edge of his garden. The hen on her nest must be violently disturbed before she will leave her eggs. The ring-necked pheasant is equally hard to flush. Relying upon protective coloration, the hen will stay on her eggs even if we pass by within a few feet of her. This pheasant commonly nests on the outskirts of small towns and near farmhouses.

In the West, the California quail provides a good example of a game bird that has become "domesticated." In *The California Quail*, A. Starker Leopold states that if suitable cover is available, this quail will nest in residential areas and that it adapts well and quickly to coexistence with people. He mentions nesting populations in brushy or wooded areas in the heart of Berkeley, California, and along riverbanks in the center of residential Reno, Nevada. According to Leopold, a tangle of blackberry vines twenty feet in diameter and six feet tall makes a perfect nesting and escape cover for the California quail. Almost equally good are ornamental plantings containing toyon (*Heteromeles arbutifolia*), pyracantha, and holly. Leopold states that although nesting success was low for suburban quail, there were usually enough young to maintain satisfactory population levels. The birds are easily attracted to feeding stations.

Some ground-nesting birds make no nest at all but scoop out a small depression to hold the eggs. In the killdeer, the male makes a number of small depressions, known as scrapes, and the female selects one of these as a place to lay her eggs. The edge of the scrape may or may not be lined with pebbles or bits of debris of various kinds. So long as the nesting site is in the open away from trees, the killdeer will use any number of habitats in or close to built-up districts. These include playing fields, vacant lots, cemeteries, parking lots, roadsides, lawns, and cultivated fields.

The ground dove of southeastern states and more southern portions of the West does not, as a rule, nest on the ground. Hal H. Harrison, in his *Field Guide to Birds' Nests,* states that of forty-five nests examined by him on Sanibel Island in Florida, none were on the ground. Nevertheless, if this exceptionally tame little dove is living near us, we can expect to find its nest almost anywhere on or near the ground.

The goatsuckers, which include the common nighthawk, chuck-will's-widow, whip-poor-will, and poor-will, build no nest at all. The eggs are laid directly on the bare ground, on pebbles, leaves, or whatever the ground may be covered with. Beginning in 1869, nighthawks were observed nesting on flat rooftops in cities. The habit spread to such an extent that rooftop nesting is now almost as characteristic of the nighthawk as chimney nesting in the chimney swift. Only if we have a flat rooftop will we have much chance of having nesting nighthawks. The whip-poor-will and other nocturnal birds in this group are best known for their repetitive calls heard throughout long summer nights. Even though the bird doing the calling may be outside our window, it is unlikely that the nest will be in our yard. A wilder, quieter habitat is required.

The horned lark nests in much the same kind of habitats as the killdeer. The well-disguised nest of leaves and grasses may be built on open ground in parks, cemeteries, golf courses, playgrounds, and airfields.

The horned lark and meadowlark have little in common except that they nest on the ground in open country. A member of the blackbird family, the meadowlark builds a dome-shaped nest of grasses which blends in so well with its pasture or hayfield habitat that it is almost impossible to see. Another pastureland species, the bobolink, may be nesting in the same field. We are unlikely to have either nesting very near us.

In the two large families to which the sparrows and finches belong, the only ground-nesters likely to nest in our yards are the towhees and song sparrow. The towhees place their nests either on the ground near cover or in low shrubs and vines. This is true of both the green-tailed towhee, a western species, and the rufous-sided towhee, a common bird found from coast to coast. The song sparrow is one of the more common nesting birds of yards and gardens. The first nest of the season is likely to be in a protected area on the ground. Later nests of the song sparrow are built in vines or lower branches of trees and shrubs. The change to elevated nesting is related to the leafing out of plants as the season advances. The birds can now find better concealment for the nests at sites above the ground.

Obviously, in a suburban garden it is not easy to duplicate conditions that will meet the needs of most ground-nesting birds. This is particularly true for small properties without much open ground. But with cavity- and ledge-nesting birds, we have far greater opportunities. One of the early experiments in attracting birds in this group was described by Gilbert Grosvenor in the National Geographic Society's *Book of Birds*. After buying a property on the outskirts of Washington, D.C., in 1913, Dr. Grosvenor set about putting up birdhouses, supplying water for birds, and, as he put it, "shooting house sparrows and driving away cats." After several seasons, the nesting bird population had increased so much that he suspected that his property might hold a national record for number of breeding birds. A census conducted by the Biological Survey proved him to be correct. The fifty-nine pairs of nesting birds counted on one acre surrounding his house proved to be a new record. Of the twelve species breeding on the one acre, seven were

*Ground nest of rufous-sided towhee*

birds that built open nests in plants: the eastern kingbird, catbird, robin, yellow warbler, orchard oriole, chipping sparrow, and song sparrow. But cavity- and ledge-nesting birds, with only five species, accounted for 73 percent of the nesting pairs listed in the count!

The reason that this group made such a spectacular showing was the presence of birdhouses. Dr. Grosvenor had set up several martin houses and a large number of wren houses. Of the cavity-nesters, purple martins accounted for twenty-six nesting pairs and house wrens for fourteen nesting pairs. The other cavity-nesters, the flicker and the bluebird, accounted for one nesting pair each. The only typical ledge-nester was the eastern phoebe with one pair counted.

By using birdhouses, we too can establish a large population of cavity-nesting birds on our property. Since Dr. Grosvenor's time, apartment-style martin houses, reminding us of condominiums, have been designed to accommodate as many as a hundred nesting pairs per house. Where such houses are fully tenanted, it is possible to have several times the nesting population that was counted on one acre on the

Grosvenor property. However, it is not only numbers but variety that is of special interest to most of us.

To lure cavity- and ledge-nesting birds we need various kinds of nesting sites. A combination of birdhouses and other artificial sites to supplement natural cavities in trees will provide something for all cavity-nesters from swallows to wrens. Not to be overlooked are any outbuildings on our property, such as a work shed, garage, or barn. If birds can gain access to such buildings through open doors or windows, they will almost certainly find crannies or ledges where they can build their nests. Likely tenants will include feral pigeons, swallows, phoebes, wrens, starlings, and house sparrows. While not all of the birds in this group may rate highly with us, we should certainly have no qualms about welcoming some of them. Cliff and barn swallows, with their swift flight and ability to catch small flying insects, are highly favored by nearly everyone. Now that old-fashioned barns are being torn down or repaired and painted, cliff and barn swallows are finding fewer places to nest. Both, to a large degree, have deserted their former cliff or cave nesting sites. When barns are painted, the wood becomes too smooth to hold the cliff swallow's mud nests. We should also have no reservations about welcoming phoebes and wrens. Both are highly insectivorous and will build their nests in interiors of sheds and other buildings. Two other cavity- or ledge-nesters, the barn owl and the kestrel, are possible tenants whose tastes for rats and mice should make them the most welcomed guests of all. Although kestrels will nest in both barns and birdhouses, it generally takes a barn or silo to accommodate the barn owl.

Decaying or partially hollow trees will attract a number of the species already mentioned as well as the screech owl, woodpeckers, crested flycatcher, chickadees, titmice, nuthatches, bluebird, and, if we are lucky, the wood duck. The woodpeckers are the architects, carving out cavities which they themselves use and which are frequently taken over later on by other cavity-nesting species. But older trees of the kind needed by birds in this group are in short supply these days. We do not come upon many trees such as the one described by Alexander Sprunt, Jr., in which five pairs of hole-nesting birds were actively nesting at the same time. As indicated in the woodpecker volume in the Bent series, the tree, in Beaufort, South Carolina, was presumably quite old and decayed, and only twenty feet tall. The occupants included two pairs of flickers and one pair each of screech owl, downy woodpecker, and crested flycatcher.

To make up for shortages of trees like this one, we can take measures to accommodate a sizable population of cavity- and ledge-nesting birds. The trick is to erect birdhouses and nest shelves. Like feeding stations and birdbaths, these entail responsibilities. We can't just put up nesting facilities and forget about them. Houses need to be cleaned, repaired, and monitored. The neglected birdhouse may be taken over by meadow mice, wasps, or birds that rate far down the list in our esteem.

Therefore, before setting up birdhouses, we should decide which species we are out to attract. Normally, if we are to be successful, we should plan around the cavity- and ledge-nesting birds we have in our neighborhood. For example, bluebirds rarely nest within the limits of towns and cities. They learned long ago that they would be subjected to too much competition from starlings and house sparrows in densely populated districts. Therefore, if we are to help the bluebirds, we must erect houses for them in rural areas. Within the last several decades, housing for bluebirds has become almost a passion with dedicated groups of bird lovers. In every state and most provinces of Canada, hundreds of bluebird trails have been established. Placing houses on fence posts and other handy sites along country roads, those managing bluebird trails frequently check their houses to determine nesting success and see that the houses are not being taken over by undesirable species. Houses are kept in good repair and old nesting material removed after the nesting season is over in order to discourage parasites. Thanks to bluebird trails, this once vanishing species is making a comeback in many parts of the country.

Purple martins, better able to withstand the assaults of starlings and house sparrows, are still common residents of many towns and cities. In the East, the purple martin has become wholly dependent upon homes erected by man; in the West this swallow primarily uses cavities in dead trees. While we can always hope to bring these birds to our yard with the help of a modern, many-compartment martin house, our luck may not be with us if there is no history of martins nesting in our neighborhood. The birds are slow to accept new localities, tending to return year after year to the same nest sites. A house placed on a pole in a broad lawn or a field or near a pond is apt to be favored over one in a more confined site. This is because martins do their feeding by gliding over open areas where they can best catch insects. In many places martins are highly valued for their services in catching mosquitoes.

Once we have determined which species we are likely to have the best luck with, we need to start thinking about houses and their placement. We can buy houses built especially for the birds we have in mind or we can build our own. Whichever the case, the house should be designed to suit the tenant. If building our own houses, we should consult plans that give measurements of the entrance hole and each piece that goes into the construction of the house. For precise details of this kind, I would strongly recommend *The Birdhouse Book* by Don Mc-Neil. In this volume, the reader will find detailed instructions on how to make houses for most cavity-nesting species and also directions for making shelf nest sites for barn swallows, phoebes, robins, and song sparrows. McNeil also provides advice on how to deal with starlings and house sparrows.

Starlings and house sparrows cannot enter birdhouses with entrance hole openings smaller than their body diameters. Houses with openings an inch and one-eighth in diameter normally exclude house

*Cliff swallows and nests*

sparrows but give access to wrens, chickadees, titmice, and nuthatches. Houses with openings an inch and one-half in diameter exclude starlings but give access to bluebirds and swallows. Therefore, we can cater to many smaller hole-nesting birds without interference from starlings and house sparrows.

The house sparrow, after reaching peak numbers during the second decade of this century, has been undergoing a steady decline. In many areas, there is no longer a danger that it will puncture eggs, kill nestlings, and otherwise destroy the nests of other birds. It has definitely become a minority species, much more subdued than it was, and often not a threat to other hole-nesting birds.

Starlings are particularly a menace to flickers, other woodpeckers, and crested flycatchers. A pair will tirelessly harass the rightful owners of a nest cavity until these birds give up and go elsewhere. Although starlings seem to be declining somewhat in numbers, their pressure upon native hole-nesting birds remains. In some places they are expanding their breeding range into wilderness areas and therefore are becoming a serious threat to nesting wood ducks.

Although colony-nesting species, like purple martins and other

*Bluebird box on fence post*

swallows, will occupy houses in close proximity to each other, most other hole-nesting birds are not this tolerant and maintain territories from which they drive other birds of the same species. For this reason, houses for bluebirds, crested flycatchers, and most other hole-nesters should be spaced quite far apart, usually at least a hundred feet apart. However, as shown by figures supplied by Dr. Grosvenor, house wrens are reasonably tolerant toward near neighbors. He had nesting pairs within fifteen feet of each other. The robin, which either builds an open nest in a tree or uses a ledge, was nesting only twelve yards apart on the Grosvenor property, with no fewer than seven pairs nesting on the one acre adjoining his house.

With few exceptions, birdhouses should be placed in open or semi-open areas, especially those for the purple martin and other swallows and the bluebird. Woodland edges, fencerows, sheltered sites near houses, and almost any other place that receives some protection from the wind as well as sunlight through part of the day are suitable sites for most birdhouses. Only a few woodland species, like the wood duck and the screech owl, readily accept houses within the forest itself. For our own convenience and also for best results generally, houses should be placed about three to five feet from the ground. Purple martin houses are an exception and should be placed on poles about ten feet above the ground. If at all possible, wood duck houses should be on poles over water for extra protection against ground-dwelling predators.

The third and largest group of nesting birds is made up of those that build in trees, shrubs, woody vines, and herbaceous plants. This group is as diverse in its choice of nesting sites as it is in makeup of species. Some, like the orioles, suspend their nests from the outer tips of branches. Others, like the vireos, construct their nests in the "V" formed by forked twigs. Others, like the catbird and the cardinal, build well within the depths of dense shrubbery. Still other birds, like the blue-gray gnatcatcher, the wood pewee, and many hummingbirds, fasten their nests to the upper surfaces of branches. But whatever site is selected, the nest is normally so well hidden that we are unlikely to know of its existence. To make the nest even more invisible, many birds use moss, lichens, and other bits of plant debris to camouflage the outside surface of the nest. Hummingbird nests are so well camouflaged with materials of this kind that they look like nothing more than a swelling or lump on the branch of a tree. Now and then a hummingbird departs from its standard lichen or moss disguise and uses something else. Hal Harrison, in his guide to western birds' nests, has a photograph of an Allen's hummingbird nest that was decorated with chips of green paint from nearby picnic tables.

Winter is the best time to look for bird nests. Except for nests in evergreens, most are now easy to see. Contrary to what we may expect, there may even be an occasional occupied nest in the middle of winter. Many hawks and owls begin their nesting activities as early as January or February. The crossbills, far northern birds with twisted, scissorlike bills adapted for extracting seeds from cones, also may nest in winter. But if we live in a more developed or urban part of the United States, any large bulky nest seen high in a tree in winter is more likely to be occupied by a squirrel than a bird.

To accommodate plant-nesting birds, we need not only a variety of trees, shrubs, and vines, but also plants in various stages of growth. Trees still in the sapling stage are favored by such birds as the white-eyed vireo, yellow warbler, red-winged blackbird, indigo bunting, and goldfinch. As the tree becomes larger, the early tenants are likely to be replaced by birds of other species, such as the eastern kingbird, robin, and orioles. Warbling vireos and cerulean warblers build very high up in tall trees. Nesting successions of this kind, with never a time when there are no potential tenants, continue throughout the life of the tree. Finally, if the tree is left standing after it dies, it becomes, as we have seen, the residence of a long list of cavity-nesting species.

For the most part, birds, unlike most insects, are able to utilize a wide variety of plant species for reproductive purposes. The robin is one of the least particular of our garden birds about where it nests. It will accept a large proportion of the trees and shrubs used in yard and street plantings; sometimes it places its nest on beams and ledges of buildings. But some of its sites may be more a matter of necessity than choice. Not always can it find the kinds of trees or shrubs that will properly support the nest and at the same time provide concealment from enemies. Given the opportunity, robins will choose American elm, box elder, maples, apple, hawthorn, Scotch pine, white pine, spruce, and closely similar trees over any others. The catbird, much more particular about its choice of nest site, will normally pick a hawthorn or multiflora rose, if any of these prickly plants are present.

Probably the best way to meet the needs of nesting birds is to supply them with a wide choice of nesting sites. To help determine the plants that will best serve their needs, I have selected four groups from the Cornell nest card records. These records, housed at the Cornell Laboratory of Ornithology, Ithaca, New York, contain information on nests and breeding data gathered from all over the United States and Canada.

The first group consists of plants that harbored at least twenty or more nesting species (all of them birds known to nest near houses). The plant name is followed by the names of any birds that nest rather consistently in that particular plant. The absence of a listing of birds after a given plant indicates that no species consistently nested in that plant.

Group II consists of plants that harbored between fifteen and nineteen nesting species; the plants in Group III sheltered between ten and fourteen nesting species. A final tabulation consists of plants known to be useful to nesting birds, but no attempt has been made to rate this group according to number of users.

### GROUP I

Apple (*Malus pumila*): eastern kingbird, blue jay, robin, cedar waxwing

Elm (*Ulmus* spp.): western kingbird, blue jay, northern oriole, American goldfinch

Hackberry (*Celtis* spp.): western kingbird, scissor-tailed flycatcher

Hawthorn (*Crataegus* spp.): black-billed cuckoo, eastern kingbird, catbird, brown thrasher, robin, wood thrush, cedar waxwing, yellow warbler, cardinal, rose-breasted grosbeak, American goldfinch

Maple (*Acer* spp.): robin, wood thrush, northern oriole, American goldfinch

Oak (*Quercus* spp.): eastern pewee, blue jay, mockingbird, wood thrush

Pine (*Pinus* spp.): Anna's hummingbird, blue jay, robin, house finch, chipping sparrow

Red cedar (*Juniperus virginiana*): yellow-billed cuckoo, blue jay, mockingbird, brown thrasher, cedar waxwing, common grackle, cardinal, American goldfinch, rufous-sided towhee, chipping sparrow

Willow (*Salix* spp.): Anna's hummingbird, eastern kingbird, yellow warbler, red-winged blackbird

### GROUP II

Ash (*Fraxinus* spp.)

Blackberry (*Rubus* spp.): cardinal, indigo bunting

Black locust (*Robinia pseudoacacia*): western kingbird, American goldfinch

Box elder (*Acer negundo*): robin

Chinese elm (*Ulmus parvifolia*): robin

Cottonwood (*Populus* spp.): western kingbird, northern oriole

Juniper (*Juniperus* spp.): Brewer's blackbird, cardinal, house finch, chipping sparrow

Spruce (*Picea* spp.): mourning dove, blue jay, robin, chipping sparrow

White pine (*Pinus strobus*): mourning dove, robin

### GROUP III

American elm (*Ulmus americana*): robin, northern oriole

Arborvitae (*Thuja* spp.): mockingbird, cedar waxwing

Blue spruce (*Picea pungens*): mourning dove, house finch

Cherry (*Prunus* spp.)

Crab apple (*Malus* spp.)

Dogwood (*Cornus* spp.): wood thrush, American goldfinch

Hemlock (*Tsuga* spp.): wood thrush

Lilac (*Syringa* spp.)

Mulberry (*Morus* spp.)

Multiflora rose (*Rosa multiflora*): catbird, brown thrasher, song sparrow

Norway spruce (*Picea abies*): robin

Pear (*Pyrus* spp.)

Plum (*Prunus* spp.): mockingbird

Poplar (*Populus* spp.): northern oriole
Privet (*Ligustrum* spp.): cardinal
Red maple (*Acer rubrum*)
Red oak (*Quercus rubra*)
Rose (*Rosa* spp.): yellow warbler
Scotch pine (*Pinus sylvestris*): robin, cedar waxwing
Sweet gum (*Liquidamber styraciflua*)
Sycamore (*Platanus* spp.): northern oriole

My final group is made up of plants reported in the Cornell nesting records, as well as plants that I have observed birds nesting in. The fact that this list comes last does not mean that these plants are less useful or dependable than the others. All are popular with nesting birds.

| | |
|---|---|
| Alder | Holly |
| Aspen | Honey locust |
| Barberry | Japanese honeysuckle |
| Birch | Linden |
| Black willow | Live oak |
| Bush honeysuckle | Mock orange |
| Douglas fir | Pyracantha |
| Elderberry | Raspberry |
| English ivy | Red pine |
| Flowering dogwood | Russian olive |
| Flowering plum | Silver maple |
| Forsythia | Sugar maple |
| Ginkgo | Sumac |
| Grape | Willow oak |
| Gray dogwood | Yew |
| Hickory | |

Looking at my four lists, I find that about 25 percent of the plants are evergreens, either cone-bearers like the pines or broad-leaved ones like English ivy or live oak. The evergreens offer a protected nesting place during the period in spring when deciduous trees are bare or not yet fully leaved. Some birds, like robins, are apt to choose an evergreen for their first nest and a non-evergreen for subsequent nests. Kinglets, as well as many warblers and finches, restrict their nest sites to cone-bearing evergreens. In the East, the purple finch confines itself entirely to nesting in cone-bearers, while in the Far West it may utilize deciduous plants as well. Common grackles usually nest in cone-bearing evergreens but sometimes spill over into maples, willows, and other deciduous plants.

The fact that some birds nest largely or solely in evergreens makes the inclusion of pines, hemlocks, arborvitae, yew, and others important in any planting scheme. But if the aim is a large and diverse nesting population, even more attention should be given to deciduous plants. My lists contain a wide selection of both to choose from. A suitable balance would be about three times as many deciduous nest plants in the yard as evergreens.

The importance of thorny plants as nest sites should not be overlooked. The hawthorns, with their sharp thorns on twigs and branches, are of first importance to many of the birds that visit our yards. The blackberries, which form dense, impenetrable tangles, make excellent nesting cover but are not well suited for landscaping. Better for decorative purposes, and also with more tempting fruit, are the raspberries. Their prickly stems also provide good nesting sites for birds. Other thorny bushes that are popular for nesting are multiflora rose, climbing roses, barberries, American holly, and pyracantha. Not entered in my lists because they are so restricted as to habitat are the cactuses with their imposing thorns. But many birds of the Southwest, including house finches and brown towhees, rely heavily upon cactus for nest sites. The giant saguaro cactus (*Cereus giganteus*) of the Arizona-Sonoran Desert is a veritable avian apartment house, with some birds, like doves, building their nests on the thorn-studded branches and others utilizing cavities excavated by woodpeckers. When a flicker or Gila woodpecker has completed its nest cavity, the gummy sap around the edges hardens, forming a perfect lining. The holes dug by the woodpeckers are occupied by many other cavity nesters, including elf and ferruginous owls.

Two other thorny plants that provide safe havens for a number of nesting birds are the honey locust (*Gleditsia triacanthos*), a native tree with a wide range in the East, and Osage orange (*Maclura pomifera*), a native small tree of Texas and Oklahoma once widely cultivated as a hedgerow plant. Not to be overlooked as a thorny ornamental for garden use is hardy orange (*Poncirus trifoliata*), a member of the citrus

*Western kingbird at nest*

family. Unlike its close relatives, it can be grown well outside the South and is reported to withstand winters as far north as Boston.

Slender, willowy branches, like those of birches, poplars, elms, and willows, make good nesting sites for a surprising number of birds. Some, like the orioles, with their woven basket nests, take advantage of outermost twigs as ideal places from which to suspend their nests. Others, like hummingbirds, kingbirds, scissor-tailed flycatcher, warbling vireo, yellow warbler, and American goldfinch, seem to prefer inner twigs and branches.

Even though the apple tree, maples, and oaks are lacking in thorns or other "security" features, they are popular with nesting birds. A possible reason is the roominess of these trees and the many crotches and forked branches that provide secure places on which to build nests. Many times, of course, the trees in question are about the only ones available. In such cases, the use of these trees is more a matter of necessity than preference.

Moderately trimmed privet, mock orange, lilac, rose, bush honeysuckle, and forsythia make good nesting sites for many of our garden birds. So long as these shrubs are not too open and scraggly or too impenetrable, birds readily use them for nesting purposes. Among the birds that find garden shrubs acceptable for nesting are the catbird, mockingbird, brown thrasher, cardinal, and towhees.

Concealment is of prime importance to some birds. The parula warbler, for example, nests only where it can find clumps of Spanish moss or *Usnea* lichen or, as I have noted along the Potomac above Washington, D.C., clusters of leaves or trash left behind in trees by floodwaters. Some birds will place their nests within the recesses of a clump of mistletoe. But selective nesting like this is far from being the rule. Most birds take their chances with the amount of concealment afforded by the leafy foliage of trees and shrubs or the needles of conifers. Red cedar, with its outer cover of prickly, needlelike leaves, makes one of the safest nesting refuges available to a large number of birds. This is good reason why this native tree is so popular with nesting birds.

Vines also make good nesting cover. Many times a vine climbing up a tree reinforces the shelter offered by needles or leafy foliage. Or again, a vine by itself climbing up a dead tree, a wall, or the side of a house may supply just the right support and protection for a bird's nest. Two of the most popular vines for nesting, as noted in the nest card records, are grape and English ivy. Among others commonly used by nesting birds are climbing rose, Virginia creeper, trumpet creeper, wisteria, and poison ivy. All but the last would be suitable for home yard planting. Vines harbor the nests of such birds as hummingbirds, mockingbird, cardinal, rufous-sided towhee, and song sparrow.

What better than a combination of trees, shrubs, and vines useful to nesting birds and the birds themselves with their song and good cheer!

# 5 / Hummingbirds and How to Attract Them

In their book *The World of Birds*, James Fisher and Roger Tory Peterson state that about a fifth of the world's birds are involved in flower pollination. To those of us who live in temperate zones and are accustomed to having our flowers pollinated by insects or the wind, this sounds like a farfetched statement. We tend to overlook the several large families of birds that visit flowers in the tropical parts of the world and, in some cases, spill over into temperate zones. The New World has its orioles belonging to the Icteridae, tanagers, honeycreepers, and hummingbirds, while the Old World has its sunbirds, honeyeaters, and flowerpeckers. Many members of the parrot family are also given to feeding extensively upon the nectar of flowers. Those of us living north of Mexico have the hummingbirds and for this we can be grateful.

*Broad-tailed hummingbird at penstemon*

Nearly everyone who feeds birds sooner or later tries his hand at seducing hummingbirds with sugary solutions. That many succeed is seen in the results of a coast-to-coast survey in 1979 conducted by the writer in cooperation with the *Nature Society News* and directed to bird lovers. Approximately 75 percent of the 300 questionnaires returned reported hummingbirds coming to flowers in the yard and 50 percent reported success in luring hummingbirds to feeders. That these tiny, swift-flying birds from the tropics should create this much of a stir seems startling until one really sees them. No other North American birds exhibit such iridescence and brilliance of coloring. But to appreciate the full glory of these feathered jewels one must see hummingbirds under proper light conditions. Only when viewed at a proper angle in sunlight is the gorgeous coloring of a hummingbird seen to best advantage. The male hummingbird is much more brightly colored than the female.

The plant kingdom not only has flowers especially adapted for pollination by bees, butterflies, or moths, but also has bird flowers. These are predominantly red, tubular in shape, rich in nectar, and odorless. The many stamens are so located in the corolla or tube that a bird probing for nectar cannot very well escape touching them and getting pollen on the head and breast feathers. Often the tube of a bird flower is shaped exactly to fit the bill of the bird that serves as its main pollinating agent. This may partly explain why there is such diversity in bill shape and size among the 341 species of hummingbirds.

The hummingbirds are highly specialized in other ways as well. With tubular-tipped or brush-tipped tongues, depending upon the species, and the ability to fly forward or backward, hover in midair, shift sideways, and fly straight up or down, hummingbirds are uniquely equipped for their special mode of existence. Their diet consists not only of nectar but of small insects and spiders, and occasionally the sap of trees and juices of fruits. A few species are said to subsist entirely upon insects.

The West, with thirteen species that breed and a number of others that wander across our border with Mexico, is by far the best part of this country for hummingbirds. Moreover, several of the western hummingbirds stay on through the winter. While this has always been true of California's native Anna's hummingbird and Costa's hummingbird in southern California, there is now an increasing tendency for other western hummingbirds to stay behind. The explanation would seem to be more garden flowers, with some of them blossoming in winter, and hummingbird feeders. Plentiful food is also the likely explanation for a population explosion among several western hummingbirds. Anna's hummingbird, for example, which rarely strayed north of Sacramento, is now found as far north as Vancouver, British Columbia. Occasional birds spend the winter in southern British Columbia, Washington, and Oregon. With help from feeding stations and small gnats, they seem to get by quite nicely. Other western hummingbirds seem more inclined to fly eastward for the winter. Numbers of them can be found in gardens all the way from Texas to central Florida.

Canada has four breeding species; the rufous is the only one that reaches Alaska. There are no hummingbirds in Hawaii. The ruby-throated hummingbird is the only breeding species found east of the Mississippi. This enterprising little bird, which makes a perilous flight of six hundred miles across the Gulf of Mexico, is the only humming-bird over much of the continent. Its breeding range extends all the way from central Alberta to the Atlantic and Gulf coasts. It is equally at home in wooded or partly wooded country or semi-shaded yards in towns and suburbs. The inner city is avoided except during migration. Margaret McKenny tells of migrant rubythroats appearing in tiny backyards in the heart of Manhattan. By late September most ruby-throats will have departed for the tropics.

Growing flowers for hummingbirds and providing food for them at feeders go hand in hand. Both help the hummingbird meet its enormous energy requirements. But for those who engage in hummingbird feeding, there are several important rules that should be followed. The most important is good sanitation. It is essential to frequently clean and rinse bottles or vials holding sweetish solutions. Fresh solutions should be supplied every few days, and aging solutions should be discarded. Normally a hummingbird will not accept a sour or fermented solution. Should a bird happen to drink from a sugar-water solution that has gone bad, it may temporarily become groggy and, for a while, will be an easy prey for a predator. Potentially a far worse hazard is a honey-water solution that has fermented. As first publicized by Dr. Augusto Ruschi of Brazil, honey solutions can lead to a fatal fungus disease in hummingbirds. He tells of the dire consequences of this disease in a 1965 issue of *Audubon* magazine. "The bird begins to stick out its tongue

*Courtship in hummingbirds*

constantly," he writes, "then, for a few days, keeps its beak constantly open and from time to time scratches the beak . . ." The disease is always fatal.

In view of Dr. Ruschi's warning, it is best not to use honey in feeding hummingbirds. Sugar is far safer and less likely to go bad. But the sugar-water solution should be no stronger than one part sugar to four parts water. Too much of a good thing in the way of sugar could lead to liver damage in these rather delicate, hyperactive birds. The water that goes into the mixture should be boiled to kill bacteria. Two or three minutes of boiling should suffice. The water itself should be free of chemicals. Several failures to attract hummingbirds to feeders have been attributed to overly chlorinated water from city water supplies.

It is best to hang feeders in shade or at least not in bright sunlight. The solution should not be left in feeders for more than three to five days. In very hot, dry weather, it may be necessary to change the solution daily. After being emptied, the feeder should be rinsed in hot water, refilled, and returned to its normal location. Mold within the feeder can be combated by scrubbing and, if necessary, using vinegar as a cleaning agent. To get at black slime that sometimes accumulates in feeding spouts and other parts of the feeder, take the feeder apart and scrub with a toothbrush or bottlebrush. Laverne A. Shaffer of San Jose, California, states that "scrupulous cleanliness of both solution and equipment is very important to slow spoilage and prevent possible sources of infection."

A wide variety of other animals have a taste for sweets and find ways of getting to solutions in feeders. Many birds are accomplished at hovering before feeders long enough to get a drink. If the feeder is provided with perches, this makes it easy for birds to take turns in much the same way as the hummingbirds. The most persistent visitors to hummingbird feeders in California and other parts of the Southwest seem to be orioles and house finches. Among other bird visitors are sapsuckers and other woodpeckers, chickadees, titmice, ruby-crowned kinglet, warblers, and black-headed grosbeak.

Not so welcome are squirrels, raccoons, and opossums who demonstrate their taste for sugar-water by pulling down feeders and lapping up the spilled residue. Feeding station operators generally get around this problem by moving feeders to less accessible locations. A much more widespread and difficult problem is competition by ants, bees, wasps, hornets, and yellow jackets. Sometimes stinging insects are so numerous at feeders that the hummingbirds will desert and go elsewhere for their sweets. That this should happen to hummingbirds, known for their aggressive behavior, seems surprising. But by using bee guards—fine-mesh covers made to fit over the feeding spout—we can often outwit the insect competitors. However, hummingbirds, when feeding, tend to splatter some of the syrup over the guards. To prevent bees and other insects from coming back, guards may have to be washed with water at frequent intervals.

If the guards do not work or are too much trouble, there is another solution to the insect problem. This is to smear just enough cooking oil, petroleum jelly, or mineral oil around feeding vents and on the wire from which the feeder is suspended to make for a highly slippery surface. Insect invaders, whether they approach by wing or, as in the case of ants, make their way by crawling, can't get a grip and fall off. While not always a complete success, the doctoring of "invasion routes" with light oils or jellies does significantly reduce insect competition.

Bees are likely to be most in evidence at hummingbird feeders when few flowers are in bloom. As soon as more blossoms are available, the bees will probably go back to their natural diet of nectar and pollen. This would suggest that flowers have a dual role when it comes to hummingbirds. They provide an alternative source of food for the birds and lure insects away from feeders. Numerous suggestions regarding good bee plants are contained in the chapter on bees and the plant list in the appendix.

Cats and plate-glass picture windows take a small toll of the many hummingbirds that visit yards and feeding stations. Like many other birds, hummingbirds see reflections of tree branches or other objects in a window and fly into the window under the illusion that they will find a place to perch or perhaps an opening that they can fly through. By pasting silhouettes of small bird hawks in the window, we can drastically reduce window strikes by birds of all kinds. It should also be remembered that hummingbirds are highly curious about anything that is red. Any red objects on the window, such as flower decals, or even red objects inside the house can lead to a window strike by a curious bird. Many times hummingbirds are not killed or badly injured on hitting a window—only stunned. We should carefully pick up any such stunned victim, keep the bird in a darkened container, and release it after it revives.

There is nothing that discourages a hummingbird more than an empty feeder or one containing sour or spoiled solution. Any initial success in attracting hummingbirds should be followed through by adhering strictly to the rules already mentioned. In the East, where there is only the ruby-throated hummingbird, chances are that applying good management practices won't prove overly taxing. But in parts of the West, hummingbirds are so plentiful that it takes considerable effort to service feeders. At times the Tucker Bird Sanctuary near Orange, California, plays host to hundreds of hummingbirds. Equally spectacular are the large numbers of hummingbirds at Mile Hi near Hereford, Arizona.

When feeding hummingbirds, it is important to know when to start and when to stop. In the East, feeders should be in place about the time rubythroats begin returning from the tropics. Along the Gulf coast and in Florida, early April is not too soon to extend our welcome. In making its flight northward, the rubythroat times its appearances with the first flowers that provide it with food. Plants to watch are the azaleas, columbine, flowering quince, red buckeye, and early phlox. The azaleas are one of the first spring flowers that begin luring the hummingbirds as they make their way northward. When the early azaleas come into bloom, it is time to put our hummingbird feeding program into operation. In the West, hummingbirds also time their appearances in spring with early flowers, such as flowering currant, eucalyptus, and tree tobacco. We can find out when to stop feeding by referring to the timetables of departure for hummingbirds in our region, which are available in literature sources such as state bird books. To prolong feeding beyond departure dates may work a hardship upon the few birds that would have left except for the inexhaustible food at our feeders. In the North, any hummingbird that stays behind may lose its life in the first severe freeze or snowstorm.

As important as it is to provide hummingbirds with extra sustenance in the form of sugar-water at bird feeders, plants play a more vital role in the lives of these energetic birds. Some, such as lichens and cinnamon fern with its downy stems, provide material for the hummingbird's artistically designed nest. Other plants are used as nesting sites. But in this chapter our interest is in the flowers that hummingbirds patronize for nectar and other foods. Most garden flowers are utilized to some extent, but some are far more popular than others.

What other foods, if any, do hummingbirds obtain from flowers besides nectar? Like honeybees, hummingbirds appear to feed to some extent upon pollen. In Bent's "life histories" mention is made of 10 and 15 percent concentrations of pollen in the stomachs of two blue-throated hummingbirds. In very early spring, when most other foods are not available, Anna's hummingbird has been seen obtaining pollen from the newly opening flowers of alder, hazelnut, and pussy willow.

Hummingbirds prey to some extent upon spiders and small insects that are found on flowers. However, the ornithologist Alexander Skutch, who has spent a lifetime in the American tropics studying birds, in his *Life of the Hummingbird* questions the ability of hummingbirds to catch insects within a flower. He points out that such insects would be invisible and difficult to obtain. Hummingbirds, he concludes, need more nectar than insects. For the most part, insects are caught on the wing by hummingbirds and consist of very small kinds such as gnats, mosquitoes, flying ants, and smaller flies. Spiders loom importantly in the diets of hummingbirds and are captured on plants or snatched from their webs. The silk of spiderwebs is much used by hummingbirds to hold together the material that forms their cup-shaped nests. But occasionally the tables are turned and a hummingbird becomes hopelessly entangled in a spiderweb.

Hummingbirds have a special predilection for red, as can be seen not only in their preference for red flowers but in their tendency to explore any red object. Hummingbirds have been observed probing red dots on a tie or scarf, investigating red markings on camera equipment, and even hovering before red lips! The hummingbird's strong predilection for red sometimes gets it into trouble. For example, during the autumn of 1983, reports began coming in of hummingbirds being killed by the current in electric cattle fences. It turned out that the birds were attracted by red insulators, and in probing the edges of these insulators with their bills contacted the "hot" wire and were electrocuted. Most mortality occurred in the Midwest and involved ruby-throated hummingbirds. Fortunately, when notified of what was happening, the manufacturer discontinued making red insulators. Wherever red insulators are still in use, they should either be sprayed with black paint or removed and replaced with ones of another color. Orange is another favorite color even though there are relatively few orange-colored flowers. The birds investigate orange-colored fruits and come to bird feeders tinted with this color. (According to Paul A. Johnsgard in his *Hummingbirds of North America*, a distinctive color is a definite aid to hummingbirds in helping them remember food sources. Hummingbirds, he writes, have excellent memories, which enable them to return to food sources they have known in previous years.)

Perhaps the best course in deciding what to plant for hummingbirds is not to rely too much on color. There are more than enough popular hummingbird plants that display a wide range of floral colors, many of them common flowers that can be grown nearly everywhere. The gardener is safe in choosing the color scheme that best suits his yard. He will, however, almost certainly want to have some red flowers for their beauty and the extra attraction they have for hummingbirds.

The first hummingbirds to arrive in spring will be eagerly searching for flowers rich in nectar. Almost anything will do at this time of the year, when so little is in bloom. But we can offer our visitors far better fare than spring bulbs or forsythia if we grow any of the following early-blooming plants:

| | |
|---|---|
| Azalea | Siberian pea tree |
| Columbine | Sweet william phlox |
| Flowering currant | Trumpet honeysuckle |
| Flowering quince | Virginia bluebells |
| Lilac | Winter jasmine |
| Red buckeye | Wisteria (in the South) |

The early azaleas and, to a lesser extent, early-blooming rhododendrons are among the most plentiful and reliable sources of food for hummingbirds returning in spring. If there is a first choice, it is pinxter flower (*Rhododendron periclymenoides*) with its pink to white blossoms which grows wild from New England to Tennessee and South Carolina. Of the early-blooming wildflowers, few seem to have more appeal to hummingbirds than American columbine (*Aquilegia canadensis*). The flowering currants, avoided by many gardeners because they are alternate hosts of the white pine blister rust, can nevertheless be planted in many areas where the susceptible pines are not present. All are useful ornamentals whose flowers open in time to supply nectar for early hum-

*Ruby-throated hummingbird at trumpet creeper*

mingbirds on their way north. One of the best to plant for humming-birds is a west coast species, winter currant (*Ribes sanguineum*). Second choice would be clove currant (*R. odoratum*). The flowering quinces are old-fashioned favorites that still find a place in many yards. The early red blossoms are eagerly visited by hummingbirds. Competing with forsythia in popularity, the lilacs come into bloom only slightly later and begin receiving attention from hummingbirds. Red buckeye (*Aesculus pavia*) is a native shrub in the South whose early red blossoms are among the first spring flowers to greet returning rubythroats. Anyone who admires Japanese honeysuckle but mistrusts the way it runs riot would do well to grow our native trumpet honeysuckle (*Lonicera sempervirens*), which is safe and even more beautiful. A twining woody vine with trumpet-shaped flowers, it has a blooming season from March until July and, like Japanese honeysuckle, is a favorite with humming-birds. For gardeners in more northern sections who are unable to grow azaleas and other more southern hummingbird flowers, Siberian pea tree (*Caragana arborescens*) is a good substitute. An extremely hardy shrub with yellow pealike flowers, the pea tree comes into bloom and invites hummingbirds in early May as they begin to arrive in southern Canada. Among early-blooming garden flowers, few have as much hummingbird appeal as sweet william phlox (*Phlox divaricata*), a good plant for the rock garden. Another early bloomer is Virginia bluebells (*Mertensia virginica*), a native wildflower whose blue flowers attract the notice of hummingbirds. In contrast to most jasmines, winter jasmine (*Jasminum nudiflorum*) thrives best in cooler climates. Its early tubular yellow flowers provide nectar for hummingbirds when little else is available. Although, except in the South, wisteria comes into bloom too late for the earliest-arriving hummingbirds, its flowers are a source of nectar for later hummingbirds or those that have taken up residence with us for the summer.

As summer gets underway, more and more flowers of the right kind for hummingbirds come into bloom and there are over twice as many to choose from. Some of them we've already met.

| | |
|---|---|
| Azalea | Columbine |
| Beauty bush | Common geranium |
| Begonia | Coral-bells |
| Canna | Daylily |

| | |
|---|---|
| Delphinium | Penstemon |
| Flowering tobacco | Petunia |
| Four-o'clock | Phlox |
| Garden balsam | Sage (*Salvia*) |
| Gladiolus | Scarlet runner bean |
| Horse chestnut | Silk tree |
| Iris | Trumpet honeysuckle |
| Japanese honeysuckle | Weigela |
| Lilac | Wisteria |
| Lily | |

Of the many azaleas and rhododendrons that begin blooming in early summer, sweet azalea (*Rhododendron arborescens*) seems in greatest favor with hummingbirds. The pink blossoms of beauty bush (*Kolkwitzia amabilis*) come into bloom just as the lilacs are fading. This is an advantage where flowering shrubs make up the largest share of hummingbird plantings. Cannas, ever popular with gardeners, delight hummingbirds and also have the virtue of a long blooming season. Kathryn R. King of Beaumont, Texas, has written of an unusual sighting of a male hummingbird, which she recognized by its bright red gorget, feeding upon pink canna blossoms in her yard around midnight. The yard was illuminated by a mercury vapor lamp. Coral-bells (*Heuchera sanguinea*) and columbine, when used together in a border or rock garden, form an irresistible combination that will almost certainly invite any hummingbirds in the neighborhood. By now our garden will be ready for European columbine (*Aquilegia vulgaris*) with blue, purple, or white flowers. Also at this season, any geraniums that we have nursed through the winter as house plants will almost certainly be in window boxes or flower beds. Their red blossoms will provide an attractive invitation to hummingbirds. Much the same can be said of another group of house plants, the begonias. Once out of doors, the white, pink, or reddish blossoms of begonia invite hummingbirds through the summer months. An old-fashioned favorite, tawny daylily (*Hemerocallis fulva*) attracts hummingbirds from late May until July. As one gardener put it: "Hummingbirds are so eager for them that they bury themselves in the blossoms." Several of the daylilies, including this one, have orange blossoms—a color not often found in garden plants. Delphiniums are perennials, whereas the closely similar larkspurs are annuals. Hummingbirds show no favoritism here, visiting the flowers of both regardless of their color. Scarlet larkspur (*Delphinium cardinale*), a native of California, is a handsome species that has great hummingbird appeal.

The flowering tobaccos, with their hanging, long-tubed flowers, offer two good hummingbird plants. One is the day-flowering sander tobacco (*Nicotiana sanderae*), an annual in the North and a perennial in the South; the other is *N. alata*, a fragrant night bloomer with white flowers. Hummingbirds find blossoms of the latter as they open late in the day. Four-o'clock (*Mirabilis*), with flowers rather similar to those of flowering tobacco, also does not open until late in the day; hence the name four-o'clock. Hummingbirds evidently find the blossoms worth waiting for; still later they will be visited by sphinx moths. Garden balsam (*Impatiens balsamina*) is a colorful cultivated variety of jewel-weed. Although the garden plant does not have quite the nectar supply that its wild cousin does, hummingbirds frequently appear at window boxes and flower beds where these popular annuals are grown.

*Cardinal flower, petunia, gladiolus*

Nothing will keep hummingbirds away from the flamboyant flowers of the gladiolus when they appear in early summer. Pink- and red-flowered plants are especially inviting. The flowers of Japanese honeysuckle, if we are willing to risk having this plant in the yard, are among the most attractive to hummingbirds in early summer. Attendance at hummingbird feeders appears to drop when there is an abundant supply of honeysuckle blossoms. After red buckeye is through blooming, there are several other buckeyes or horse chestnuts that will take its place. All have flowers that are highly attractive to hummingbirds. There are so many cultivated irises that it would be hard to say which ones have the most hummingbird appeal; those with blue flowers seem as good as any for the garden. The lilacs will still be in bloom in early June and getting some attention from hummingbirds. If there are lilies in the garden, it will now be their turn. Two of the best for attracting hummingbirds are Turk's-cap (*Lilium superbum*) and tiger lily (*L. tigrinum*).

The penstemons are largely western flowers—native to the West and grown, for the most part, in western gardens. The flowers seem especially made for hummingbirds and, as we might expect, are well patronized by them. The fact that petunias are seen in gardens everywhere, and often in window boxes, doesn't make them any less popular with hummingbirds. Old-fashioned single petunias are preferred, especially ones with red flowers. By now one or two other species of phlox will be in bloom and providing color for the rest of the summer. The two that seem best suited to our garden and the needs of hummingbirds are annual phlox (*Phlox drummondii*) and garden phlox (*P. paniculata*).

Early summer is when the sages, those delightful members of the mint family, start coming into bloom. At least one sage in the garden is a must for anyone catering to hummingbirds. One of the best for hummingbirds is the ever popular scarlet sage (*Salvia splendens*), whose solid ranks of red can fill the entire flower bed and dazzle the eye. Sages that come in white, blue, or purple seem almost as popular with hummingbirds. For something different in the way of ornament, scarlet runner bean has much to offer. Grown mostly in the North, the scarlet flowers rate highly with hummingbirds and we can eat the beans that ripen later on. The more southern silk tree or mimosa (*Albizia julibrissin*) with its hundreds of fuzzy pink flowers is such a hummingbird attraction through the summer months that feeders take on a secondary importance. A single tree can accommodate a dozen or more humming-birds at a time.

The trumpet honeysuckle that came into bloom in spring will still be producing coral-red flowers through the summer. This is a good vine to grow on a fence or trellis. Weigela is the name of a group of flower-ing shrubs with pink, red, or sometimes white flowers. Good hum-mingbird plants, they come into bloom about the time the lilacs shed their blossoms. In more northern states, we will see the last of the wis-teria blossoms in June.

As summer flowers begin to fade, a whole new display is required to meet the needs of late-season hummingbirds, including migrants that will be passing through. Of the flowers listed below, some will have been in bloom since midsummer.

| | |
|---|---|
| Bee balm (bergamot) | Jewelweed |
| Butterfly bush | Nasturtium |
| Cardinal flower | Rose of Sharon (shrub |
| Catmint | althea) |
| Crape myrtle | Spiderflower (cleome) |
| Fuchsia | Trumpet creeper |
| Glossy abelia | Zinnia |
| Hollyhock | |

Bee balm is one of the most popular of hummingbird plants and has the added attraction of inviting bees and butterflies. Both in the wild and in gardens, hummingbirds seem partial to the red-flowered species while bees are more likely to go to those with lavender flowers. Either bee balm (*Monarda didyma*) or wild bergamot (*M. fistulosa*) can be grown in the garden and both are outstanding hummingbird plants. Much the same can be said of butterfly bush (*Buddleia*), whose charm for butterflies is matched by an equal charm for hummingbirds. The species to grow for late summer is orange-eyed butterfly bush (*Buddleia davidii*) with red, pink, purple, or white flowers, depending upon the variety. Cardinal flower is a moisture-loving plant that grows along shady streambanks, but it can be successfully introduced to the flower garden. With its brilliant red tubular flowers and rich nectar supply, it is a perfect example of a bird flower. As in wild columbine and trumpet creeper—both of them also bird flowers—its flowers are scarlet on the outside and yellow within.

Catmint (*Nepeta cataria*), whose taste and fragrance are dear to the hearts of cats, has considerable hummingbird appeal. Betty N. Meisner of Peru, New York, has reported that it wasn't her hummingbird feeders or garden flowers that attracted the attention of hummingbirds but a hedge of wild catmint. Others, too, have had good success with this modest-looking plant with its small tubular white flowers with pink or purple dots.

The next three plants are flowering shrubs whose late summer blossoms appear at a time when hummingbirds are putting on weight for their long flight southward. Crape myrtle, with its red, pink, or lavender flowers, is a good plant for southern gardens. Fuchsia is a year-round outdoor plant only in frost-free parts of the continent. Whether out of doors on a temporary or permanent basis, it is a hummingbird plant par excellence. The hanging tubular flowers, often a vivid red, seem made for hummingbirds. Far less striking are the small whitish tubular flowers of glossy abelia (*Abelia grandiflora*), but this popular hedge plant is also well patronized by hummingbirds.

Hollyhock, with its long summer-fall blooming season, is not as popular with hummingbirds as many of the other plants mentioned, but the large, showy blossoms give them something to fall back on when little else is in bloom. Jewelweed is a wildflower adapted to damp woodlands. Unless we have suitable habitat for it, we might as well leave its spotted orange or yellow flowers for hummingbirds living a wilder existence. Nasturtium is a far easier plant to grow. The long spur at the base of the flower contains a copious supply of nectar that attracts both bumblebees and hummingbirds—just one of several reasons to grow this popular annual with its yellow, orange, or red flowers. For those who admire the gaudy, colorful flowers of hibiscus, so much a part of the tropics, there is a close relative that we can grow even if we live as far north as Massachusetts. This is rose of Sharon (*Hibiscus syriacus*), whose striking white, red, pink, or bluish purple flowers are attractive to hummingbirds.

For an annual whose blossoms will last well into fall, we can try spiderflower (*Cleome spinosa*). Although better known as a bee plant, the spidery white to rosy-purple flowers have considerable humming-bird appeal. Trumpet creeper will begin opening its red funnel-shaped flowers toward the end of summer. Its blossoms are so large that the rubythroat cannot reach the nectar by hovering. It plunges into the tube. Like the petunia, the zinnia is one of the most widely grown annuals. It satisfies our need for color and, at the same time, attracts butterflies and hummingbirds. The flowers are of the composite type, made up of numerous small florets, each containing enough nectar to invite the attention of hummingbirds.

By late fall, hummingbirds and their favorite blossoms will be found only in more temperate parts of the continent. In these milder sections there will be a new group of flowering plants, many of them tropical in origin, to supply the needs of wintering hummingbirds. The plants listed below are primarily adapted to the conditions of southern Florida and southern California in winter. But some can be grown farther north or in warmer parts of Texas and the Southwest.

| | |
|---|---|
| Agapanthus | Hibiscus |
| Banana | Lantana |
| Bottlebrush | Orange |
| Bougainvillea | Pentas |
| California fuchsia | Powder puff |
| Camellia | Red-hot poker |
| Cape honeysuckle | Scarlet bush |
| Chuparosa | Shrimp plant |
| Firecracker plant | Tree tobacco |

Subtropical plants, the two species of agapanthus seen in this country are suited only for outdoor planting in warmer parts of Florida and the Southwest. The blue flowers attract hummingbirds. The flowers of banana are rich in nectar and much visited by nectar-feeding birds in the tropics. Banana plants growing in southern Florida or southern California are likely to receive attention from hummingbirds. Bottlebrush (*Callistemon*) is widely planted in California and has a reputation for being a good hummingbird plant. Bougainvilleas are evergreen shrublike vines from the tropics. Where grown in Florida and California, the blossoms attract butterflies and hummingbirds. A native of California, the California fuchsia with its trumpet-shaped scarlet flowers is so popular with hummingbirds that the plant is often called hummingbird's trumpet. Not to be confused with the true fuchsias, this

*Feeding young*

plant belongs to the genus *Zauschneria*. Camellias range as far north as Vancouver and, in the East, to Delaware. In more southern sections, the large waxy flowers appear from October to April—good timing for wintering hummingbirds. A native of South Africa, Cape honeysuckle (*Tecomaria capensis*) has about the same hummingbird appeal as our native trumpet creeper. The orange-red trumpet-shaped flowers of this shrublike vine appear through the winter wherever the plant is grown in Florida or California. Chuparosa (*Justicia californica*) is a native of southern California and Arizona. Like those of the shrimp plant, to which it is related, its flowers are highly attractive to hummingbirds.

Except for the small red tubular flowers that may cover the entire plant, firecracker plant (*Russelia*) is a low shrub without any noteworthy features. But the flowers, especially when hummingbirds are flitting from blossom to blossom, make the plant a valuable addition to gardens in southern Florida. As already noted, both hibiscus and rose of Sharon have colorful flowers and are attractive to hummingbirds. The plant that is most often called hibiscus is Chinese hibiscus (*Hibiscus rosa-sinensis*), a tropical shrub suited for the out-of-doors only in warmer parts of Florida and the Southwest. Lantana is often found growing side by side with Chinese hibiscus. Its clusters of small yellow, orange, or red flowers have both hummingbird and butterfly appeal. In its semi-tropical setting, lantana blooms the year round.

The sweet-scented blossoms of the orange tree attract both bees and hummingbirds. Some years ago, while visiting an orange grove in southern Louisiana on the early date of March 28, I found ruby-throated hummingbirds visiting the blossoms. The tiny birds may have just completed their long return flight across the Gulf of Mexico. Pentas (*Pentas lanceolata*), a two-foot-tall shrub with colorful star-shaped flowers, can be counted upon to produce blossoms the year round. Where this plant is grown in Florida, it is known for its hummingbird appeal. The pink and white or red blossoms of the powder puffs (*Calliandra* spp.), tropical shrubs with an apt name, have a fluffy appearance and are largely composed of elongated stamens. The plants have a long blooming season in the Deep South and rate highly as hummingbird plants. For something exotic to embellish far southern yards, there is red-hot poker (*Kniphofia uvaria*) with its candelabralike spikes of orange-red flowers. The nectar-filled flowers attract both orioles and hummingbirds. A native shrub that deserves far more use as an ornamental, scarlet bush (*Hamelia patens*) of southern Florida has tubular orange-red flowers that are followed by red berries. Ruby-throated hummingbirds throng to the flowers. Chuparosa's relative, the shrimp plant (*Justicia brandegeana*), is an important winter food plant for hummingbirds in southern Texas and other parts of the Deep South. The small white flowers have purple dots and are enclosed in showy red bracts. The plant is well named since the flowers with their bracts do look like shrimps. Tree tobacco (*Nicotiana glauca*) is the last of the Deep South hummingbird plants on my list. A tree from South America, growing to about eighteen feet, tree tobacco has become widely naturalized. Its green-to-yellowish blossoms are among the most important winter sources of nectar for hummingbirds in southern California and Arizona. The plant blossoms more or less continuously throughout the year. Tree tobacco is not to be confused with the previously mentioned flowering tobaccos, although both belong to the same genus.

As can be seen below, annuals and perennials figure significantly in my treatment of hummingbird plants. Flowering shrubs are of major importance, while flowering trees and vines, although represented by only a few species, include several outstanding plants. Plants that grow from bulbs or corms are few in number but well worth considering. Many other good hummingbird plants could be added to my list, but the ones I have noted seem to be among the best for garden use. They are both ornamental and seasonally popular with hummingbirds.

ANNUALS
- Annual phlox
- Flowering tobacco
- Four-o'clock
- Garden balsam
- Larkspur
- Nasturtium
- Petunia
- Salvia
- Scarlet larkspur
- Scarlet runner bean
- Scarlet sage
- Spiderflower
- Zinnia

PERENNIALS
- Agapanthus
- American columbine
- Banana
- Bee balm
- Begonia
- California fuchsia
- Canna
- Cardinal flower
- Catmint
- Common geranium
- Coral-bells
- Delphinium
- European columbine
- Flowering tobacco
   (in the South)
- Garden phlox
- Hollyhock
- Jewelweed
- Penstemon
- Red-hot poker
- Summer phlox
- Sweet azalea
- Sweet william phlox
- Virginia bluebells
- Wild bergamot

FROM BULBS OR CORMS
- Daylily
- Gladiolus
- Iris
- Tiger lily
- Turk's-cap

FLOWERING TREES
- Horse chestnut
- Orange
- Silk tree
- Tree tobacco

FLOWERING VINES
- Bougainvillea
- Cape honeysuckle
- Japanese honeysuckle
- Trumpet creeper
- Trumpet honeysuckle
- Wisteria

FLOWERING SHRUBS
- Azalea
- Beauty bush
- Bottlebrush
- Butterfly bush
- Camellia
- Chinese hibiscus
- Chuparosa
- Clove currant
- Crape myrtle
- Firecracker plant
- Flowering currant
- Fuchsia
- Glossy abelia
- Lantana
- Lilac
- Orange-eyed butterfly bush
- Pentas
- Pinxter flower
- Powder puff
- Red buckeye
- Rhododendron
- Rose of Sharon
- Scarlet bush
- Shrimp plant
- Siberian pea tree
- Weigela
- Winter currant
- Winter jasmine

# 6 / Entertaining the Mammals

Our native mammals rank somewhere in popular esteem between birds and the reptiles and amphibians. On the whole, we like them so long as they do not disturb us or our property. If, as sometimes happens, they make a nuisance of themselves, we tend to lose our patience rather quickly. It is their appetites that cause the most trouble. Nearly all mammals have an overpowering way of demanding and taking food. They tip over garbage cans early in the morning or uproot plants and make inroads on our

*Cottontail gnawing bark*

flower beds and vegetable garden. If we in the East find our woodchucks, raccoons, and squirrels bothersome, what about the residents of some Los Angeles suburbs who have coyotes to contend with? Not only do the coyotes tip over garbage cans and take fruits and vegetables of many kinds but they are also known to prey upon smaller breeds of dogs and house cats. People also complain of being awakened at night by their howling!

The answer to a mammal problem is to protect our plants and property as best we can with screening, repellents, and the like. There are many products on the market that serve to ward off everything from small rodents to deer. While some measures may not prove to be completely effective, they will at least help tide us over the period when a particular species is making a nuisance of itself. Most mammal problems are seasonal in nature or occur only when there is intense pressure on the food supply because of overpopulation.

No matter where we live, there will be native mammals in our neighborhood as well as introduced ones. If the animal is a good climber or fleet-footed, it is likely to show itself during the day. Species that are not so agile in escaping enemies stay hidden for the most part. We are scarcely ever aware of the presence of native mice, voles, and shrews. Yet these small inhabitants of wood piles, stone walls, and underground burrows may be the most abundant mammalian residents of our neighborhood. Larger, better-known mammals, such as the skunks, opossums, and raccoons, are for the most part nocturnal and therefore seldom seen although present in cities and suburbs. Even though a mammal is seen infrequently, it often leaves traces in the form of footprints, droppings, and even hair caught on wire strands of a fence. Shrews rarely show themselves, but bodies of dead ones provide evidence that they are in the neighborhood. The lowly mole that digs its tunnels just below the surface reveals its presence by the soil it has pushed up.

Censuses of mammal populations in various habitats in North America show that mammals do indeed live almost everywhere. It seems hard to believe that crowded Central Park in the heart of Manhattan can claim no fewer than thirteen species of native mammals. Of these, four are visitors—the big brown bat, little brown bat, red bat, and hoary bat. The remainder—the eastern mole, short-tailed shrew, woodchuck, red squirrel, southern flying squirrel, gray squirrel, eastern cottontail, raccoon, and muskrat—are residents.

Mammals, like birds, respond readily to food offerings. Whether invited or not, they often appear at bird feeders and take food meant for birds. This is another reason why certain of the mammals, especially squirrels, are not regarded highly by many people. But there are some who supply food to mammals as willingly as they do to birds. Louise Mullen of Brattleboro, Vermont, plays host to striped skunks and raccoons at night and birds, red squirrels, gray squirrels, and chipmunks during the day. Night visitors are given a choice of chicken necks, dog food, and sunflower seeds. On one occasion, a stray house cat appeared and ate with the skunks. An opossum, close to the northern range limits for this species, joined the other guests for most of one winter. But harmonious relationships do not always prevail at the feeding places. Red squirrels chase the grays, and if a skunk is pushed too far by a raccoon, it will retaliate by releasing its odoriferous spray.

In a recent survey conducted by the Long Point Bird Observatory in Ontario, no fewer than twenty-two species of mammals were recorded in winter at bird feeders. No one yard had close to this many species, but with the snowshoe hares in several yards, the flying squirrels in others, and sightings of weasels, martens, raccoons, striped skunks, cottontails, meadow voles, gray squirrels, red squirrels, chipmunks, mice, shrews, and woodchucks, mammals clearly were patronizing the feeders almost as much as birds. Since most of the mammal guests appeared at night, only the normal amount of competition occurred at the feeders during the day.

If anyone holds a record for the number of mammalian species coming to food offerings, it is Helen Hoover, who in a 1960 issue of *Audubon Magazine* wrote of the many animals that came to food at a wilderness cabin on the Minnesota-Canada border. She tells of over sixteen species making an appearance during a one-year period. Even the fisher, a wary member of the weasel family, could be enticed to feed from the hand on cold winter days. Suet or red meat lured fishers and weasels while three species of shrews came for bacon grease. Food put out for birds attracted the eastern chipmunk, least chipmunk, red squirrel, flying squirrel, and snowshoe hare.

Judging from the enthusiastic way in which Helen Hoover and others have written about the joy of attracting mammals to their yards, it would appear that this wildlife hobby deserves more attention. Little extra effort is needed, and if we accept the testimony of those who have tried it, we will have fewer problems from mammals, not more—the theory being that well-fed mammals are less destructive.

The requirements of mammals are much the same as those of birds—living space, shelter, food, and water. Therefore, the wildlife gardener who has been catering to birds will not have to add many new enticements. Aside from feeders especially for mammals, the only two recommendations I would make would be nest boxes for squirrels and more nut and oak trees than we would normally plant for birds. Oaks, pecans, hickories, and walnuts will provide food for squirrels and, if the harvest is good, may even keep them from competing unduly at the bird feeder. If acorns are plentiful, the oaks not only will keep squirrels and chipmunks well supplied but will furnish food for the opossum, eastern cottontail, raccoon, and gray and red foxes. Although not ideal for ornament, the persimmon is another tree whose fruits rate highly with mammals, including foxes. Gray squirrels often turn from nut-meats to sample the fruits of pyracantha, yew, hollies, hawthorn, cotoneaster, and flowering crab apple. Studies showed that fruits of the common privet (*Ligustrum vulgare*) made up as much as 60 percent of the diet of raccoons in Alabama during the months of November and December.

Finally, if we are to lure more furtive mammals, such as deer, we must do what we can to ensure a peaceful environment. This does not mean an end to dogs romping or children playing. But it does mean peaceful times of the day when activity of this kind is at a minimum. Our mammal visitors often know our habits better than we do and time their visits to the early morning or dusk or any other period when little outside activity is taking place. A tight fence is probably the best solution to keeping the neighborhood dogs from entering our yard and creating a disturbance. Deer can easily jump most fences.

The rewards of having mammal visitors are much the same as those we obtain from having birds. There is the life and gaiety they add on dull days when we long for something to distract us. One squirrel chasing another endlessly around the yard, a chipmunk with a smug look on its face, cheeks bulging with food and scampering away with tail in the air, a woodchuck sitting on its haunches, surveying the landscape, and suddenly diving back into its hole, are a few of the sights that greet us if our yard is a haven for mammals. Even city dwellers can enjoy these sights. Out of necessity, mammals are moving into cities and suburbs as habitats in more rural areas are being destroyed. Can we achieve a peaceful coexistence with these fugitives from the wild? They bring us problems as well as grace, beauty, and a sense that something that was once missing is now restored. After comparing their faults and virtues, most of us will agree that we can live peacefully with these new neighbors of ours and also with those that have been with us all along. But we need to be on our guard in case some of them misbehave. There are harmless steps that we can take in the event of misdemeanors.

## OPOSSUMS

Shuffling along under cover of darkness with its nose to the ground looking for garbage, the opossum is one of the least prepossessing of the small mammals that visit our yards. But, like the skunk, the opossum proves itself a valuable asset by eating beetles, grasshoppers, and other harmful insects. It also eats mice and other small rodents and, in the capacity of a scavenger, cleans up carrion along roadsides. Not so creditable is its habit of visiting garbage cans and strewing the contents far and wide. Of the relatively little plant food taken, pokeberries, grapes, persimmons, apples, and corn make up the largest share. Although I have found possums in the henhouse under suspicious circumstances, Ralph S. Palmer in his *Mammal Guide* states that "alleged damage to poultry [by possums] is a considerable overstatement of known facts."

In spite of its reputation for being dim-witted, the possum has been amazingly successful in mastering every major habitat, including built-up districts in towns, cities, and suburbs. The environment most to its liking, though, is the old-fashioned farmstead with its outbuildings, apple orchard, vegetable garden, and overgrown fencerows. Intrepid pioneers, possums over the last several decades have been moving ever farther northward and are now well established in parts of southern Ontario. Lacking the complete furry covering of northern mammals, possums are subject to frostbite and this presumably limits their range expansion northward. Its ability to rear large families is one factor in the possum's success. Palmer states that the litter size is from eight to eighteen with about seven surviving the period when the brood is confined to the pouch. As the young grow older, they may sometimes be seen using their mother as a form of conveyance, riding on her back with their prehensile tails wrapped around her tail as she holds it arched forward over her back.

*Opossum mother feeding on persimmons*

When attacked, the opossum resorts to one of two stratagems. It may play dead, rolling over, closing its eyes, and allowing its tongue to hang out. This ruse seems to be fairly effective. The other tactic is to pretend to be a fierce fighter. By hissing, salivating, and opening its mouth wide to show its teeth, it tries to frighten the attacker off.

I have occasionally seen possums wandering about in broad daylight. When living on a farm in Virginia, I surprised a possum early one morning up in a small tree containing a robin's nest with one egg. I climbed the tree in order to take in the situation better. The possum simply glared at me and I climbed down, leaving things very much as they were. Returning later in the day, I found the possum curled up sound asleep on a branch near the nest. The next day the possum was gone. The robin's nest now contained two eggs, proof that the possum had not been up to any mischief.

Possums do not hibernate during the winter, but in colder sections they prepare for winter by gorging during the fall. The extra fat they store helps them get through periods of inclement weather. At such times, the animal holes up in a den. Except for far northern sections of this country, the opossum is found throughout the East; it occurs in the Plains states and Texas and in parts of California, Oregon, and Washington.

# MOLES

Not many people have a good word to say for moles. In tunneling just below the surface in search of food, moles push up the sod in such a way as to disfigure the lawn. Also it is wrongly supposed that they destroy bulbs and eat the seeds of garden plants. This strong indictment scarcely holds for most species. Moles are primarily carnivorous, preying upon earthworms and underground insects. Although we need earthworms for the good they do in aerating and enriching the soil, the toll that moles take of insect larvae, including those of the Japanese beetle, should put these small mammals in a more favorable light. Like the earthworm, the mole also deserves praise for its role in aerating the soil.

When speaking of moles, we usually think of the eastern mole, whose range covers most of the East and the eastern Great Plains. I. Sanderson, in his *How to Know the American Mammals,* writes favorably of this nearly blind, fossorial mammal with its huge front paws for digging, velvety fur, tiny tail, and long snout. He states that any damage they do to lawns and plants is quite trivial compared to the good they do by eating tons of garden insect pests every year. The amount of vegetable matter that the common mole consumes is so minute that it can scarcely be accused of eating seeds or bulbs. The blame, if there is damage to plants, probably falls on the meadow vole, which habitually uses mole tunnels for foraging. On the other hand, Townsend's mole, a large blackish mole of coastal Washington and Oregon, is not quite so innocent. Studies of its food habits show that it does eat bulbs of tulips and other plants. It is such a voracious bulb eater that it constitutes a significant threat to bulb growers.

Two other moles—both of them found in northeastern states and adjacent parts of Canada—deserve mention. The star-nosed mole, with a strange rosette of twenty-two fleshy appendages on its nose, is a wetland species and is unlikely to appear in yards. The hairy-tailed mole, with blackish fur and hair on its tail, has about the same habits and habitat preferences as the common mole.

If moles seem to be getting the upper hand, we can apply certain non-lethal methods to deal with them. Beatrice Trum Hunter, in her *Gardening without Poisons,* states that by growing caper spurge (*Euphorbia lathyrus*) we can deter moles. Also called mole plant or gopher plant, this spurge has a milky sap which is poisonous and caustic. Small burrowing mammals, like moles and gophers, could well experience discomfort on coming into contact with the roots of this plant. We are advised by Hunter that castor beans and mothballs serve as mole repellents. Both should be placed in mole tunnels. Mothballs are a well-known mammal and insect repellent; therefore, I would be tempted to place more confidence in them than in castor beans, which are poisonous but not generally regarded as repellents.

## SHREWS

Of some two dozen species of North American shrews, only the short-tailed shrew is enough of an inhabitant of yards and gardens to deserve mention. Four to five inches long, this nervous, highly active mammal differs from other American shrews in secreting poison when it bites. The poison quickly paralyzes its victims, making it easier for the shrew to subdue animals larger than itself, including mice and small snakes.

Although shrews are said to be insectivores, it might be more appropriate to call them omnivores. Almost any prey that is small enough is attacked and eaten. The list of garden animals that fall victim to the short-tailed shrew includes those mentioned as well as snails, slugs, salamanders, frogs, insects, spiders, centipedes, and even the young of ground-nesting birds. If we were aware of all this slaughter around us, we might be much more ill disposed toward shrews than moles. Shrews also eat carrion and some vegetable matter.

Although active at almost any hour of the day or night, the shrews are seldom seen. They make their homes under logs, stones, and leaf litter and for the most part use the tunnels of other animals in order to get from place to place. The one piece of evidence that tells us of their presence is the body of a dead shrew. A year or two is about the maximum age for these hyperactive animals. Dead shrews are often found in the open and more often in fall than any other time. Their musk glands make them unpalatable to cats and other carnivores; therefore the corpses are likely to remain untouched.

Food on the ground at bird- or mammal-feeding stations gives us our one opportunity to catch more than a fleeting glimpse of a living shrew. As previously mentioned, Helen Hoover, using bacon grease, attracted three species of shrews to her northwoods feeder. The short-tailed shrew, found from the eastern Great Plains to the Atlantic, is the most likely species to make an appearance. Its tastes run to sunflower seeds and anything containing peanut butter. Active the year round, our shrew visitors may turn up at any season. But they will be in too much of a hurry to allow us anything but a brief look.

## BATS

Attitudes toward bats are slowly changing. Victims of absurd charges and a folklore that pictured them as instruments of the devil, the bats have fared poorly at our hands for centuries. Presently a great deal is being written about bats showing that they are not such bad creatures after all. The vampire bats of the American tropics, represented by three species, are exceptions, however. Small to medium-sized, they single out cattle, horses, pigs, and other animals (only rarely humans) for attack. After biting a victim, the vampire laps up the blood; it does not suck blood, as was so often thought. The real danger is not so much from the loss of blood but from the diseases the bat transmits. A carrier of rabies, the vampire itself is highly resistant to the disease.

Having such unpleasant bats as the vampires to the south of us has cast an aura of suspicion over all bats. Their ghostlike flight and their ugly faces haven't helped improve their image. But it is a long way from the tropical rain forests of the vampires, and our North American insect-eating bats are so small and innocuous that it is a pity they are so universally mistrusted. The little brown bat, also called little brown myotis, is the species most commonly seen pursuing insects in the sky toward twilight. It sometimes comes out in broad daylight. The little brown bat is found as far north as Alaska and from coast to coast in

Canada and the contiguous states. Frequently found in towns, it roosts in buildings, caves, or hollow trees. This bat and other members of the genus *Myotis* are something of a nuisance when they use our attics as domiciles. They leave a musty odor and a greasy spot where they hang. But these are minor inconveniences and scarcely reason to call the exterminator. Small bats like the little brown are incapable of transmitting rabies through their bite. Their teeth cannot pierce our skin.

There are plenty of rumors about bats carrying rabies but virtually no documented cases of deaths to humans in the United States. But the rumors nevertheless raise the specter of the diabolical and unwholesome bat. However, as we gradually overcome our prejudices about bats, we will discover that they are in many ways as interesting as any of the other visitors that come to our yards. Echolocation, which permits bats to avoid objects, including ourselves and our hair, is one of nature's most clever adaptations. The same high-frequency sounds are used by bats to locate their prey. Night-flying moths constitute one of the most important sources of food of North American bats. In the absence of flying insects during cold winters bats either hibernate or migrate to a warmer climate. The little brown bat is one of the species that hibernates; the hoary bat and red bat, two other common species, migrate southward.

An interest in bats can open up a new field of nature study, but not many people care to enter the caves and other dank places where they live. This is just as well since bats thrive best where they are not disturbed. Yet from our doorsteps we can often view the first of the bats taking wing toward twilight. As more of them leave their daytime roosts, they circle and dart on erratic courses in pursuit of small insects. There will be fewer biting insects about at dusk if we play host to these much-abused small mammals.


# RACCOONS

Of all the small mammals that have invaded suburbia in recent years, the raccoon can be said to be one of the most troublesome. It is also the most lovable and entertaining. Not everyone is aware of its presence, for raccoons are largely nocturnal, and they haven't yet spread as far into cities and suburbs as the gray squirrel. The tipped-over garbage

*Bat catching insects toward dusk*

can is a good sign that there are raccoons in the neighborhood. If they would only confine themselves to scavenging out of doors, we wouldn't have any very serious complaints about them, but there are more and more reports of raccoons getting into houses and committing small depredations. With hands and fingers almost as dexterous as those of monkeys, raccoons can turn knobs, lift latches, pry open windows, unscrew bottles, pull corks, and turn faucets. Having learned these skills gradually over the years, raccoons are now entering houses and turning and pulling anything that will come open. Sometimes it is the door of the refrigerator. The feast that follows is a nightmare for the homeowner. In a story that strains our credulity, A. B. C. Whipple tells of a raccoon that would announce its arrival by first ringing the doorbell. At least this gave the human occupants time to put the food away and bolt the cupboards.

While some tales about raccoons border upon folklore, there is no question about the tendency of raccoons to enter houses. Friends of ours who lived in a Chicago suburb tell of a family of raccoons that made their home in the chimney directly above the damper. Seldom seen in the house proper, the raccoons made their way to and from their abode through the chimney. At around six in the morning, there was always a raccoon perched at the top of the chimney surveying the landscape. Another report, which I can vouch for, was of a raccoon that entered a suburban home on the outskirts of Washington, D.C., and, of all things, chose for its fare a potted cactus plant, devouring it, thorns and all. This animal's appetite can be compared with that of the southern Florida raccoons which are known to eat oyster plants (*Rhoeo discolor*). The oyster plant, a perennial herb grown for ornament, contains a toxic juice which causes stinging, itching, and irritation to human eyes.

Although I have owned pet raccoons, I have never to my knowledge had a wild one enter my house. I have often found raccoons prowling outside my tent at night when camping in parts of the South. On one occasion, while I was sleeping, a raccoon opened the lid of my food chest and removed a carton of milk and the bacon. Although it made away with the bacon, I appreciated the fact that it set the milk carton upright on the ground without spilling a drop.

There is very little that a raccoon won't eat. Everything from fresh corn to crabs and crayfish is eaten with the gusto of a gourmet. Although greedy and often destroying more than they eat, raccoons do maintain a certain decorum in how they eat their food. Normally they dip their food in water and wash it before it is eaten. At a California raccoon-feeding station, animals habitually took unfamiliar food to the birdbath and washed it. Even bread and cake were washed until nothing was left but tiny sodden pieces. At a Milton, Massachusetts, feeding station for raccoons, it was observed that some of the animals dunked and washed their food while others rarely, if ever, did this. Manners here were poor. Parents always ate first, chasing off their young ones. Certain stubborn individuals would sit in the food bowl and cover the food so that other animals couldn't eat. Through the night there was a great deal of squabbling and roughhousing accompanied by barks, growls, and churring noises.

Opinions differ as to why raccoons wash their food. The best explanation I know of is that in the wild raccoons obtain much of their food on mud flats and along streams. In order to remove impurities and see what they are eating, they resort to washing their food. The habit is so ingrained that they go right on washing food even if it is something they find away from water.

In the fall, raccoons eat even more than usual. Some of them become so fat that they look like butterballs. Whereas the average weight of a raccoon in the summer is about fifteen pounds, the weight in the fall almost doubles. Raccoons, in common with other animals, are larger in the North. A recorded weight of sixty-two pounds was probably of a raccoon in the fall near the northern limits of the range. Raccoons are found from southern Canada southward and from coast to coast. There are few habitats or parts of the country that do not have this animal, which is aptly called the "masked bandit." Raccoons remain in their dens for varying periods of time in the winter but they do not hibernate.

Can the wildlife gardener safely invite this entertaining rogue to his yard? The same inducements that bring birds will encourage raccoons. A feeding station, water, and a den where the raccoon can raise its young and find shelter are the basic requirements. So long as the gardener does not raise sweet corn there should be no serious conflicts between his interests and that of the raccoon. Sweet corn in the milk stage is too much of a temptation to put in the way of a raccoon or, for that matter, a squirrel. The raccoon also has a weakness for watermelon. Through a hole in the rind only the size of a silver dollar, a raccoon with its paws can scoop out the entire contents. Grapes are another favorite. In California raccoons made well-beaten paths to fig trees when the fruit was ripe. Although no loss to any of us, I have discovered that raccoons in Maryland have a liking for the ill-smelling fruits of the ginkgo tree. So far as ornamental shrubs are concerned, raccoons eat the fruits of pyracantha, hollies, and privet, but most of the harvest is left for the birds.

If the wildlife gardener can put up with these annoyances, there is no reason why he shouldn't invite this animal to his yard. A porch or deck is a good place to leave scraps for hungry raccoons that come at night. Sweets as well as sunflower seeds, chicken necks, suet, bread, and other kitchen scraps will be more than welcomed by the nocturnal visitors. The birdbath will ordinarily supply raccoons with all the water they need. As for a den or nesting box, Palmer recommends a box in a tree made of sound wood. The box should be 14 inches square and 36 inches tall and have an entrance 5 by 6 inches on the side near the top.

Raccoons pay us back by eating many garden pests. They are particularly fond of grasshoppers and crickets. They also make inroads upon the mouse and rat population. Although we may be nervous about what they will do next, we can't help but admire this resourceful animal that is so familiar with us and our ways. As put by a correspondent of mine in Canada who had his share of troubles from raccoons: "Coons are interesting and my bursts of anger over them are rather brief."

## WEASELS AND SKUNKS

Of the mustelids, as weasels, skunks, and their allies are called, only the skunks are of any importance to the wildlife gardener. Weasels are solitary animals that are experts at staying out of our way. Their one crime is getting into the poultry house and going on a killing spree. Killing as much for pleasure as for food, a single weasel may slaughter up to sixty or seventy chickens in a night. I recall the trouble my grandfather had with weasels getting into his henhouse. As a small boy I once happened upon a long-tailed weasel near the poultry yard in broad daylight. Ignoring my presence, the animal sat upright on its haunches looking around in every direction. This member of the weasel family is found from southern Canada southward and from coast to coast.

Upon hearing distress cries of birds and small mammals, long-tailed weasels are apt to run out into the open to investigate. In several reported instances, this weasel has scampered up the legs of persons holding squeaking birds. Killers that they are, the weasels are useful in controlling rats, mice, ground squirrels, and other small rodents. In a survey conducted by the Long Point Bird Observatory in Ontario, three species of weasels were recorded at bird feeders. The animals not only took kitchen scraps and suet but preyed upon squirrels and meadow voles that came to the feeders. No mention was made of their taking birds.

The skunk that everyone knows, if only through the scent that it releases, is the striped or common skunk. With a range that includes most of North America, it is an example of a mammalian success story. Less well known is the much smaller spotted skunk with a range from Florida through the West and Midwest. This skunk weighs only a pound or two but is just as accomplished as the striped skunk in using its spray to repel enemies. In positioning itself to release its spray, it stands on its two forefeet and raises its body vertically: at the same time, it turns its back to its enemy. The hooded and hog-nosed skunks are found in parts of our Southwest and southward through Mexico.

The striped skunk makes its home nearly everywhere, including barns, outbuildings, and any space it can find beneath houses. Relying upon its odoriferous discharge, it takes few precautions except to restrict its foraging largely to the nighttime. The horned owl is a major predator upon this skunk and other skunks as well, but the motor vehicle takes a deadlier toll. Skunks and opossums, in my experience, are the most frequent highway victims in more eastern states.

As a rule, skunks need to be severely provoked before they discharge the fine spray which is so effective in routing enemies. The spray comes from glands near the anus. Highly accurate in their aim, skunks can hit a target twelve to fifteen feet away. A science teacher who was an acquaintance of mine learned the hard way that skunks can direct their discharge even when the tail is not elevated. Among the remedies recommended for ridding oneself of skunk odor is to wash portions of the body receiving spray with any of the following: gasoline, vinegar, tomato juice, or ammonia. Clothing should be washed in a solution of ammonia and water. For a dog that has been sprayed, the remedy is washing with ketchup or tomato juice. Dogs never seem to learn to stay away from skunks and therefore, much to the discomfort of all concerned, are forever having encounters with neighborhood skunks.

Mothballs or naphthalene flakes are the only repellents I know of for ridding the premises of skunks. As might be expected, the animals

*Spotted skunk using its spray effectively*

are immune to most bad odors. They can also withstand far stronger dosages of natural poison than most animals. They demonstrate their impunity by fearlessly robbing bee and wasp colonies. According to Grzimek's *Animal Life Encyclopedia,* a hog-nosed skunk was bitten ten times by a bushmaster, an extremely poisonous snake, and yet survived apparently unharmed.

Skunks are friends of the gardener. If we can overlook the slight risk of their discharges, we can welcome this animal with open arms. Its services as a mouser and consumer of beetle grubs make it one of our most valuable wildlife allies. Since scarcely any vegetable food is consumed, we have nothing to fear from the skunk so far as flowers and the vegetable garden are concerned. The best aspect of the skunk's services is their thoroughness. Leonard Lee Rue III calls the striped skunk "nature's vacuum cleaner." He tells how this skunk goes over every foot of ground to dig out grubs and turns every stone in its search for beetles.

If we put out food for mammals at night, skunks may appear along with opossums and raccoons. All three may eat together but usually there is friction, with raccoons trying to dominate the other two. Skunks are less accomplished than raccoons when it comes to getting into the garbage. If successful, they eat as much as they can hold and scatter the rest. Skunks may disappear for days at a time in cold, wintry weather, but they are out again foraging for food when the worst is over. They put on extra weight in the fall but do not hibernate.

As with some other mammals, there is always the danger of rabies. A skunk that is acting queerly and is abroad at an unusual time of the day may be infected with this deadly virus. The safest course is to stay well clear of such an animal and call the police, the ASPCA, or some other appropriate agency. Most of us would not go near a skunk anyway and therefore our chances of being bitten by a rabid one are slight indeed. However, such animals can be dangerous to dogs and cats.

# WOODCHUCKS

In many parts of our northern and central states, it is not unusual to see a large rodent feeding at the grassy edges of highways. Its brownish coloration, flat head, and habit of standing on its haunches tell us that it is a woodchuck. Also called groundhog, this stocky animal is abroad during the day, especially early in the morning and toward dark. Never far from entrances to underground burrows, the woodchuck beats a hasty retreat when a dog, a fox, or any other potential enemy makes an appearance. Before running for cover, the woodchuck often emits a loud whistle as though warning others of its kind. For those of us who live in the East and see few wild mammals along our roadsides, the woodchuck offers a pleasant treat. It can be called the common roadside mammal of our scenic parkways.

But the gardener may view the woodchuck in a different light than the motorist. Few animals can create as much havoc in a vegetable garden in a shorter period of time. A vegetarian, with the habits of a grazing animal, the woodchuck is quick to trade its diet of meadow grasses and clovers for the spoils of the garden. Friends in Illinois tried to divert a family of woodchucks from their vegetable garden by offering them all the food they could eat in another part of the yard. Each day no less than three pounds of carrots, two pounds of apples, and four bananas were offered as a bribe. The woodchucks gratefully consumed all this food and then went right back to feeding in the vegetable garden.

By the end of the summer, my friends had counted no less than six full-grown woodchucks and two younger ones coming for food. The animals had burrows at the edge of the yard and throughout the day appeared at a feeding place below a large willow tree. After the first heavy frost in October, the woodchucks disappeared. They had gone to underground sleeping chambers and would remain in them sound asleep through their period of winter hibernation. But it was too late for my friends. Their lettuce, celery, cauliflower, beans, and peas had served only to fatten a large family of woodchucks. Animal lovers that they were, they took their losses philosophically, saying that the woodchucks were there before they were.

Woodchucks are sedentary animals not given to wandering far from their burrows. Normally their home territory extends less than a radius of fifty yards. The burrow, with openings near rock piles or in brier patches, may be up to thirty feet long. Dirt dug from the burrow is heaped in a mound at the entrance. The woodchuck uses this hillock as an observation post. A number of other mammals, including skunks, opossums, raccoons, and rabbits, use woodchuck burrows as refuges or living quarters. John O. Whitaker, Jr., in his *Audubon Society Field Guide to North American Mammals,* points to little-appreciated contributions that woodchucks make to the soil. Their diggings loosen and aerate the soil, letting in organic matter and moisture. He reports that over 1,600,000 tons of soil are turned over each year in New York State alone.

The home gardener will probably prefer having earthworms perform these services. If woodchucks are close neighbors, he will almost certainly have to fence in portions of the garden that might be tempting to this animal. A wire-mesh fence two and a half feet tall and extending eight inches below the surface will prove helpful in protecting the garden but can't be guaranteed to keep the animals out. Planting nasturtiums at strategic locations in the yard may prove helpful. The plant, with its spicy foliage, is disliked by woodchucks, rabbits, and other vegetable eaters.

Still another method of coping with woodchucks was described in a 1984 issue of *The Conservationist.* All one has to do is pour some gasoline in a small receptacle, place the receptacle a short distance inside

*Woodchuck on guard at tunnel entrance*

the burrow, and wait for results. According to those who have tried this tactic, the woodchuck, objecting to the unpleasant fumes, soon leaves the premises. This method sounds almost too simple to be true!

# SQUIRRELS

Of the several species of squirrels found in North America, only the gray, fox, and red squirrels are of special interest to the wildlife gardener. Engaging, lively animals that make their presence known, squirrels are found almost everywhere. Gray and fox squirrels are among our closest wildlife neighbors and are as much at home in densely populated districts as they are in wilderness areas. The red squirrel is more of a wilderness animal, but nevertheless makes itself at home around farmsteads and sometimes penetrates into towns and suburbs. Its real home is the coniferous forests of Canada and more northern states. Gray and fox squirrels are partial to deciduous woodland and have adapted well to rural areas and the shade trees of towns and cities. Flying squirrels, although common in the North and wooded parts of the East, are retiring, nocturnal animals that may be our close neighbors without our knowing it.

## Gray Squirrel

The western gray squirrel of the Pacific coast and the common gray squirrel of the East are familiar to everyone living within their respective ranges. Gray squirrels are the common squirrels of city parks, yards, and gardens. The two gray squirrels look alike and have much the same habits. It is somewhat misleading, however, to call the gray squirrel gray. In summer the predominantly gray pelage is tipped with brown and the underparts are white or pale gray. The fluffy tails of gray squirrels, their most conspicuous physical characters, are sometimes held by the animals over their heads like umbrellas when it rains.

Although we hear a lot about the nuisance that squirrels make of themselves, most people will admit to liking them. On a questionnaire that I sent to over three hundred persons, many of them bird lovers, over 70 percent indicated a favorable attitude toward the gray squirrel.

Fox, flying, and red squirrels received equally good or more favorable ratings. My findings were in accord with those of a survey taken in Ontario in which squirrels, chipmunks, and cottontail rabbits were found to be liked by urbanites.

The main complaint about gray squirrels is that they appropriate far more food at bird feeders than we think they are entitled to. A better climber than the fox squirrel and with a tenaciousness that can scarcely be matched among our native small wild animals, gray squirrels have a reputation of being able to get to some of the best-protected bird feeders. But, contrary to popular opinion, gray squirrels rarely get past a well-designed squirrel guard or reach a squirrel-proof feeder, *unless they have found a way to jump from a nearby tree limb, post, part of the house, or the ground*. And extraordinary jumpers they are! In a recent experiment, I tried moving a feeder attached to a post fitted with a squirrel guard farther and farther away from the railing from which a squirrel was making successful jumps. After the feeder had been moved to a position requiring a leap of four and a half feet at an upward angle, the squirrel seemed to sense that the distance might be beyond his capacity. He (if I correctly diagnosed the animal's sex) began to study the situation carefully. Positioning himself at various points from which leaps could be made, he seemed to be estimating distances and finally decided, correctly, that the railing was still the best bet. Back at the railing, he hesitated for some time and then, flexing his muscles, made a successful leap, landing with some room to spare. After the feeder was moved still farther away—this time requiring a leap of four feet ten inches—the squirrel once again carefully studied the situation and again made a successful leap from the railing. At five feet—only two inches farther—the squirrel seemed temporarily unsure of himself. But the very next day he cleared the five-foot gap with a powerful leap and was seen at the feeder contentedly eating sunflower seeds.

Squirrel-proof feeders that I have tested include the Droll Yankee Garden Pole Feeder, the Droll Yankee hanging feeder called the BJ–Jr, and a make by another company called the Presto Galaxy Feeder. As effective as these feeders and others are in thwarting squirrels, I would also suggest using a simple inexpensive proofing device that we can make ourselves.

Secure a strong nylon fishing line between the house and a tree or post, first stringing at least a dozen empty film cartridges or empty wooden thread spools on the line. Hang a feeder or feeders midway on the line, with an equal number of spools or cartridges on either side but at some distance from each other so that they will not all jam together. Clothespins or rubber bands can be used as separators. A squirrel will ordinarily have no difficulty tightrope walking along the nylon fishing line, but as soon as it puts its weight on the spools or cartridges, they will spin, tumbling the squirrel to the ground. The only injury the squirrel will suffer will be to its dignity. It will sit for a while with its tail twitching violently and then go back to plotting another course of action.

I have experimented with the fishing line/spool or cartridge method for over two years and found it to be 100 percent effective in keeping squirrels from feeders. But the line and its feeder must be high enough from the ground and far enough from other vantage points to prevent squirrels from reaching their goal by making long leaps.

One need not feel sorry for outwitted squirrels. Usually enough food falls from hanging bird feeders to keep squirrels and ground-feeding birds well supplied. Moreover, many people scatter food on the ground or have a special feeder for squirrels where corn is the main item on the menu.

We have no choice but to keep gray squirrels from bird feeders. They not only eat much of the food but sometimes wreck the feeders as well. There are even cases of this squirrel drinking sugar-water at hummingbird feeders and in the process smashing the glass or plastic vials. The appetite of the gray squirrel is enormous. Edwin Way Teale tells of a gray squirrel that in a half hour ate twenty unshelled peanuts, two pecans, a Brazil nut, and three almonds. A correspondent of mine in North Carolina reported that six gray squirrels in cold, wintry weather spent an entire day eating at her bird feeder. We are apt to conclude that the squirrels prefer our foods to anything they can find in the wild. The truth of the matter, however, is that the gray squirrel is quite content with its natural fare and normally makes use of our food only when there has been a poor harvest or competition is particularly keen for its favorite acorns and other nut crops. During the fall harvest season, when gray squirrels are eating all they can and storing the rest for use later on, other busy gleaners are also gathering their share. Besides other species of squirrels, the gray squirrel must compete for acorns with woodpeckers, jays, nuthatches, titmice, and other birds. During the frenzied harvesting period, which may last from late summer until late fall, the squirrels may scarcely notice our bird feeders.

Burying nuts for the winter food supply is a habit that has endeared the gray squirrel and its fellow food hoarders to all of us who love trees and want to have more of them. The many acorns and nuts that are buried, lost, and forgotten are a potential source of renewal for woodlots that have been badly cut over. The gray squirrel shoves each nut it wishes to store into a separate hole it has dug, fills the hole, and tamps down the fresh dirt with its forepaws and nose. During a good harvest season, a single gray squirrel may bury several thousand nuts. These supplies normally carry the squirrel population through the winter. The squirrels remain active and even dig for hidden nuts when there is a heavy snow cover on the ground. They locate their own nuts and those of other squirrels through their keen sense of smell. Nevertheless, only a fraction of the nuts are retrieved.

There are occasions when gray squirrels make lemminglike emigrations from their home territories. During the previous century a number of these mass movements were so spectacular that they gave rise to lurid accounts of squirrels swimming rivers and lakes in great hordes and devouring entire fields of corn and wheat. Eugene Kinkead tells of an emigration of this kind from Wisconsin in 1842 in which millions of animals were reportedly involved. During this century, several large movements occurred in the mid-thirties when squirrels left New England in a southwesterly direction and in the course of their departure swam the Connecticut and Hudson rivers. During the fall of 1968, squirrels were on the move throughout most of the Atlantic coastal region. The squirrels were found to be well fed, healthy, and under no psychological stress. A smaller movement in New England during the fall of 1978 was more easily explainable. There had been a complete failure of the acorn crop. Helen Bates of Springfield, Massachusetts, writes me that as the famished squirrels passed through her area they stripped hollies, hawthorns, crab apples, and other ornamental shrubs of their fruits. In a short time, they had ruined food supplies that might have lasted birds through the winter.

The squirrels that embark on these mass movements subject themselves to great risks. As with the lemmings of Scandinavia, whose periodic mass movements sometimes end in the sea, the ranks of the gray squirrel hordes are thinned by predators, starvation, drowning, and, since the beginning of this century, the motor vehicle.

Hunting pressure has long been a factor in keeping squirrel populations under control. But in the absence of hunting, squirrel populations frequently outgrow the food supply. Under these conditions, we can expect increased pressure on bird feeders and more destructive activities than usual, such as digging up and eating flower bulbs, gnawing into overhead cables, and getting into the attic. About one gray squirrel to an acre and a half of good mature woodland in or near the suburbs is about within the normal carrying capacity of a habitat. This figure was arrived at by Dr. Vagn Flyger, who trapped, marked, and released gray squirrels in a wooded suburb on the outskirts of Washington, D.C. Kinkead, who cites this figure, also tells of a park census in New Haven, Connecticut, showing as many as ten animals to an acre, and reports that in portions of Central Park even higher densities were found. Here the squirrels tended to concentrate around park entrances because this was where they could expect the most generous handouts from people who supplied them with food.

In addition to eating the standard peanuts offered by park strollers, gray squirrels exhibit other sophisticated tastes. In city parks, they eagerly accept all the snacks offered them by lunch-hour strollers. These may consist of anything from candy to popcorn, Fritos, and pizza. Whether a steady diet of artificial food of this kind is good for them is another matter. There is some evidence that city squirrels living largely on peanuts become scrawny-looking. Even more questionable is the effect of too many sweets. Gray squirrels are fond of chocolate candy bars and individual squirrels have even learned how to rob candy vending machines. Coconut meat is a great favorite. I once saw a gray squirrel in Kensington Gardens in London frantically trying to chew through a hole in a coconut that had been hung for birds. Our gray squirrel was introduced to England in 1876. The population has grown and spread and, at the same time, the animals have proved to be more destructive over there than in their native home. They are about as unpopular in Britain as the introduced starlings and house sparrows are in this country.

Like squirrels of other kinds, the gray squirrel is fond of mushrooms and takes full advantage of this food whenever it is available. Fruits and berries also seem to offer a welcome change. The halved oranges and apples and the grapes that I put on my feeders for birds are, as often as not, consumed by squirrels. The older and more rotten this food is, the better the squirrels seem to like it. Fresh corn is a delicacy that takes gray squirrels only too often into cornfields and vegetable gardens. If whole corn is put out for birds or squirrels, it will be noticed that the gray squirrel eats only the germ and leaves the rest. As we find from bitter experience, sunflower seeds and mixtures containing peanut butter are consumed so quickly that birds do not get their share. When in late spring sunflower plants begin springing up in odd places in the garden, we know that they have been planted by either jays or squirrels. Fortunately the gray squirrel has little use for suet; not having the carnivorous tastes of the red squirrel, it normally does not plunder the nests of birds. Sometimes gray squirrels make modest inroads upon the fruits of yew, holly, and pyracantha. Showing an almost birdlike taste, a gray squirrel that I chanced upon was stripping a poison ivy vine of its fruits. Of concern to those who wish to have tidy lawns and sidewalks, gray squirrels go on twig-cutting binges that leave our grounds as littered as if there had been a violent windstorm. The squirrels nip off the twigs in order to better get at buds, blossoms, seeds, fruits, or nuts. After eating whatever has attracted them, they drop the twigs to the ground. The tree gets a good pruning but we are left with the cleanup job. Twig cutting can occur almost any time during the warmer months of the year. Some years it is more prevalent than in others.

If we can forgive this animal for its misdeeds, we may want to give it a helping hand. Almost as important to squirrels as food and water are nesting dens. Unless there are a good many older trees in the neighborhood, there is likely to be a shortage of cavities where the squirrels can rear their young. We can make up for this deficiency by erecting nesting boxes. A squirrel box should be constructed of good timber or half-inch to one-inch plywood and should be about 20 inches high, 8 inches wide, and with an entrance hole 3 inches in diameter about 2 inches from the top of the box. It should be placed ten feet or more from the ground in a sizable tree—preferably an oak, hickory, or beech. Either the top or front of the box should be removable in order to permit inspection and cleaning. One box per acre is adequate for a normal squirrel population.

On the other hand, if squirrels are too much of a nuisance, we have the option of live-trapping them and taking the animals to the countryside for release. For most of us this is too much trouble. It is easier to learn to like them.

### Fox Squirrel

From the Great Plains region eastward, many people play host to the fox squirrel. This squirrel looks much like the gray squirrel (it sometimes takes careful study to determine which it is) but is larger, with a squarish head, and in much of its range it exhibits a tawny brown pelage without any white showing below. To complicate matters, in parts of its range the fox squirrel has altogether different color patterns from the one described, running from wholly black, except for white on the nose, lips, and ears, to a gray phase in which the underparts are white. The gray squirrel also has different color phases—albinos occurring in some localities and melanistic animals in others. But in the gray squirrel these are only isolated cases, not whole populations. In the fox squirrel each part of the range has its dominant color phase with intermediate phases also being found. These differences pose problems in making proper identifications.

The fox squirrel is nowhere near as widespread as the gray squirrel. Although common in some areas, the fox squirrel is rare or absent in parts of its original range. The same factors that have aided the gray squirrel haven't always worked so well for the fox squirrel. Indeed, one race, known as the Delmarva fox squirrel, has been listed as endangered and occurs naturally only in four counties on the Eastern Shore of Maryland. But in the Midwest the fox squirrel, for the most part, still flourishes and here it has taken well to living in towns and cities.

Not as quick or agile as the gray squirrel, the fox squirrel is more easily discouraged from taking food at bird feeders. In Denver, Colorado, where the fox squirrel has been introduced, I once had the opportunity of testing its food preferences at a feeding station. Besides liking sunflower seeds and other typical bird foods, the squirrels eagerly took peanuts, bread, grapes, and banana. If anything, banana was the favorite. Like the gray squirrel, the fox squirrel has little use for suet.

Fox squirrels exhibit typical squirrel fondness for nuts, fruits, berries, corn, and mushrooms. Hickory nuts are perhaps their preferred nuts, followed closely by pecans, walnuts, and acorns. Corn from the milk stage onward is a great favorite. Fox squirrels living near cornfields make use of this crop from midsummer until the last ears left after the harvesting have disappeared. Each ear is carried to a safe eating place in a tree at the edge of the field. The ground beneath these feeding spots becomes littered with piles of corncobs. As with gray squirrels, only the germ is eaten; the rest of the kernel is discarded. By early fall, the fox squirrel commences putting food away for the winter. Like the gray squirrel, it buries the nuts individually rather than in large caches in the manner of the red squirrel.

The fox squirrel is a late riser, foraging mostly during the midday hours. In this way, it avoids competing with the gray squirrel, which typically feeds early and late in the day. But those gray squirrels that have taken up residence in cities and suburbs have changed their times of feeding, foraging throughout the day instead of only at their former early and late hours. Their feeding hours thus coincide with those of the fox squirrels. Where the two find themselves eating together, they tend to show an aloof indifference. In Ithaca, New York, I watched to see what would happen when a fox squirrel joined half a dozen gray squirrels consuming food that had fallen from a hanging bird feeder. Keeping as much to itself as possible, the fox squirrel sat stolidly in one place, eating steadily with its back turned to the grays. The gray squirrels moved about as they ate and from time to time one would chase after another. Finally, when a gray squirrel got too close to where it was eating, the fox squirrel came to life and began pursuing the gray.

Unless we happen to be corn growers, we will normally have little reason to find fault with this squirrel. It plants trees in the same way as the gray squirrel and is a handsome, interesting addition to our outdoor menagerie. Plenty of oaks and other nut-bearing trees are to its liking, and its nesting dens, if you want to build them, should be to the same specifications as for the gray squirrel.

*Red Squirrel*

Weighing about half a pound, the red squirrel makes up for its small size by being the noisiest and most excitable of all our squirrels. As soon as a dog, cat, or other trespasser appears in its territory, the red squirrel commences an incessant chattering, and jumping from limb to limb, it follows the intruder, scolding, hurling insults, and letting all the world know of its disapproval. If we live in Alaska, Canada, mountainous parts of the East or West, or more northern states, we may find ourselves playing host to this plucky little squirrel that is capable of withstanding the coldest winter temperatures. A red squirrel on the west coast has yellowish or orange underparts instead of the typical white and is called the Douglas squirrel. Whichever one of these animals we have for a neighbor, we will soon find that we have to match our wits with it. The red squirrel has all the perverse ways of the gray squirrel but, if anything, is more given to chewing holes, digging bulbs, and getting into attics. There have been many instances of red squirrels chewing birdhouses to pieces, especially ones constructed of plywood. It is believed that they chew into the plywood in order to get a taste of the glue that holds the strips together. After a bird feeder in Vermont was squirrel-proofed, a red squirrel took its frustration out on the nearby house, chewing holes in the siding and window ledges.

The red squirrel has the same food preferences as other squirrels and a few additional ones. More carnivorous than the others, it is fond of suet, meat scraps, and, sad to say, baby birds. Taking advantage of its northwoods habitat, the red squirrel makes full use of the seeds of conifers. Even before cones have opened, the squirrels are busily gnawing into them in order to obtain the seeds. Mushrooms figure as importantly in the red squirrel's diet as in those of other squirrels. The mushrooms are gathered, hung on limbs of trees, and, after they have dried, stored along with other foods for future use. The deadly amanitas are consumed without apparent ill effect.

Food is taken to special locations where it is either consumed or stored for future use. A stump, rock pile, or low limb may serve as a dining hall. At sites such as these, chewed-off fragments may accumulate over the years to form large heaps or middens, which often serve as caches for winter food. Dorcas MacClintock tells of middens that were as much as twenty feet long, twelve feet wide, and three feet high. Middens of this size must be the work of several generations of red squirrels.

Like the gray and fox squirrels, the red remains active through the winter. To provide for the thin times that lie ahead, it spends much of the fall storing food. Objects are buried separately or are placed in underground storage chambers. As much as a bushel of green cones from spruce and pine trees has been found in one of these chambers. With the arrival of spring, sap from maples, birches, and other trees provides a welcome change in the diet. Sap is obtained from sapsucker drillings or from holes that the squirrel itself cuts in the upper surface of limbs of trees.

You need a placid disposition to put up with the red squirrels' mischievous antics on your property, but if it is any consolation, they can be kept from bird feeders with only a modest amount of shielding. Also, they are highly territorial, with a pair laying claim to an acre or two. No other red squirrels are allowed in this holding, and the owners, usually without any noticeable degree of success, try to defend the territory against intrusion by gray squirrels. Of course, this happens only in more southern parts of the range where both species exist side by side. Although the two species are constantly at odds with each other, they sometimes settle their differences by coming to food at different times of the day.

*Chipmunks*

Small striped squirrels, the chipmunks form a homogeneous group of close to twenty species that are difficult to tell apart. Ordinarily there are no more than two species of chipmunks occupying any one habitat. Like the tree squirrels, the chipmunks are active during the day and have a taste for nuts, fruits, berries, seeds, bulbs, mushrooms, snails, insects, and occasionally the eggs and young of birds. Not nearly as proficient at climbing and jumping as tree squirrels, the chipmunks spend most of their time running about on the ground when they are not in their burrows. All but one of the chipmunks are westerners. Living for the most part in wooded, mountainous country, the western chipmunks are not commonly seen about the homes of man. They should not be confused with the ground squirrels, which often share the same habitats with them and look and act like chipmunks. (The golden-mantled ground squirrel is well known to those who hike and camp in the western mountains. It accepts food at campsites and picnic tables and looks for all the world like an oversized chipmunk.)

Throughout much of the East there is only one chipmunk—the eastern chipmunk, a small largely reddish-brown animal with two black stripes running along each side and whitish underparts. There are no chipmunks in far southeastern sections, and in the western Great Lakes region the range of the eastern chipmunk overlaps with that of the least chipmunk, a predominantly western species. The perky eastern chipmunk is often seen scampering about the lawn and darting into holes in rock piles or old stumps. If we let them, the chipmunks in our yards can haul away almost as much food from our bird feeders as the tree squirrels. Making trip after trip to the feeder to gather food in its ample cheek pouches, a chipmunk will work all day to put food away for the winter. MacClintock states that an eastern chipmunk can hold as many as thirty-one kernels of corn or from sixty to seventy sunflower seeds in its cheek pouches. Fortunately, it is easy to shield bird feeders from chipmunks; also, the small animals sleep through colder parts of the winter and therefore are not on hand during the height of the bird-feeding season.

The eastern chipmunk has the same capacity as the gray squirrel for developing a taste for exotic foods. One pet chipmunk was fond of peach ice cream and even enjoyed taking sips of coffee from a cup, particularly relishing the sugary residue at the bottom. Edwin Tunis states that corms of violets, crocus bulbs, and pansy blossoms are among the chipmunk's favorite foods and that even tomatoes, especially the small cocktail kind, are sometimes eaten. A taste for tomatoes is unusual in mammals. At one of my bird-feeding stations, chipmunks showed a liking for the pulp of halved oranges.

Chipmunks are also fond of butterflies and sometimes show skill in catching them. Early in July at Ithaca, New York, I discovered mourning cloak butterflies thronging to fermented sap oozing from the base of a large oak tree. A chipmunk was sitting nearby, seizing butterflies one by one whenever they came close enough. Judging from the pile of discarded butterfly wings at the foot of the tree, the chipmunk had had good hunting.

Chipmunks lead a precarious existence and therefore seldom reach the high population levels attained by tree squirrels. House cats take a heavy toll and so do weasels wherever these relentless carnivores are found. Other enemies include hawks, snakes, and foxes.

In the event that chipmunks are numerous enough to become a problem in the garden, we can safeguard our bulbs in early spring by laying quarter-inch hardware cloth over beds where they are planted. When the bulbs sprout, we can remove the hardware cloth and hope that by then there will be enough other foods to distract the chipmunks' attention. Also, as with tree squirrels, chipmunks occasionally get into the house and rummage for food. If we can excuse such breaches of good behavior, we can enthusiastically welcome these engaging little animals as additions to our garden for wildlife.

## MICE, RATS, AND VOLES

For the most part, our native mice, rats, and voles are secretive, nocturnal prowlers whose presence we seldom suspect until we see signs of the damage they have done. One of the most widespread and abundant of these rodents is the meadow vole or meadow mouse. Along with other members of the genus *Microtus*, meadow voles are found over much of the continent except for more southern sections. We can distinguish them by their brown to blackish coloration, longish hair, stout bodies, and beady black eyes. If our young fruit trees are girdled and plants and bulbs near mole runs damaged, we are seldom wrong if we put the blame on the voles. But not until the vole population climbs to epidemic proportions is the damage likely to be severe. About every four years vole populations peak and soon thereafter begin to decline. If it weren't for predators like possums, skunks, foxes, weasels, hawks, and owls, these small rodents would overrun the countryside and cause incalculable damage. We should also give credit to house cats and dogs for the part they play. Several of the dogs I've owned turned into very good mousers.

On the other hand, we should also recognize the importance of voles and other small rodents as a vital link in a food chain that begins with plant life and climbs upward to carnivores and finally to man himself. Our aim should be to encourage the predators that control the number of small rodents and, at the same time, find ways to limit the damage the rodents do. To protect fruit trees and any other woody plants subject to damage from rodents gnawing bark near ground level (girdling)—a frequently encountered problem with young trees—encircle the trunks with a quarter-inch hardware cloth cylinder, which should be two feet high with the base buried two to three inches in the soil. Use stakes to keep the cylinder upright. This device will serve to protect plants from gnawing by mice, voles, and rabbits.

## HARES AND RABBITS

The terms "hare" and "rabbit" have been applied so loosely that we can be excused if we do not use them properly. In rabbits, the young are born naked and helpless, with eyes closed; in hares, the young are born covered with fur, with eyes open and capable of moving about shortly after birth. Under this definition jackrabbits and snowshoe rabbits are hares. The familiar cottontails, found from coast to coast, are rabbits. Chances are good that the grayish or brownish "bunny" that enters our yard, with ears standing straight up and a fluffy white tail, is a rabbit called a cottontail. The eastern cottontail is found from the western Great Plains eastward; the desert cottontail and mountain or Nuttall's cottontail are western relatives.

If it weren't for the damage they inflict on young trees, shrubs, and garden plants, the cottontails would probably be the most popular of the small mammals we see in our yards. They oblige us by appearing during daylight hours. They are most active at dawn and again toward sunset, using the fading hours of daylight to feed and sometimes to run, jump, and cavort about in a playful manner. During the breeding season these displays or dances are related to courtship; during the winter the rabbits are sometimes seen engaging in playful antics on the snow. But for the most part rabbits stay close to cover, ever watchful for danger from their innumerable enemies.

My friends in Illinois whose garden vegetables were devoured by woodchucks also played host to a family of eastern cottontails. Whatever the woodchucks had spared of the lettuce, cabbage, beans, radish tops, and cucumbers was eagerly consumed by the cottontails. The rabbits also found their way to the bird feeders and there ate whatever grain and seeds had dropped to the ground. Apples fallen from trees in the yard rounded out the rabbits' rich bill of fare. My friends complained that the only item in the garden spared by the cottontails and wood-chucks was onion tops. They found little consolation in this, however, since the neighbors stole the onions.

Most of us would not have allowed events to reach such a drastic conclusion. There are several ways in which we can protect our plants from rabbit damage. A standard method is to fence the garden using chicken wire or other mesh with openings no larger than one and one-half inches. The fence should be two feet high and extend to a depth of six inches below the surface. If fencing sounds like too much of a chore, we can try rabbit repellents. By sprinkling repellents such as blood meal, tobacco dust, and powdered aloes liberally about the garden, we can hope that the rabbits will be discouraged and go elsewhere for their food. Still another method is one suggested by Betty C. Winfree in the March–April 1979 issue of *The Garden Club of Virginia Journal*. She reports that a visiting horticulturist saved her pansy bed, where twelve dozen pansies had been nibbled to the ground by cottontails. Under shrubs near the beds she buried empty pop bottles so that only the necks were exposed. Air passing across the tops of the bottles made a faint sound that frightened the rabbits, and the next crop of pansies was un-disturbed.

Experiences like those of my friends in Illinois and Betty C. Win-free are somewhat exceptional. Many of us rarely have the problem of rabbits overly cropping our garden vegetables or flowers. Typically, cottontails nibble a little of this and that and then move on. We scarcely miss the few lettuce leaves or carrot tops they may have taken. If the lawn contains tender grasses, clovers, and dandelions, this is normally where the cottontails will concentrate their attention.

When winter comes, cottontails in more northern sections make up for the absence of green food by eating twigs and bark of shrubs and young trees. If there is any plant at this season that has more appeal to them than any other, it is sumac. During a hard winter with deep snow cover, sumacs may be stripped of their bark from ground level to three or four feet up the trunk. The rabbits stand on their toes to reach up as high as they can. To prevent them from giving a similar treatment to young fruit trees, we are often obliged to encase the trunks in wire-mesh cylinders of the kind used to deter mice and voles. If a tree is completely girdled, it will almost certainly die.

The degree of hospitality we extend to rabbits is likely to depend upon the amount of gardening we do and whether or not we grow fruit trees. If there is nothing much for them to damage, we might even go so far as to plant a rabbit garden containing clovers, kale, lettuce, and rape. In lieu of a brier patch where rabbits can take refuge and, in relative safety, raise their young, we can offer a brush pile. If there is adequate escape cover available, rabbits can flourish in yards where dogs romp and cats do their hunting. With its enormous reproductive capacity and ability to outrun and outdodge predators, the rabbit has demonstrated that it can live almost anywhere.

# DEER

With the opening up of forested lands through lumbering operations, roads, pipelines, power lines, and settlement, there has been an enormous increase in the kinds of food available to browsing animals. Sunlight reaching what had once been dark forest floor has stimulated the growth of early succession plants—young trees, shrubs, and grasses. As a result, the deer populations of North America have rebounded from a low point reached earlier in this century. As their populations increased, the deer have turned to other foods besides those of forest clearings. They have come into pastures and hayfields to graze, and in the East the white-tailed deer feed so heavily on soybeans that their flesh has taken on a different flavor. In addition, deer have taken to raiding gardens close to the woodlands where they make their home.

The species that is best known and has seen the most spectacular population increase is the white-tailed deer. Found from the Pacific Northwest to the Atlantic, the whitetail lives up to its name by lifting its tail as it bounds away to show the fluffy white fur of the underside. The buck or male grows antlers; the doe or female does not. The mule deer, found from the western Great Plains westward, looks very much like the whitetail but is on the average a trifle larger and its tail is tipped with black.

For the most part, people are so pleased to see the return of these graceful animals that they forgive them for the damage they do. Probably the biggest worry is not so much deer eating crops and garden plants but the plight of the deer when their numbers become too great. The result is often mass starvation. Of necessity, when winter comes to more northern regions, the deer change over from feeding upon the rich harvests of summer and autumn to a diet of bark, twigs, and needles. As they exhaust their winter food supply and snow impedes their movement, starvation begins to take its toll. This sad fact mars what otherwise would be the remarkable success story of animals returning from near oblivion to abundance.

Few other animals would feed upon plants that the whitetail takes delight in eating. According to an article on white-tailed deer in New York State in a 1980 issue of *The Conservationist*, the preferred foods for winter browsing were yew, arborvitae, hemlock, and apple. The article recommends wire-mesh cylinders over plants such as small arborvitaes and hemlocks. The deer can still browse on twigs protruding through the wire mesh but they can't destroy the entire plant.

One must marvel at the digestive powers of the white-tailed deer which allow it to live on plants that would kill other mammals. The foliage of yew is toxic and highly dangerous to most animals, but the deer eat it with impunity. The same is largely true of mountain laurel and rhododendron, both of which are safely eaten by white-tailed deer. Odd plants and even garbage are eaten by the deer as they forage about the homes of man. A correspondent of mine in Durango, Colorado, states that the deer browse on rose bushes in her yard and eat such extras as apples, citrus rinds, and banana skins. In a suburb of Baltimore, white-tailed deer were accused of eating the flowers and foliage of rose bushes, leaves of English ivy, tomato vines, and violets.

If the gardener wishes to gear his plantings toward species the deer won't eat or will eat only under exceptional circumstances, he should consult a list contained in the *New Western Garden Book*, published by Sunset Books. The list of fifty-eight plants or groups of plants considered relatively unpalatable to deer includes irises, lupines, narcissus, poppies, rosemary, tulips, and zinnias. But it should be added that several of the plants on the Sunset list for western gardens are freely eaten by white-tailed deer in the East.

Should deer become a nuisance in the garden, it may be necessary to resort to repellents. Blood meal sprinkled on the ground or placed in cloth bags hung in shrubs is said to be effective in keeping deer at a distance. Still another repellent—this one working on the principle that deer shy away from anything smelling of *Homo sapiens*—is human hair. Collect hair from the hairdresser's or barbershop, place it in small bags, and hang them in likely spots about the yard or garden. Another substance said to repel deer is fresh creosote. The theory here is that the smell smothers other odors—something that deer, ever on the alert for the odor of man or other potential enemies, can't tolerate. Deer depend as much upon their sense of smell as upon their vision for their safety. Plants that are said to repel deer are foxglove and the castor bean plant.

If nothing else works, a tall fence should be erected. A six-foot fence will deter most deer, but it will take a seven- or eight-foot fence to keep out the most venturesome ones with good leaping powers.

Whenever we have a problem from deer or any of the other mammals mentioned, there is nearly always a harmless solution. First of all we should try the solution that is easiest and least costly (if this does not produce the desired results, we try others). For example, a separate feeder for squirrels often leads them away from bird feeders. For those

*White-tailed deer in garden*

who live in the woods and have a porcupine problem, there is a simple way of dealing with this rodent's habit of chewing into ax handles, canoe paddles, and other objects that have a trace of salt on them from human perspiration: provide a special "salt lick," where they can obtain all the salt they want without damaging our belongings.

# 7 / Bees—Our Best Friends Among the Insects

Of the more than 3,500 species of bees that occur in North America, the wildlife gardener need concern himself only with the social bees which include the introduced honeybee and our native bumblebees. Although the solitary bees, which constitute the vast majority of the species in the family, visit flowers, they are too few in number to be of much help in pollination. For this vital function we rely upon the honeybees and bumblebees and whatever added help we receive from hover flies, butterflies, moths, and hummingbirds. Normally we take the services of bees for granted, but should a cool, wet spring keep bees from visiting flowers, we may well have disappointing harvests later in the season.

*Bumblebees visiting red clover*

I recall the wet spring of 1983, when few bees were on the wing at the time beach plum bushes were in bloom on the island of Nantucket. That fall my wife went out as usual to gather beach plums for the annual ritual of making beach plum jelly. She could find barely enough to make half a dozen jars. In other years, she put up three or four times as many jars. The only lucky gatherers that season were persons having access to bushes within a hundred feet or so of hives of honeybees. The bees had gathered nectar from the flowers of these nearby bushes in spite of the bad weather.

Not only does the honeybee assist us by pollinating flowers but excess honey from its hive provides the world with the delicious substance that has been called the nectar of the gods. Because of its added services in supplying us with honey and beeswax, honeybees have received vastly more attention than the equally hardworking bumblebees. Bumblebees store honey, but only enough is put away to supply the colony while it is active during the warmer months of the year. So unless we belong to the fraternity of beekeepers, hardy individuals who risk being stung as they solicitously care for their hives, we might as well regard all social bees in the same light. They are essential pollinators for many groups of plants, taking pollen from male flowers and, as they go from blossom to blossom, accidentally depositing some of it on female flowers. Some plants do not require services of this kind, either having flowers that are self-pollinating or dependent upon the wind for pollination. But if it were not for the tireless travels of social bees, our cherry, peach, apple, pear, and plum orchards would bear little fruit, and the raising of clover, alfalfa, and other forage crops would be impossible. Also, both the quality and the quantity of our vegetable harvest would be drastically reduced.

Jasmine Edline of Birmingham, England, in a letter that appeared in a 1981 issue of *Birds*, gives honeybees credit for making her yard a better habitat for wildlife. After installing a bee hive, she noted a dramatic improvement in the ecology. The bees "enthusiastically pollinated everything within a three-mile radius of the hive." According to the writer, this led to a great increase in seeds, berries, and nuts for wildlife. The resultant growth in bird, mouse, and gray squirrel populations provided more food for predators. Owls and kestrels made an appearance for the first time.

Although the writer may have overstated the contributions of her bee hive, she does show a good understanding of the interrelationships among the various forms of wildlife that inhabit suburban yards. With a plentiful food supply, smaller animals increase in number and, in turn, are preyed upon by foxes, hawks, and owls. The honeybee plays an important role in maintaining food chains of this kind through the part it plays in pollinating flowers.

Keeping honeybees is not only a way to ensure pollination and earn an income but also a very popular hobby. Many people enjoy the small chores entailed in beekeeping and it is an especially enjoyable hobby for those who grow flowers or raise vegetables. Gardening and beekeeping go hand in hand. We have a better garden with bees, and the more flowers we have, the more honey available from the hive. According to Roger A. Morse, about 300,000 people in the United States keep bees. The majority are hobbyists who maintain from one to ten hives. The amateur beekeeper can pursue his hobby almost anywhere. Even a backyard in a city can support a hive or two. But if the production of honey is the main goal, either beekeeping should be conducted in an agricultural area or the bees should be moved from time to time to fields or orchards so as to be on hand for peak blossoming periods.

Among the crops that supply the beekeeper with the most honey are clover, alfalfa, buckwheat, cotton, mustard, and soybeans. Orchards and citrus groves are another good source of honey. Important weed and woodland nectar-producing crops, according to Morse, are basswood, tupelo, goldenrod, and aster. He states that about half the honey produced in the United States comes from non-agricultural crops. While there appears to be no estimate available as to the amount that comes from garden flowers and vegetables, the combined total from such sources must be large indeed. For the hobbyist beekeeper, there usually need be only sufficient honey to sustain his one or more hives and provide enough for table use.

Honeybees fan out to distances of two or three miles in search of pollen and nectar and sometimes much farther. They are attracted to flowers partly by their color. Bees are drawn to blue, violet, and pink, and they also see well in the ultraviolet range. However, other factors besides color play equally important roles in luring bees to the flower. A great deal depends upon the ease with which the bee can collect pollen and nectar. Long-tubed flowers, like those of the nicotianas, present an insurmountable obstacle to the honeybee with its short tongue. So do those with tight openings like the snapdragon. Honeybees in their busy lives haven't time to probe and explore. Lured by fragrance, color, and the examples of their fellows, they take whatever path is easiest.

One often sees a honeybee with the baskets on its hind legs bulging with pollen. Not used in making honey, pollen is stored in special cells and is eaten by members of the colony. Pollen supplies bees with their sole source of protein as well as some minerals and vitamins. A number of plants yield pollen but no nectar. This is largely true of poppies, most roses, St.-John's-wort, lupine, and some species of clematis.

However, nectar, the main ingredient of honey, is produced by most flowers. Some yield much more than others. A good bee flower is one that produces large amounts of nectar and grows abundantly enough to satisfy the needs of bees. Morse states that three dozen plant species supply 90 percent of the honey. In any given locality, he writes, there are usually no more than two or three plant sources from which the bees can make more honey than they require for their own sustenance. Although none of our garden flowers are normally grown in great enough quantities to meet Morse's standards of a good bee flower, many can compete with agricultural crops when it comes to nectar secretion.

In early spring, when many bee colonies are half starved, the willows, with their fuzzy blossoms, provide a much-needed source of food. No other early-blooming flowers are said to yield so much pollen and nectar. In our flower garden, we can make a contribution to bees in

*Worker returning to hive with pollen*

early spring by planting pussy willows. Maples also come to the aid of bees in early spring. The red maple outdoes nearly every other tree in this respect. I have seen honeybees coming to the blossoms of this tree in Georgia in late January. Still another tree that is a good source of nectar in early spring is the redbud. The pink blossoms, appearing about the same time that flowering dogwood comes into bloom, add a gorgeous background of color to a garden that is just coming to life. Among the other plants in our garden that assist honeybees in early spring are common crocus, wallflower, daffodil, primrose, February daphne, and flowering quince.

Even though we might have a number of the early-flowering plants favored by bees, there may not be enough sustenance for them if the weather does not cooperate. Unseasonably cool or damp weather in spring can deliver a severe setback to the beekeeper. Normally the air temperature has to be close to 60° F. for honeybees to make short flights and five degrees warmer for them to make long flights. But some colonies fly at lower temperatures than others. Flights cease altogether if the wind is over twelve miles an hour or if rain sets in. Even in the best of weather, some flowers are stingy with their nectar. In bad weather, they are apt to offer nothing at all. One of the very best bee plants, buckwheat, yields nectar only in the morning.

When summer arrives, our garden is likely to have much more to offer. Bees will be visiting most of the flowers. The only drawback is that our yard, no matter how well planted, cannot supply the needs of a hive with a population of as many as 70,000 bees. A hive of this size requires fields or orchards full of flowers. Nevertheless, the combined contribution of our flowers and those of our neighbors can add quite a few pounds of honey to the beekeeper's harvest. Moreover, many of our flowers, including ones not highly esteemed by beekeepers, help tide colonies over during scarce periods. Although I have never kept bees, I like to think that my flowers are helping a neighbor, even a distant one, who is keeping them.

There are so many flowers supplying honeybees with nectar and pollen through summer and early fall that it would take a sizable publication to treat them all. Perhaps the best approach, if we wish to attract bees to our garden, is to think of combinations of flowers that will suit them and ourselves as well. We should remember that it takes a whole bed of flowers or several shrubs and trees in bloom to come close to meeting the daily needs of a hive. Even if we think we have the right combination of flowers, the bees will not always oblige us by coming when we think they should. They can easily be lured away by plants that we disapprove of and that produce inferior honey. I recall seeing very few honeybees at the herb garden on the Cornell University campus in Ithaca one summer. While strolling about the campus when our son was a student there, I had been in the habit of noting which flowers the bees were coming to in greatest numbers. Although an apiary with a number of hives was near the herb garden, the bees had gone somewhere else. I found them close to a mile away. By the hundreds they were visiting the ill-scented blossoms of privet. The flowers of this hedge plant are so attractive to honeybees that they will desert the flowers of what to our way of thinking are far better plants from the standpoint of honey. Not even an herb garden or the tempting flowers of linden, also known as basswood or lime, seem able to lure bees away from privet when this plant's blossoms are yielding good supplies of nectar. This preference is not at all to the liking of beekeepers. Privet nectar has a strong, bitter taste and a dark color. If bees bring enough of it to the hive, it will ruin any honey with which it is mixed.

Fortunately, the period in summer when privet leads bees astray is relatively short. Soon the bees are back gathering pollen and nectar from plants that produce better honey. If we have an herb garden, this is where bees will be busiest during much of their harvesting year. Honeybees are strongly attracted to most of the plants in the herb garden, especially the sages. Frank C. Pellett states that "the quality of sage honey is the best and not excelled even by the clovers and linden." He also points out that they have a long blooming season and sometimes produce phenomenal quantities of honey for the beekeeper. But to have sages in bloom over the longest possible period of time, we need early bloomers, like autumn sage (*Salvia greggii*), and late bloomers, like pineapple sage (*S. elegans*). For the East, Pellett particularly recommends garden sage (*S. officinalis*) as a good honey plant; for western gardens, black sage (*S. mellifera*) and purple sage (*S. leucophylla*).

However, we do not need to rely exclusively upon the sages for honey, fragrance, and culinary uses. The herb garden has other good bee plants in sweet marjoram (*Origanum marjorana*), winter savory (*Satureja montana*), lemon balm (*Melissa officinalis*), lovage (*Levisticum officinale*), thyme (*Thymus* spp.), hyssop (*Hyssopus officinalis*), mints (*Mentha* spp.), lavender, and borage (*Borago officinalis*). If we also include the heathers, which are suited for either the herb or the rock garden, we may find that we have the most popular bee attraction for miles around.

It should be remembered, however, that bees require whole fields of flowers if they are to lay aside enough honey to meet their own needs and at the same time reward the beekeeper. Therefore, we need other sources to help them fill their quotas. Almost overlooked in this day of tidy gardens and well-cut lawns is the lawn itself. If this valuable space is to be as helpful to bees as it is to robins, the grass should not be cut so short as to blight the clovers. Pellett calls the clovers by far the most important American honey plants. In addition to clovers belonging to the genus *Trifolium*, which includes white clover, crimson clover, and red clover, there are several others, and as a group, in the words of Pellett, they are probably the source of more surplus honey than all other plants combined.

If only for their nitrogen-fixing properties, clovers should be added to the grass seed we use in reseeding our lawns. Add to this the value of clovers in attracting bees and butterflies and they become a must for the wildlife gardener. White clover (*T. repens*) is the best one to plant for honeybees. Moreover, it can withstand fairly short clipping and still produce flowers. Red clover (*T. pratense*), on the other hand, is more of a bumblebee flower. With their longer tongues, bumblebees can reach the nectar in the deeper blossoms of this clover more easily than can honeybees. When either of these clovers begins blooming pro-

*Honeybee brushed with pollen of blue sage*

fusely in any part of my lawn, I avoid these areas with my lawn mower. Later on, when the blossoms have died down, I begin cutting again. Unfortunately, sweet clover (*Melilotus alba*), which grows to a height of anywhere from three to ten feet, is usually regarded as a weed. Nevertheless, it ranks with the other clovers as one of the best sources of pollen and nectar for honeybees.

Another good bee plant, the dandelion, has also been regarded as a weed. But if we properly appreciated the many virtues of this plant, we would not see a need to eradicate it from our lawns. The attractive yellow flower heads appear from early spring onward and are sometimes used in making wine; the leaves can be eaten as greens. Bees visit the flowers chiefly during the forenoon, when the plants produce the most pollen. In addition, the seeds of the dandelion are taken by birds. So if we can forgive this plant for its weedlike persistency in invading lawns and flower beds, we can elevate it to the status of a worthwhile garden flower.

One reason dandelion has a bad reputation is that it is often mistaken for cat's-ear (*Hypochaeris radicata*), a stubborn lawn plant with small yellow flowers. I have been trying to eradicate this aggressive little plant from my lawn for years without any conspicuous signs of success.

Before honeybees return to the hive to spend the winter, they will have one last fling, so to speak, if English ivy is growing anywhere in the vicinity. Saving its small greenish blossoms for September or later, English ivy is one of the last of the good bee plants to flower. John Crompton, in *A Hive of Bees*, says that, unlike fickle summer flowers, those of ivy yield nectar at all temperatures and under nearly all conditions. He calls the plant a godsend to bees short of honey in late fall. The flowers also attract butterflies, bumblebees, wasps, and a number of nectar-loving flies. There is so much buzzing and activity around the blossoms on a warm autumn day that one wonders how the tiny flowers can accommodate so many guests.

Although it is said that bees collect honey from flowers, this is not strictly true. They collect nectar, the sweet liquid in flowers that they turn into honey. Not until the moisture content of nectar has been greatly lowered and chemical changes have taken place do we have the prized substance that is called honey. An enzyme in the bees' saliva is added to the nectar, changing sucrose into glucose and fructose. The bees lower the moisture content by attaching small droplets of nectar to surfaces within the hive. After the moisture has sufficiently evaporated, the bees collect the residue and place it in storage cells. With aging, it becomes the honey we eat.

Most honeys are blends derived from the nectars of a wide variety of flowers. There is usually a dominant taste, which may come from the flower species that contributed the most nectar. Thus we have orange blossom honey, tupelo honey, sweet clover honey, goldenrod honey, mesquite honey, and many others. But no matter what the name, the bees have gathered at other flowers as well.

Water is another substance that is brought back to the hive. It is used to dilute honey that is fed to young bees and to cool the hive in warm weather. Ages before man thought of air conditioning, bees were cooling their hives by fanning their wings over droplets of water. With enough bees engaged in this activity, the inside temperature of the hive is effectively lowered.

When there is a dearth of pollen because cold or wetness has resulted in fewer blossoms than usual, bees sometimes turn to other substances, including such useless ones as particles of sawdust, coal dust, fine earth, or small bits of grain from the bird feeder. Here the honeybee's normally trustworthy instinct has gone astray.

The same unfavorable conditions that limit the amount of pollen available also apply to nectar yield. If nectar is in short supply, bees often turn to honeydew, a sweet liquid exuded by aphids and some other insects. When aphids are abundant on the foliage of street trees, some of the honeydew rains down to splatter sidewalks and parked cars, causing us to wonder about the source of the small sticky dots that besmear our cars. Beekeepers are even less pleased. Honey from honeydew is strong-tasting and finds few patrons in this country.

Bees use a substance called propolis in much the same way that we use putty. Consisting of resins or gums from trees, propolis is used by bees to fill cracks or openings in the hive and to smooth over rough surfaces.

The outdoor activities of honeybees can be observed in our yard almost any day in summer. We can watch as the bees go from flower to flower gathering nectar or pollen. We may see them licking up honeydew that has fallen on the leaves of trees. Or we may find a small cluster of bees collecting water at the edge of the birdbath. Even the bird

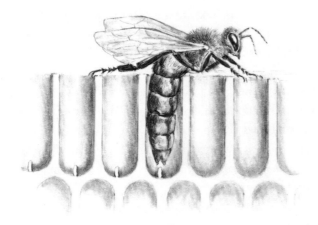

*Queen laying eggs*

feeders may be visited by these ever inquisitive, probing insects. Once a hummingbird feeder is discovered, the bees may become a nuisance by clustering around feeding vents to drink the sugar-water, thereby, in some cases, keeping the hummingbirds away. If the bees are coming to feeders containing seeds or grain, it may be that they are gathering fine bits of chaff as a substitute for pollen. In any case, it is fascinating to watch the bees as they make their rounds. We can never be sure where we'll find them next.

Once the bees enter the fastness of their hives, their lives become a mystery to us. It has taken centuries to unravel the complicated social structure within the hive, the methods bees use in communicating with one another, and how the colony perpetuates itself from one generation to another. Egg laying, rearing young, making honey, storing honey and pollen are some of the activities that take place in the hive and are not seen by us. Few governments are run more smoothly than the way bees run their colonies. Their whole aim is perpetuation of the species and not, as is so important in the human species, the fulfillment of goals of the individual.

The focal center of all this activity is the queen bee. Attended by a retinue normally made up of from ten to twelve nurse bees, she is looked after and cared for with a solicitude that would be the envy of any human monarch. Should she vanish from the hive, the thousands of occupants become utterly demoralized. Sanity returns to the colony only after another queen is installed.

During warmer months of the year, the queen spends her time laying eggs. When her egg laying is at full capacity, she may produce as many as 1,500 eggs a day. Her yearly output may exceed 200,000 eggs. As if this weren't enough of a chore, she must wander about the hive looking for empty cells or compartments in which to lay her eggs (one egg to a compartment). Once the eggs have been laid, the workers do the rest.

Worker bees are non-reproductive females that are responsible for virtually every duty required by the colony. Only mating and egg laying are left to others. During the summer, they literally work themselves to death. The life span of a worker at this season is about four to six weeks. During the colder months, when there is much less to do, a worker may live as long as six months. Finally there are the drones, male bees whose one function in life is to mate with a virgin queen. Successful suitors die through the violence of the mating act. Drones that do not participate in mating live on through the summer, waited upon and cared for by the workers. But with the coming of cold weather, they are turned out of the hive to die in the frosty cold.

When a worker finds a worthwhile source of food, she announces her discovery to other workers by performing a dance on her return to the hive. The bees watching her are able to interpret her movements. If the food is less than a hundred yards from the hive, the dancer performs what is known as the round dance; greater distances call for the more elaborate tail-wag dance, which gives the audience important clues concerning the distance and direction of the food source. There are still other clues that assist the onlookers. The flower's fragrance will have attached itself to the returning bee. The others take note of this as well as the odor of the nectar that has been brought back to the hive. In this way the workers learn what kind of flowers to look for and where to find them.

Since the workers perform their dances on honeycombs within the hive, this is one of the many activities of honeybees that go unseen by most of us. The fact that bees communicate with each other by this means was unknown until research conducted around the middle of this century by Karl von Frisch, an Austrian. His findings were a notable contribution to our knowledge of honeybees and how they live.

Some trips are made primarily for pollen and some primarily for nectar, but often the bees come back with a mixture of the two. For plant pollination, the important requirement is that the bees stay for a period of time with the flowers of a particular species and do not jump from one species to another. Honeybees pass this test with high marks. So long as the flower furnishes the ingredients the bee is looking for, there will be no crossing over on any given foraging trip to plants of other species.

Some of the pollen from the first flower a worker bee visits will become attached to the forked hairs covering its body. At the next flower, the same thing happens. Only this time some of the pollen from the previous flower will fall off and become attached to the sticky female organ of the flower called the stigma. As the bee continues on its way, it may visit dozens of flowers before filling its honey sac with nectar. Hundreds of bees, all doing the same thing, will effect the pollination of a vast number of flowers. "Bee flower" is the term that is applied to flowers that, through their structures and other qualities, particularly invite the services of bees. To advertise its wares, the flower flaunts bright colors and a fragrance that attracts bees and delights our senses. The visiting bee is often aided by lines, like those on a map, imprinted on the flower that lead it directly to the source of the nectar. The guide lines, as they are called, are meant only for bees and are often invisible to us. This is one way that flowers reserve their nectar for bees and discourage other would-be visitors.

Compared to the honeybee, the bumblebee leads a simpler and more democratic existence. The queen begins the spring season by doing all the work herself. She, and she alone, survives the winter. Having mated the previous fall, she goes about building a nest and rearing young. She establishes her colony in a deserted mouse nest or an old bird nest. The site can be below the ground or at the surface. Once her first brood takes wing and begins bringing back nectar and pollen, she lays more eggs until the strength of the colony reaches about eighty to one hundred individuals, or sometimes more.

Bumblebees start work earlier in the day than honeybees, work faster and later, and they are able to probe deeper into flowers. They are also out foraging in cooler or damper weather than their rivals venture out in. Therefore, in many ways they are superior to honeybees in carrying out the vital function of flower pollinator. Before the arrival of

*Honeybees at apple blossoms*

the white man, and with him the European honeybee, bumblebees were doing the largest share of flower pollination on this continent and apparently doing it very effectively. But agricultural lands, highways, and cities took away the wilder areas where bumblebees made their homes and in many places pesticides killed them. As a result, their numbers seem to have decreased drastically. The wildlife gardener can do something about the decrease in bumblebees by setting aside undisturbed areas on his property where grasses, weeds, small trees, and shrubs can provide the kind of habitat that will enable the bees to establish their nests. Michael Tweedie, in his book *Pleasure from Insects,* supplies detailed instructions on making artificial nest sites for bumblebees. I suggest that this book be consulted by those who want to see more of these useful insects visiting flowers in the garden.

Since what little honey the bumblebees produce is quickly used up by members of the colony, there has never been any incentive to rear these bees in the same way as honeybees. But, on the whole, they are likable insects—in the words of Tweedie, "large, clumsy, furry insects, and general favourites despite the fact that they can sting severely if molested."

It is fear of being stung that dampens the enthusiasm of many of us for bees and their close relatives, the hornets and wasps. But we ordinarily have nothing to fear from honeybees and bumblebees so long as we do not disturb their hives or nests. To be stung by a bee anywhere else is a sheer accident. For example, inadvertently stepping on a bee when going barefooted may well result in a sting. A honeybee normally pays for its impetuosity with its life; in attempting to withdraw its barbed sting, it suffers internal damage. An individual bumblebee, on the other hand, can sting many times without harming itself.

Not to be mistaken for bees are other nectar-feeding insects known as hover flies or syrphids. Belonging to the order Diptera, the hover flies give away their identity by hovering in one spot on rapidly whirring wings and then quickly darting off to visit a flower or move to some other spot. I have often had to look twice at a hover fly to make sure that I wasn't watching a honeybee or bumblebee. Hover flies do not bite or sting.

The mixed assemblage of bees and beelike insects that appear in our yards when flowers are in bloom have several qualities in common. All visit flowers for nectar, and some for pollen as well, and all contribute to the pollination process. We should be very grateful for this service and especially to the honeybee for the exquisite product for which it is famous. No other guests to our flower garden repay us quite so well.

# 8 / Butterflies and Their Flowers

As we have seen, many of our garden flowers are ideally suited for attracting hummingbirds and bees. This is somewhat less true when it comes to the butterflies. Highly specialized in their requirements, the butterflies seek out only a limited number of plants for their use during the several stages in their life histories. In many instances, the immature or larval form of the butterfly requires an entirely different plant than the adult. Whereas the immature feeds on plant leaves, the adult in many butterflies is a nectar-feeder that seeks the special flowers that meet its requirements. To achieve the kind of garden that will attract butterflies in all stages of their life cycle will take time and thought, but the effort will be well worth it. Few forms of wildlife have such pleasing beauty and few are so free in displaying their beauty where we can easily see it. What is more colorful than our garden flowers in full bloom and attended by throngs of brightly colored butterflies?

Both butterflies and moths go through a series of transformations

*Painted lady at thistle blossom*

known as a metamorphosis. The first stage is the egg. From eggs laid on leaves and other surfaces emerge small wormlike forms that undergo a series of molts until they become recognizable as caterpillars. Often fearsome-looking, the caterpillar bears little or no resemblance to the adult butterfly.

When large numbers of caterpillars are devouring leaves, the results can be devastating. But, on the whole, serious defoliation is the work of certain moths and only rarely butterflies. As pointed out by H. M. Kulman, entomologist with the University of Minnesota, in a paper on butterflies, very few butterflies are economic pests. Some, in fact, benefit man by feeding on injurious plants or insects, and many assist in the pollination of flowers.

Before the ungainly caterpillar turns into an attractive butterfly, it must go through an inactive stage. Fastening itself to a twig or some other object, the caterpillar builds a chrysalis or protective shield around itself and outwardly goes into a state of limbo. But inside the chrysalis important changes are taking place. The organs of the caterpillar are breaking down and being replaced by the various parts and organs of the adult. After a period of time, the adult emerges and soon flies away to its brief and seemingly merry career as an adult butterfly.

Most butterflies live only a few weeks or, at the most, a few

*Cloud of monarchs heading south*

months. But some, including the well-known monarch, live considerably longer. The monarch regularly flies south to wintering grounds where vast numbers collect within time-honored territories. Monarch butterflies from central and eastern parts of the continent make a spectacularly long flight to mountain forests of the Sierra Madre in mid-central Mexico. It wasn't until 1976 that the major Mexican wintering ground was discovered. In December of that year, a research team led by Dr. Lincoln P. Brower discovered a mountain forest where more than 14 million monarchs overwinter.

Thanks to the studies of Brower, other aspects of the life history of the monarch have been clarified. For example, it was long known that the monarch in both its larval and adult stage was distasteful to birds. A bird ingesting any part of a monarch normally experiences a painful upset and refuses thereafter to touch one of these butterflies. Moreover, the bird is likely to avoid any other butterfly that even looks like the monarch. The viceroy, which has no such taste defense against birds, mimics the monarch and gains a sizable measure of protection. But in a paper by Brower and Linda S. Fink in the May 1981 issue of *Nature,* it was reported that monarchs on the Mexican wintering grounds, in spite of their supposed immunity, were heavily preyed upon by a native oriole and the black-headed grosbeak. Research into the cause led to the discovery that the wintering monarchs were not so ill-tasting to birds after all. During the larval stage the monarch feeds exclusively upon milkweeds. Some milkweeds contain a heart poison or, in scientific terminology, cardiac glycosides; these are absorbed by the caterpillar and the poison is carried over to the adult monarch. A single monarch caterpillar dining upon one of the more poisonous milkweeds takes in enough cardiac glycosides to kill five people. Blue jays eating any part of the caterpillar or adult promptly vomit and in this way get rid of the bad-tasting morsel.

But no such reactions were seen in birds feasting upon overwintering monarchs in the mountains of Mexico. What was the reason? Brower and his associates discovered that very little of the distasteful cardiac glycosides was present in the tissue of these butterflies. It was concluded that a large proportion of the monarchs wintering in the Mexican mountains had fed as larvae upon non-poisonous milkweeds. According to Brower and his associates, with the spread of common milkweed (*Asclepias syriaca*) and showy milkweed (*A. speciosa*), both of which do not contain the poisonous glycosides, not as many monarchs are gaining immunity to bird attack. These two milkweeds are spreading as a result of present land-use practices. Similarly, monarchs wintering along the California coast have insufficient protection. About half contained no poison at all in their tissues.

But in spite of heavy losses due to predation, unfavorable weather, and, in some cases, the activities of man, millions of monarchs survive the winter and begin to mate as soon as warm weather arrives. It would be a mistake to believe that an individual monarch that passed the winter in Mexico or along the coast of California returns north in the spring to grace fields and pastures it left some eight months earlier. The female that has survived the winter travels only a relatively short distance and lays her eggs on the leaves of a milkweed. She soon dies, but after her eggs hatch, a new generation is ready to resume the flight northward. It may take four breeding cycles before we see the return of monarchs to more northern states and Canada.

According to Robert Pyle in his *Audubon Society Field Guide to North American Butterflies,* only the monarch has an annual true migration from breeding territory to wintering grounds and back again. Of course, the same individuals do not complete the cycle. Other species, according to Pyle, emigrate in vast swarms because of population pressure, or other, unknown reasons, and do not return. In most longer-lived species, the adult goes into a state of hibernation at the approach of cold weather. The mourning cloak, reminding us of the chipmunk, rouses itself on warmer winter days and may show itself for a while. I once found a hibernating mourning cloak in a woodpile. The butterfly was so rigid and lifeless in appearance that I thought it was dead. When I brought it indoors, however, it began to show some signs of life after several hours in a warm place. But it was not fully active until after about two days. Most butterflies at our latitude overwinter as larvae.

The first step, and the hardest one, in bringing butterflies to the yard is finding the right food plants for the larval form. Not only does each butterfly species have its special food plants but often these plants will all be members of a single group, such as the milkweeds. Among the important larval food plants are the milkweeds and also grasses, nettles, clovers, vetches, and violets. Woody plants, among them wild cherry, oak, black locust, honey locust, willow, poplar, elm, and hackberry, are food plants for a number of species. Some of our herbaceous garden plants also support larvae, but the number is so limited that we usually have to encourage or bring in additional plants if we are going to play host to a large butterfly population. Lack of suitable plants for the larval stage is a prime reason why butterflies are generally uncommon or absent in urban or semi-urban areas.

One way to encourage butterflies is to let a portion of the yard revert back to the wild. By this I do not mean that we should aim at having a jungle of trees, shrubs, and vines. As likely as not, we will already have an assortment of suitable woody plants in our yard or nearby. It is the herbaceous plants, many of them weeds, that make the difference between an average butterfly garden and an outstanding one. While gardeners may shudder at the thought of letting some part of the yard grow up in weeds, this is not really a disaster. We may be pleasantly surprised when a neglected piece of soil is claimed by sweet clover, vetches, milkweeds, mustards, and chicory. If less desirable weeds begin to show themselves, we can eradicate them. Even thistles and nettles have a place in the butterfly garden if we are willing to tolerate them.

As unlikely as this may seem, weeds will eventually be crowded out by other plants that are even more vigorous. Weeds are pioneers, taking over disturbed soil and flourishing for a few years. Sooner or later, seedlings of woody plants will make their appearance. In time, the young saplings will grow large enough to shade out the original weedy growth. To prevent a succession of this kind, we may have to turn over the soil at the end of each growing season. The weeds will be back again and as thick as ever the following spring.

The list below, based upon information in Robert Pyle's butterfly guide, contains names of common butterflies and their major larval food plants. As can be seen, there is a limited range of plants to choose from.

| BUTTERFLY | LARVAL FOOD PLANT |
|---|---|
| American painted lady | Everlastings (*Gnaphalium*) |
| Black swallowtail | Carrot, Queen Anne's lace, celery, parsley |
| Buckeye | Snapdragon, plantain, sedum |
| Comma | Hops, nettle |
| Common sulphur | Clover, vetch, lupine |
| Dainty sulphur | Marigold |

| BUTTERFLY | LARVAL FOOD PLANT |
|---|---|
| *(continued)* | *(continued)* |
| Giant swallowtail | Prickly ash, hop tree, citrus trees, gas plant |
| Great spangled fritillary | Violet |
| Gulf fritillary | Passionflower |
| Monarch | Milkweed, dogbane |
| Mourning cloak | Elm, willow, poplar |
| Painted lady | Everlasting, thistle, hollyhock |
| Pearl crescent | Aster |
| Pipevine swallowtail | Dutchman's-pipe |
| Question mark | Elm, hackberry, basswood, nettle |
| Red admiral | Hops, nettle |
| Red-spotted purple | Willow, poplar, plum, quince |
| Regal fritillary | Violet |
| Silver-spotted skipper | Black locust, wisteria |
| Spicebush swallowtail | Spicebush, sassafras, sweet bay |
| Spring azure | Flowering dogwood, sumac, spirea |
| Tiger swallowtail | Wild cherry, poplar, ash |
| Viceroy | Willow, poplar |
| Wood nymph | Grasses |
| Zebra swallowtail | Papaw (*Asimina*) |

Growing the right food plant does not necessarily ensure the presence of a desired butterfly. We may live in too urban a setting, or some other factor, such as the use of strong pesticides, may prevent butterflies from taking hold. Nevertheless, there are many examples of success with beautiful butterflies. East of the Rockies, the chances are good that the black swallowtail will come to our yard if we plant any of the following: carrot, dill, caraway, celery, Queen Anne's lace, parsley, or parsnip. Neal Leydens of Pella, Iowa, writes me that he attracts this butterfly yearly by planting a seven-foot row of parsley in his garden. The colorful larvae are soon followed by the immaculate-looking adults

*Life cycle of the monarch*

that seem to float over the yard during the summer months. Usually parsley is the best and easiest plant to grow to attract this butterfly.

Another butterfly that responds well to the presence of a food plant is the pipevine swallowtail. Requiring one of the pipevines during its larval stage, this butterfly hatches out into a blackish swallowtail with a green or blue wash on the hind wings. Thanks to the widespread use of Dutchman's-pipe (*Aristolochia durior*) to shade porches and climb up the sides of houses, the eastern form of the pipevine swallowtail has expanded its range westward by about a thousand miles. But whenever the vine loses popularity, the butterfly soon begins to decrease. The larva also accepts the leaves of the less frequently planted Virginia snakeroot (*A. serpentaria*).

Another swallowtail, the largest butterfly in North America, may appear if we happen to have one or more of the right food plants. The giant swallowtail is chiefly a southerner, whose larva eats the leaves of citrus. The orange dogs, as the larvae are called, are sometimes harmful to the trees. Sometime after the introduction of citrus to southern California, the giant swallowtail made an enormous leap westward and appeared in the Imperial Valley. But with the help of other food plants, including hardy orange, prickly ash (*Zanthoxylum*), hop tree (*Ptelea*), and gas plant (*Dictamnus albus*), we can sometimes coax this butterfly into yards quite far north in the eastern United States.

Kulman suggests that the Baltimore, a small black butterfly with light spotting on its wings, could benefit from the same kind of practices that so often are successful with the swallowtails. The Baltimore normally occurs only in wet places where its favorite food plant, turtle-head (*Chelone glabra*), is found. Should this wildflower be transplanted to the garden, Kulman predicts, the Baltimore would soon follow. He points out that a better candidate for upland situations would be a close relative, *C. lyonii*. This plant and also occasionally American fly honey-suckle (*Lonicera canadensis*) have been accepted by larvae of the Baltimore. But apparently more experiments are needed if we are to be successful in luring this butterfly from its wetland habitat.

The adult monarch visits a wide variety of flowers for nectar but reveals its attachment to its larval food plant by continuing to patronize milkweeds and dogbane. I recall failing to find monarchs one year in early summer on Nantucket, where this butterfly is normally quite common. Finally, in late July, I found a single monarch, feverishly, it seemed, drinking nectar from the blossoms of a common milkweed. The butterfly was so absorbed in its task that I could have picked it up between my fingers.

That August, finding leaves of common milkweed partly eaten, I investigated and found that the culprit was a gaudy-looking caterpillar about two inches long with white, yellow, and black bands. Pairs of longish filaments at the head and rear gave the creature a grotesque look. Amazingly, the caterpillar in the next stage of its metamorphosis would be a bright green chrysalis with golden dots. Dangling from its place of attachment, the chrysalis would in time turn into an adult monarch butterfly.

By late summer the monarch population on the island had increased to the point that every yard containing flowers was being visited by a few of these butterflies. Unlike many of our other butterflies, which restrict their nectar drinking to only a few plants, the monarch visits almost every flower that will conveniently hold its weight and easily offer it nectar. Red, yellow, orange, and purple seem to be the floral colors that are most favored. Pat Murphy of Reno, Ohio, tells me that she has seen about one hundred instances of monarch butterflies being attracted to the yellow-orange line found in the middle of many highways.

Whatever preference the adult monarch may have for flowers of other kinds, it remains loyal to milkweed. Distant parts of the world have been populated by this butterfly and only because these regions offered adequate supplies of milkweed. Advancing westward across the Pacific during the last century, the monarch reached New Zealand and Australia and there found its favorite food plant. Moving eastward across the Atlantic, the monarch has reached the Canary Islands and is at home there because of the presence of milkweed. Should Europe provide the proper food plants, we could anticipate prompt colonization in Britain and on the Continent. Either wafted by wind or aided by passage on shipping, the monarch appears on the far side of the Atlantic almost as regularly as some of our birds.

Over the many years since the butterflies came into being, plants have responded to their presence by offering flowers that are ideally suited to their needs. Butterfly flowers, as they are called, are tubular, rich in nectar, often fragrant, and have a flat rim where the butterfly can perch while it feeds. The composite family, with its goldenrods, asters, dahlias, marigolds, and zinnias, contains good examples of butterfly flowers. The flower heads provide suitable perching space and each small tubular floret can be easily probed by the butterfly for its nectar. The same convenient features can be found in the verbenas, milkweeds, and butterfly bushes (*Buddleia*), to mention a few others. Colors favored by butterflies include red, purple, lavender, yellow, orange, and white.

Butterflies are like hummingbirds in that they do not always adhere strictly to the flowers that seem best suited to their needs. There is a certain amount of testing of any flower whose scent or color attracts them. Some butterflies have departed entirely from flower feeding and live on sap from trees or the liquid they find in carrion, excrement, and rotting fruit. Clive Farrell, writing about butterfly food habits in *The Butterfly Gardener*, states that some butterflies prefer rotting fermenting fruit or bird droppings to nectar. "An à la carte selection," he writes, "includes dung, decaying mushrooms or fungus, decomposing animal remains, honeydew, pollen, sap from wounded trees, mammal urine, mud-puddle cocktail or even human perspiration."

The mud-puddle cocktail that Farrell speaks of could be almost any mud puddle where rainwater collects in a dirt road or a path. The largest concentrations of butterflies are normally found drinking at the edges of such puddles. Austin H. Clark explains the habit in his volume on butterflies of the District of Columbia. These drinking parties, he explains, are made up of the males of many species that come together at favorable places whenever there is a problem of population pressure. The "clubs," as he calls them, are made up of young males fleeing from the tyranny of older, more experienced males. In the absence of competition for females, the young males live together harmoniously and spend many hours siphoning up water from mud or wet soil. If the water is contaminated by feces or urine, so much the better.

Farrell explains that liquid from mud puddles often contains sodium salts but their effect upon feeding butterflies is unknown. It is thought that the many non-nectar sources of food provide protein and salts lacking in the butterfly's normal diet. Whatever the answer may be, I've had good luck attracting a variety of butterflies to my yard in Nantucket with a bait composed of fermented fruit to which sugar and some wine or beer had been added. The mixture was mashed up and placed in small containers in various parts of the yard. Butterflies attracted to my concoction included the red admiral, question mark, wood nymph, red-spotted purple, and mourning cloak. Several of these species I had not seen in my yard until the bait was offered. No doubt the butterflies had been lured by the odor emanating from the strong-smelling potion. Although no monarch butterflies came to my offering, this species may occasionally feed from sap oozing from trees. I've had one report of monarchs feeding on sap from a huge dying weeping willow.

The tiger swallowtail, one of our most common butterflies, which feeds on a wide variety of flowers, also has lowly tastes. Carrion and manure are on its menu and it is sometimes attracted to cigar smoke. Aretas A. Saunders, in his *Butterflies of Allegany State Park*, tells of how a tiger swallowtail came to a cigar he was smoking and, alighting upon it, remained a half inch from the burning tip for several minutes. He states that this butterfly's preference is for cigar smoke, not pipe smoke.

The tiger swallowtail is also attracted to mud puddles and sometimes appears at such places in large numbers. Anne Mahone of New Martinsville, West Virginia, writes me that tiger swallowtails swarm by the hundreds to the wet mud in her barnyard where domestic turkeys have left their droppings.

The less savory tastes of butterflies are taken advantage of by butterfly collectors. For luring hackberry and tawny emperor butterflies, Austin Clark recommends a dead snake suspended about five feet above the ground. Piles of decaying fruit, especially grapes, are effective in enticing some species, according to Clark, and the result may be the mass intoxication of the diners. After their senses have become blurred, the butterflies are easily captured. Among the most avid feeders on fermented fruit are the comma and question mark butterflies among the anglewings and the goatweed butterfly among the leafwings.

As we have seen, food plants for the larval stage are the key to building up a sizable butterfly population. To hold the adult butterfly and bring in still others from the outside is a somewhat easier assignment. As likely as not, some of the flowers already growing in our garden will help meet the nectar requirements of our guests. Garden favorites like the asters, cosmos, dahlia, daylily, fall crocus, forget-me-not, fuchsia, gaillardia, garden balsam, iris, marigold, lavender, petunia, phlox, pinks, sweet william, verbena, and zinnia will be patronized to varying degrees. Perhaps the best advice about familiar garden flowers comes from L. Hugh Newman in his *Create a Butterfly Garden*. He states that butterflies on the whole prefer small, rather simple flowers and ignore ostentatious ornamentals like enormous gladioli and dahlias, chrysanthemums and begonias, or expensive lilies and irises. He finds that roses have no attraction for butterflies and that any old thistle is better than the sterile head of a hydrangea.

I am convinced from my own observations that butterflies, with their keen olfactory perception, are attracted to flowers as much by scent as any other factor. Everything else being equal, butterflies will go to strongly scented blossoms and bypass others. I have noticed this many times in gardens with a large variety of flowers but only one or two that have the required degree of fragrance. If there are sweet-scented lilacs in the yard in spring, this is where most of the butterflies will be. The same kind of clustering will occur as other plants with fragrant flowers come into bloom. In England in late spring, wallflower (*Cheiranthus cheiri*) with its sweet-scented flowers is an outstanding butterfly plant. We have our sweet mock orange (*Philadelphus coronarius*), which comes into bloom soon after the lilacs. The fragrant flowers immediately begin attracting butterflies. Common heliotrope produces flat clusters of bluish-white flowers from May to September which are favorites with butterflies. The flowers exude a vanilla fragrance that seems to be stimulating to both man and insects. By the time the privets, with their sickly sweet fragrance, are through blooming in early July, butterflies can turn to butterfly bush or buddleia.

One of the most alluring plants of all to butterflies, buddleia has a honeylike scent that can be perceived even by our insensitive nostrils from distances of ten to twenty feet. The first of the buddleias to come into bloom is fountain buddleia (*Buddleia alternifolia*). Its lilac-colored blooms appear in mid-May. The bright globular orange flowers of globe butterfly bush (*B. globosa*) appear for a short period in June and are followed by the midsummer blossoms of orange-eyed butterfly bush (*B. davidii*). All three species exude fragrance and attract almost every butterfly that visits our gardens. The orange-eyed is the most commonly planted buddleia and, with some help on our part, will stay in bloom

*Butterflies at buddleia*

for nearly two months after the first blossoms appear in late July. Depending upon the variety, the flowers of this bush are white, pink, red, or purple. Miriam Rothschild, in *The Butterfly Gardener,* calls this buddleia a "butterfly pub" and tells of counting no fewer than a dozen species of butterflies at this bush on a single day in July. The garden Rothschild described is in England, where buddleia not only is widely grown in gardens but has escaped into the wild.

To make the most of our buddleias, we should cut the bushes back almost to the ground in April. This pruning will lead to vigorous shoots that will later support a full quota of flowers. As flowers wilt, they should be cut off—a measure that prolongs flower production.

Chaste tree with its fragrant lilac or violet flowers comes into bloom in August in more northern states and attracts butterflies from the start. Lantana and pentas, grown as greenhouse plants and put outside in summer, are also excellent butterfly flowers. Clive Farrell calls lantana the number one nectar plant for all flower-feeding butterflies and recommends the red-flowered variety. This tropical shrub does well out of doors in Florida and attracts such predominantly southern species as the southern cloudy wing, zebra, polydamas swallowtail, and giant swallowtail. The pentas, represented by *Pentas lanceolata,* are second only to lantana, according to Farrell, in attracting butterflies. Like lantana, the pentas are tropical shrubs that flower the year round.

Many other good butterfly plants grow in the wild in more northern latitudes. Most should be left where they are to adorn the countryside. But butterfly weed (*Asclepias tuberosa*), favored by the monarch as a larval food plant, has often been brought into cultivation and holds its own among our most beautiful garden plants. This milkweed is visited not only by the monarch but also by the closely related queen, a butterfly of the Deep South. Many other butterflies throng to the orange-yellow blossoms. With a long flowering season from late June through September, butterfly weed has a distinct advantage over plants with shorter seasons. It is a roadside plant that does well in dry, sandy soil.

William H. Frederick, Jr., writes that many meadow flowers, including butterfly weed, joe-pye weed, ironweed, coneflowers (*Rudbeckia*), and goldenrod deserve more attention for garden use. All are excellent butterfly plants and have ornamental value as well. I would be tempted to add a few more meadow plants to Frederick's list of those worth trying in the garden.

My first choice would go to the milkweeds and their close relatives the dogbanes (*Apocynum*). Both have milky sap, cylindrical seed
pods, and small flowers that usually grow in clusters. As we have seen,
the milkweeds and dogbanes constitute the sole larval food plants for
the monarch butterfly. Although butterfly weed is the only member of
the group that is commonly planted in gardens, we might consider common milkweed as an edge plant; its greenish-white or greenish-purple
blossoms on three-to-five-foot-high plants might add an exotic look.
This milkweed is sometimes seen growing in neglected yards and now
and then is adopted as a garden flower. But its main attraction lies in
its appeal to butterflies. I have a list of thirty species seen coming to
the flowers. If there is a wet place near our garden, we might give
swamp or red milkweed (*Asclepias incarnata*) a try. Growing to a height
of two to four feet, this milkweed shows its red or rose-purple flowers
throughout the summer. The butterflies seem as eager for the flowers
of this milkweed as they are for the others.

One of the largest gatherings of butterflies I've ever seen was in a
patch of dogbane on the Arkansas River in Arkansas. Besides at least
twenty species of butterflies, there was a throng of other nectar-feeders,
including hummingbird moths. Others have also reported seeing large
numbers of butterflies at the small greenish-white blossoms of this
plant. My list for dogbane now stands at thirty-eight species, the highest total I have for any plant genus and good reason to plant dogbane.
The plants sometimes appear in neglected yards and edges of small
woodlots. There may be a wilder part of our yard where dogbane would
fit in quite nicely.

Among other meadow plants, we should consider the thorough-
worts. Joe-pye weed (*Eupatorium maculatum*) has domed clusters of
purple flowers and grows in wet environments. Boneset (*E. perfoliatum*)
is a meadow wildflower with white flowers in summer. Mistflower (*E.
coelestinum*) is the only thoroughwort with bluish flowers. All attract
butterflies when they are in bloom and make suitable candidates for the
herbaceous border or wild garden.

Oxeye daisy and yarrow are other meadow plants that deserve a
place in the wild garden. The oxeye daisy, which grows so plentifully
in neglected fields and pastures, has at least twenty-five butterfly patrons, according to my list. I have seldom seen a butterfly on any of the
cultivated yarrows, but the wild yarrow (*Achillea millefolium*) is visited

*Black swallowtail at Queen Anne's lace*

by at least fifteen species in New York State alone. Queen Anne's lace, almost elegant enough for the garden, is a fair butterfly plant, while the seldom tolerated goldenrods are even better. My list for the goldenrods stands at sixteen species. The flowers of goldenrods are much visited by the monarch butterfly as it wings its way southward in early fall. Red clover, with no fewer than thirty-four butterfly users on my list, appears in lawns and neglected flower beds with little help from us. Much the same is true of white clover, for which I have fourteen butterfly patrons. Even the little self-heal (*Prunella*), a mint with purple flowers that arrives in our garden uninvited, has twenty-one butterfly visitors on my list.

Much the same story is repeated with weedlike plants that most of us would scarcely mention in the same breath with our handsome garden flowers. Pearly everlasting, hawkweed, daisy fleabane, burdock, and teasel are like the thistles in being much too uncouth for the garden. But if there is a meadow near us or we let wild plants take over a corner of our yard, these are plants to encourage and leave for the butterflies.

As sources of food for both the larval and adult stages, wild plants in general have more butterfly appeal than cultivated ones. This is why I have recommended introducing certain wild plants to the butterfly garden and also letting a portion of the yard go wild wherever this can be done without harmful effect. At the same time, there are measures we can take to make our existing plants more appealing to butterflies. We can prune flowering plants in early spring so as to encourage more blossoms. Equally important, many of the larval food plants of butterflies can be trimmed back in spring and summer in order to stimulate new tender growth. The old growth sometimes becomes too tough for even the voracious appetites of caterpillars.

Attracting butterflies, although it takes more time and effort than we normally devote to nectar-feeders, is rewarding in itself. But in addition, many of the plants that attract butterflies are suitable for day-flying moths, bees, and hummingbirds. This is particularly true of the buddleias and butterfly weed, two plants that should be in every wildlife garden.

# 9 / *Welcome Visitors Among the Moths*

For those who enjoy the
color and graceful flight of
the butterflies, there
is always the temptation
to go a step further and
become acquainted with
the moths. Learning
about moths is not
very difficult, for
they are found
almost every-
where and in
both the larval
and adult stages
are among the most
common insect visitors
to our gardens. Some are
like butterflies in being ad-
dicted to the nectar of flowers.
Many, including some of the largest and most beautiful, are attracted
to lighted windows at night. While not
likely to reveal themselves as openly as butterflies,
the moths are well worth our attention. Contrary to popular opinion,
the moths are not all chewers of fabrics and foliage. By far the largest
number are neutral in human affairs; they neither harm our interests

*Luna moth*

nor do much to advance them. So why not enjoy them for the same reasons that we enjoy butterflies?

The first step in identifying moths is learning to distinguish them from butterflies—not always an easy task. Moths have a way of imitating or mimicking other insects and even birds. In the tropics, and to a lesser extent in temperate zones, certain moths fly by day, are brightly colored, and look for all the world like butterflies. The clear-winged moths, with their narrow, partly transparent wings, look like wasps. The hawk moths have the appearance of miniature hawks and some of them can easily be mistaken for hummingbirds and others for bumblebees.

If we pick up a moth or a butterfly, a powdery substance will rub off on our fingers. Under a microscope the specks will be seen to be minute scales. The moths and butterflies, constituting the order Lepidoptera, are the only insects with scaled wings.

Butterflies have threadlike antennae that usually have a clublike knob at the tip. Moths are more likely to have plumed or feathery antennae. When at rest butterflies hold their wings above the back in a vertical position. Moths at rest either spread the wings out horizontally from the body or fold them against the body. Butterflies are active only during the day, whereas moths of most kinds are active only at night. Once we have learned these elementary distinctions, we should be ready to begin identifying some of the more than nine thousand species of moths that are found in North America. A fair share of this number can be looked for in almost any backyard or garden. I mentioned in an earlier chapter that Dr. Frank E. Lutz achieved the amazing tally of 1,402 insect species in a suburban yard in New Jersey. Of these, 442 were moths and 35 were butterflies. Equally impressive numbers of moths and butterflies have been recorded in parks and gardens in England. For example, Miriam Rothschild reports in *The Butterfly Gardener* that 344 species of Lepidoptera were recorded in the garden of Buckingham Palace in the heart of London. It seems probable that at least 300 of these were moths.

For those who would like to become better acquainted with the moths that visit their yards, I would recommend concentrating at first only upon the more conspicuous and easily recognizable species. By consulting such aids to identification as *A Field Guide to the Moths of Eastern North America* by Charles V. Covell, *The Moth Book* by William J. Holland, the Golden Guide's *Butterflies and Moths* by Mitchell and Zim, and *The Audubon Society Field Guide to North American Insects and Spiders* by Milne and Milne, we can identify many of the moths as easily as we can the butterflies.

The best place to look for day-flying moths is the flower garden. Many sip nectar from flowers and will either alight upon the rim of the flower like a butterfly or hover before the flower in the manner of a hummingbird. By nightfall, we will have a whole different assemblage of moths to look for. By far the greatest number will be found coming to the bright beams of light that shine from windows and doorways. If a window or door is left open on a warm summer night, moths begin fluttering about inside the house. Most will be small, nondescript gray, brown, or white moths that only an expert entomologist could identify. But any large, colorful moths may well be giant silk moths—a group that is so well marked that we can make accurate identifications. But rather than open our house to night-flying moths, and maybe mosquitoes as well, we can sally forth into the night and seek out moths in more natural settings. One technique is to bait various sites with a sugary mixture that attracts many kinds of moths. When we turn our flashlight beam on the places we have "sugared," we may be greeted by a throng of moths, including some that are quite colorful.

Like butterflies, moths go through a metamorphosis of several stages: egg, caterpillar, pupa, and adult. It is only during the caterpillar or larval stage that destructive moths do their damage. In the East, tent caterpillars defoliate wild cherry, apple, pear, and hawthorn. An even worse pest, the gypsy moth caterpillar during its irruptions defoliates whole forests in the Northeast.

At the end of its larval stage, the caterpillar spins a cocoon and undergoes the changes that transform it into an adult moth. During the adult stage, silk moths and some others do not eat at all, but in most species the adults subsist on such foods as the nectar from flowers, sap from trees, and decaying fruit.

## GIANT SILK MOTHS

The giant silk moths, which go by such names as io, polyphemus, cecropia, cynthia, luna, and promethea, are known for their silken cocoons. Should we find a cocoon and later on see it hatch, we would be rewarded with a beautifully colored moth that sadly has only a short time to live. The giant silk moths have no mouthparts and therefore are incapable of feeding. They live only a few days—barely time to mate and for the female to lay her eggs.

Each of the giant silk moths has something distinctive about it. The io, more than the others, is supposed to confound would-be assailants by opening its wings and showing relatively enormous eyespots. The spots, located on the hind wings, are believed to startle the enemy and give the moth enough time to escape. But Edwin Way Teale, in his *Grassroot Jungles*, suggests that the eyespots in the silk moth draw the attention of a predator to that part of the moth's anatomy. As the predator seizes the rear wings with the spots, the wings are torn away, and the moth escapes little worse for the encounter.

We can begin looking for cocoons of the silk moths in winter when leaves are off the trees. Like the butterflies, the silk moths have specific food plants where the larvae feed and where the cocoon is usually attached. The books I suggested as aids to identification also contain information on where to look for cocoons of the more common species.

The io caterpillar, a formidable creature covered with highly irritating poisonous spines, spins a thin, papery cocoon on the ground. The larvae feed on a variety of plants, including corn and roses.

The cocoon of the polyphemus may be found suspended from a twig or branch of a food plant—oak, hickory, elm, maple, birch, and others. The parchmentlike cocoon often falls from the tree during the winter; therefore we should look for it on the ground as well as on lower limbs of trees.

The cecropia, the giant among this family of large moths, has a wingspread of up to 6.3 inches. Unlike the cocoons of other silk moths, the cecropia's does not always hatch out the first spring, sometimes delaying until the following spring. The large cocoon is attached lengthwise to twigs and may be found on lower limbs of such trees as apple, ash, birch, elm, maple, and willow. It is not unusual to find the cocoon on trees lining city streets or on trees in city parks. This colorful moth has invaded towns and cities to such an extent that it is well established along Lake Shore Drive in Chicago, miles from the nearest countryside.

The cynthia moth, very similar to the cecropia in appearance, is

*Io moth startling white-footed mouse*

also well adapted to city conditions. One of the moths used in the silk industry in the Far East, it was brought to this country to serve the same purpose. Although nothing came of this expectation, the moth, thanks to the abundance of ailanthus, its larval food plant, is well established in many eastern cities.

The luna, a pale green moth whose hind wings taper off into long, streamerlike tails, is undoubtedly the most spectacular moth in the family. Unlike the two preceding species, it is to be looked for only in rural settings. Sweet gum, hickory, walnut, birch, and persimmon are the main larval food plants. The papery cocoon of this moth is more often found on the ground than anywhere else. On summer evenings, the luna sometimes joins the host of smaller moths that flutter outside the lighted windows of farmhouses. During the day, the adult luna flattens itself against a limb or tree trunk and there stays motionless until darkness falls. Like most other silk moths, this one is active only at night.

The promethea moth, like the butterfly called the spicebush swallowtail, uses spicebush (*Lindera benzoin*) and sassafras as larval food plants. Because of its special liking for spicebush, this moth is sometimes called the spicebush silk moth. Tulip tree and wild cherry are two other food plants used by the promethea. The cocoon is always suspended from the food plant and is conspicuous enough to be easily seen in winter.

## THE HAWK MOTHS

In contrast to the giant silk moths, the hawk moths are streamlined swift flyers, are relatively long-lived, and have keen olfactory powers. They are found over much of the world and sometimes appear on ships far out at sea. They also make themselves at home in yards and gardens. Striking in appearance and resembling, in some cases, bees or hummingbirds, this group has caught the fancy of a number of distinguished entomologists. J. H. Comstock, in his *Introduction to Entomology,* comes close to calling them "the most beautifully arrayed of all the Lepidoptera." He speaks of their "high-bred tailor-made air" and "quiet but exquisite colors." Their coloring, he adds, is "a perpetual joy to the artistic eye." This is quite a tribute from one of our earlier entomologists not often given to bestowing praise of this kind.

To have these moths visiting flowers in our garden is almost as much of a treat as having hummingbirds. Indeed, in this case bird and insect are so much alike in their feeding habits and appearance that we often have to look twice to make sure which one we are observing. The nineteenth-century naturalist Henry Walter Bates, when collecting in South America, admitted to being easily fooled by the close similarity between the two. On several occasions, he shot hawk moths, mistaking them for hummingbirds.

The illusion that we are looking at a hummingbird extends even to the noise and rapid vibrations of the wings as the hawk moth probes a flower. With a rapid buzz of its wings, it feeds briefly at a flower by hovering before it and then suddenly dashes away to another flower or disappears from our line of vision. With its long tongue, the hawk moth can probe into deep-throated flowers in much the same way that the hummingbird, with its long bill and tubular tongue, can probe into flowers of the same sort. In some hawk moth species, the tongue is twice as long as the body. With so much that is similar between the two, we can only wonder at the powers of convergent evolution that have brought bird and insect so close together.

Even though the British do not have hummingbirds, they have recognized the similarities between these New World birds and hawk moths. They have a hummingbird hawk moth and it is attracted to tubular flowers and bright-colored objects in much the same way that our hummingbirds are. L. Hugh Newman, in his *Create a Butterfly Garden,* states that this moth investigates such bright objects as brass doorknobs, painted croquet sticks, artificial flowers, and exotic orchids.

Perhaps one of the most baffling things about the hawk moths is how easily, in their various stages of metamorphosis, they remind us of other entities. This is reflected in the common names given to the caterpillar and adult moth. Hummingbird moth is only one of many names that owe their inspiration to the peculiarities of this group of moths. The name "sphinx moth," applied to individual moths and sometimes the entire group, refers to the sphinxlike attitude of the caterpillar when it hunches itself up, as it frequently does, with head pointing downward. It takes only a little imagination to see a resemblance between the caterpillar in this posture and the Egyptian sphinx at the foot of the Great Pyramids. Some hawk moth caterpillars have a hornlike appendage at the rear end, giving them the name "hornworm." For example, we have tomato hornworms and tobacco hornworms, both of which eat the leaves of the plants in question. Hummingbird moth, one of the most appropriate names of all, has been applied to several species and at times to the entire group. Finally, the name "hawk moth" derives from the swift, direct flight of these moths and their slender, pointed wings. Actually falcon moth would be more appro-

*Hummingbird moth at Japanese honeysuckle*

priate since it is the falcons that have these flight and wing characteristics.

However these moths strike us, it is a pleasure to watch them—
the diurnal species visiting our flowers in much the same way that hummingbirds do, and those that appear after darkness sets in moving
swiftly from flower to flower like fast-moving shadows. The hummingbird moth (*Hemaris thysbe*), also called common clearwing, is the most
likely species to visit our garden flowers during the day. With a wide
range throughout the East, this small moth clearly has the ways and
look of a hummingbird. Like several other members of its genus, the
hummingbird moth visits flowers during the day and is the moth most
likely to be seen competing with bees, butterflies, and hummingbirds
for nectar at flowers. Somewhat smaller than a hummingbird, this moth
frequently touches down on the flowers it is visiting with its two front
legs and even, sometimes, the second and third pair of its six legs. But
even when it does alight, its wings continue to vibrate and so fast that
we usually cannot make out the transparent "windows" in them which
give the moth its name "clearwing." Its habit of crawling over flowers
is distinctly beelike. Indeed, a smaller member of this genus, the bumblebee clearwing (*Hemaris diffinis*), looks even more like a bumblebee
and is approximately the same size as a large one. The bodies of the
clearwings are covered with loose down scales and this, too, is a characteristic that reminds us of bees. Like bees, the hummingbird clearwings, as well as other hawk moths, play a useful role in pollinating
flowers.

By far the most common clearwing, in my experience, and the one
to look for most often in our garden, is the hummingbird moth. It has
both the beelike characteristics I've mentioned and the ways of the hummingbird. Its curiosity often takes it to flowers that it does not visit for
nectar. We can cater to this daytime visitor by growing food plants for
the larval stage and suitable flowers for the adult stage. Among its larval
food plants are snowberry, coralberry, European cranberry bush (*Viburnum opulus*), hawthorns, cherries, and honeysuckles.

I have drawn chiefly upon my own notes for the following list of
garden flowers visited by this moth:

Bee balm (*Monarda didyma*)
Butterfly bush (*Buddleia* spp.)

Buttonbush (*Cephalanthus occidentalis*)
Common heliotrope (*Heliotropium arborescens*)
Common milkweed (*Asclepias syriaca*)
Dame's rocket (*Hesperis matronalis*)
Dogbane (*Apocynum* sp.)
Garden petunia (*Petunia hybrida*)
Garden phlox (*Phlox paniculata*)
Glossy abelia (*Abelia grandiflora*)
Ground ivy (*Glechoma hederacea*)
Iris (*Iris* sp.)
Purple loosestrife (*Lythrum salicaria*)
Showy evening primrose (*Oenothera speciosa*)
Sweet mock orange (*Philadelphus coronarius*)
Thistle (*Cirsium* spp.)
Verbena (*Verbena* sp.)
Weigela (*Weigela* sp.)
Zinnia (*Zinnia* sp.)

The hummingbird clearwings make up only one small group in the large family of hawk moths. The other hawk moths, which are best known as sphinx moths, are strong flyers and are most active from about twilight onward. Even more hummingbirdlike in actions and appearance than the clearwings, these moths largely escape notice because of their nocturnal habits. But one species, the white-lined sphinx (*Hyles lineata*), is often seen during the day. It visits many of the same flowers as the clearwings do and some others as well. Hummingbird flowers, such as daylily, trumpet creeper, and petunia, are on its itinerary as it makes the rounds of our garden. It is strange to see this moth hovering before the same flowers patronized by hummingbirds and moving from blossom to blossom in typical hummingbird fashion. It is no wonder that the white-lined sphinx is often mistaken for a hummingbird. It also feeds at night and is sometimes seen thronging about outdoor lights in sizable numbers.

Flowers of the night-flying sphinx moths are typically white or nearly white, strongly scented, and long-tubed. The pale coloring serves to make the flower stand out in the darkness, and the fragrance is a signal that brings the moth pollinator in from long distances. Most sphinx moth flowers do not begin emitting their fragrance until about dark. J. H. Lovell, in *The Flower and the Bee*, tells of an experiment in which a sphinx moth was released at a distance of three hundred yards from one of its flowers. The moth instantly sped toward the plant, a honeysuckle with very fragrant blossoms. He adds that moths belonging to this group are among our most efficient flower pollinators. Like the honeybee, they tend to confine their visits to a single species of flower. These moths make their rounds regardless of weather conditions. Some of them, according to Lovell, fly only on the rainiest and darkest nights.

Even if we fail to see the sphinx moths as they visit our garden at night, we will enjoy the fragrance of the flowers that attract them. Sweet scent on the night air is reason enough to grow some of the flowers in the list below. All of them are well patronized by the night-flying sphinx moths.

> Bouncing bet or soapwort (*Saponaria officinalis*)
> Common heliotrope (*Heliotropium arborescens*)
> Common jasmine (*Jasminum officinale*)
> Dame's rocket (*Hesperis matronalis*)
> Evening primrose (*Oenothera biennis*)
> Four-o'clock (*Mirabilis jalapa*)
> Madonna lily (*Lilium candidum*)
> Night-blooming nicotianas (*Nicotiana* spp.)
> Night-flowering catchfly (*Silene noctiflora*)
> Night-scented stock (*Matthiola bicornis*)
> Primroses (*Primula* spp.)
> Woodbine honeysuckle (*Lonicera periclymenum*)

## OWLET MOTHS

With some 3,000 North American species, the family Noctuidae, the owlet moths, is almost certainly represented in every yard and garden. But not many reveal themselves during the day. An exception is the eight-spotted forester (*Alypia octomaculata*), whose appearance at garden flowers during the day reminds us of the hummingbird clearwings. But this moth alights upon the flower and probes for nectar without vibrat-

*Sphinx moth caterpillar*

ing its wings. Though it is easily mistaken for a butterfly, we can readily recognize the forester by its spotted black wings and black body and its nearly two-inch wingspan. Each forewing is decorated with two large yellow spots and each hind wing with two white spots—making a total of eight spots. This moth comes to many of the flowers patronized by butterflies and bees. I have seen it on the flowers of butterfly bush and dogbane. The larvae eat the leaves of grape, porcelain vine (*Ampelopsis brevipedunculata*), Virginia creeper, and Boston ivy.

Identifying even a few of the many small white or brownish moths that belong to the noctuid family is beyond the capabilities of most of us. All that I could learn about a small whitish moth with conspicuous silvery marks on each wing which was visiting flowers at the herb garden at Cornell was that it was a noctuid and that the larva was a cutworm. Recalling how cutworms damage plants by cutting the stems at ground level, I somehow couldn't become very enthusiastic about this little moth flitting about the garden in full sunshine.

If one is to become better acquainted with this large family and meet some of its more colorful members, baiting and visits to bait sites at night are the answer. Years ago, collectors discovered that these moths throng to sugary baits to which an alcoholic beverage has been added. The mixture is smeared onto the bark of trees and the sites are visited at night with the aid of a flashlight. Ray F. Morris, in his *Butterflies and Moths of Newfoundland and Labrador,* recommends brown sugar and molasses mixed with mashed bananas, overripe peaches, and stale beer or fermented fruit juices. This bait, he adds, is more attractive if left to ferment overnight; a pinch of yeast may be used to accelerate the process. Two important considerations mentioned by Morris are that the mixture be stiff enough so as not to run off tree trunks where it is smeared and aromatic enough to give off the odor of alcohol and esters. This concoction is almost guaranteed to bring a fair sampling of the noctuid family and sometimes moths belonging to other groups.

P. B. M. Allan, in his *Moths and Memories,* goes a step further and recommends adding cinnamon and a little grated nutmeg to a mixture containing port. However, he admits to sipping some of the bait himself before going out on a cool autumn night to do his collecting. He adds that another tumbler or two is exceedingly pleasant on one's return. But whatever the motives of the collector may be, chances are good that noctuids will respond. The most prized ones are the underwings belonging to the genus *Catocala.* The hind wings of some of these moths are brightly colored.

*Cecropia moth and cocoon*

The baits used to lure moths at night are frequently discovered by other insects and even mammals. Moth collectors have recorded such midnight guests at their baits as deer mice, flying squirrels, and raccoons. Allan, when baiting moths in pastures, was troubled by horses and cows consuming his well-spiced mixtures. When one considers the ingredients that go into moth baits, it is little wonder that they are so eagerly consumed by moths and other animals.

# 10 / The Other Insects

My authority for insects in the yard is Dr. Frank E. Lutz, who, as we have seen, compiled the amazing total of 1,402 species in his small yard in New Jersey. Yet this number is relatively small compared to the approximately 15,000 species that Dr. Lutz states can be found within fifty miles of New York City. For most of us, the thought of only a few of these insects in our yard is worrisome. We tend to remember the unpleasant side of insects and overlook the good they do.

*Walkingstick*

We have encountered this problem with other groups of animals, but with insects our fears are more deeply ingrained. We have a vision of locust hordes eating everything in their paths and trees completely defoliated by gypsy moths. Yet this kind of devastation is an exception and the work of only a very few species. Before we can understand insects and gain an appreciation of their role in nature, we need to look at them all, helpful species as well as harmful ones. In this chapter I will survey "the other insects," the ones we know less about.

Some of the other insects are the gardener's best friends; some are his worst enemies. Most, however, are neutral, so far as we are concerned, not doing much to help or hinder. It may come as a surprise that insects classified as harmful comprise the smallest group of all. According to entomologists, only about 1 percent of the insect species fall into the harmful category. Of the remaining species, about half prey upon other insects and therefore provide nature's best check upon populations that otherwise would burgeon and get out of hand. Dr. Lutz reminds us that insect control of other insects has been "shamefully overlooked." He could have added that nature's controls, for the most part, are vastly superior and more effective than the sloppy methods we use.

Of the many species that appeared in his yard, he found very few that conflicted with his gardening or other activities. The life histories, habits, and strange appearance of insects, good and bad, were an unending source of entertainment to him. We, too, can enjoy this aspect of the insect world if we would change our attitude toward these creatures. Instead of placing our whole emphasis on their economic impact, we might take Dr. Lutz's advice and treat them as another interesting part of the world around us. With few exceptions, the insects in this chapter are ones he recorded in his yard and are likely to occur in ours as well. Some of the insects, like so many other forms of life, have adapted well to man and his environs and appear wherever he builds his home or tills the soil.

## ORDER ODONATA

The dragonflies and damselflies are infrequent-to-common visitors to yards. Dr. Lutz recorded ten different species during the course of his survey. Our luck with these colorful insects depends to a large extent upon how far we live from water. The larval or nymphal stage of the insects in this group is spent in the water. Upon hatching, the adult takes to the air and begins a useful career of catching flies, mosquitoes, and other small flying insects. Whereas the damselfly is a delicate insect whose weak flight seldom takes it far from the body of water where hatching took place, dragonflies are strong flyers and several species perform long migrations. We can lure both damselflies and dragonflies to our property if we have a small pond.

# ORDER ORTHOPTERA

Including the walkingsticks and mantids (sometimes placed elsewhere), the Orthoptera make up one of the more obvious groups of insects to appear in our yard. Dr. Lutz's tally for this group was twenty-nine species. We rather like the crickets, even though they may invade our homes. Their tuneless chirping provides us with a form of companionship as we work or relax indoors. The walkingsticks and mantids are such strange-looking insects and have such strange ways that we hardly know what to make of them. Like the crickets, the grasshoppers and katydids are musicians of sorts but too fond of green vegetable food to be trusted.

The house cricket, with an almost worldwide distribution, was described by the eighteenth-century British curate and naturalist Gilbert White as a thirsty insect, showing a great propensity for liquids of all kinds. As a way to get rid of them, he suggested setting out a container half full of beer. They would crowd in and drown until the container had been filled with them. He goes on to tell of the harm they do. They gnaw holes in wet woolen stockings and aprons hung before the fire and eat yeast, salt, bread crumbs, and kitchen scraps. On a more positive note, he calls them the housewife's barometer, informing her when it will rain. As Dr. Lutz points out, this cricket also gives us an approximate reading of the air temperature. If we count the number of chirps a cricket makes per minute, divide the result by 4 and add 40, we have our reading.

The tree crickets (*Oecanthus* spp.) can be a nuisance in their nymphal stage by feasting upon garden plants and as adults by keeping us awake at night with their constant monotonous chirping. But the adult compensates by preying upon aphids and caterpillars. Toward the end of summer and through the fall, we may be treated to a loud chorus of crickets that lasts with little pause throughout the night. This is one of the loudest insect sounds we are likely to hear. The performers are male snowy tree crickets (*O. fultoni*), pale green insects with transparent wings. The males, high up in trees and shrubs, keep time with each other, with never a discordant note made by any one of them. The females, said to be deaf, can scarcely be impressed by these performances. I am not bothered by cricket chirping. There are far worse sounds we have to put up with from human neighbors. But I do object to the egg-laying habits of the black-horned tree cricket. Females of this species cut slits in the twigs or canes of raspberry bushes, using the incisions as places in which to deposit the eggs. Portions of the stem above the incisions soon die and the whole plant will die if heavily infested. The remedy is to cut off the dead canes and burn them in early spring before the eggs hatch.

Walkingsticks look like something a child might create with some wire, a few pins, and a toothpick. They are green or brown, depending upon their age, with long, very slender bodies, tiny heads, long legs, and long antennae. Their stretched-out bodies, up to almost four inches in length, are in sharp contrast to the compact bodies of daddy-long-legs and spiders. The walkingsticks are so well camouflaged against the green background of the plants on which they feed that we scarcely notice them. Normally they are not numerous enough to cause harm. When egg-laying time comes around, the females, high in trees, begin laying almost in unison. The eggs are not deposited but dropped to the ground. According to Dr. Lutz, the sound of large numbers of eggs dropping onto the dry leaves below resembles that made by falling raindrops. The eggs remain on the ground, covered by leaves, until hatching takes place in spring.

The mantids, best represented by the Chinese mantid from Asia and the praying mantis from Europe, are reasonably well regarded because of their tastes for butterflies, moths, flies, bees, and caterpillars. However, this menu, for the most part, contributes little to the ecology of the garden. The mantids have a sinister habit of stalking hummingbirds and sometimes capture these tiny birds as well as mice and small snakes. They take their prey through stealth. Looking very much like a part of the plant on which they are resting, these grotesque and fearsome insects, with their beady eyes, triangular heads, powerful forelegs, and elongated bodies, wait for intended victims to come within reach. Then the forelegs flash out and grasp a victim before it can escape. Other mantids are captured and eaten with as much gusto as any other insect. In fact, mantids are so highly cannibalistic from the time the eggs hatch onward that populations never become very large. Cannibalism reaches its most repulsive climax at mating time. The male, helpless while embracing his strapping companion, as the French entomologist J. Henri Fabre called the female, is often devoured while mating is in progress. The head may be the first part to go, then the neck, and finally the body. Fabre tells of a captive female praying mantis that ate seven mates within a two-week period. But perhaps the mantids should not be unfairly singled out for condemnation. In ant lions, many ground beetles and spiders, the female takes the precaution of eating her mate. Not to do so might subject the newly hatched young to the risks of being eaten by their father.

Because of their predominantly vegetarian diets, the katydids and grasshoppers are likely to be regarded with suspicion by gardeners. We recognize these insects by their two pairs of wings, large compound eyes, chewing mouthparts, and long, powerful hind legs which are used for jumping. The katydids are handsome green insects with somewhat the look of both the cricket and the grasshopper. It is the true katydid that regales us in summer with the *katy*-DID and *katy*-DIDN'T song. The grasshoppers are also musicians of sorts, rubbing together rough places on the wings or legs. Rarely are grasshoppers numerous enough in yards and gardens in the East to constitute a nuisance. The famous locust plagues in the West are outbreaks of a western species known as the Rocky Mountain locust. When huge swarms of these grasshoppers are on the move, they eat every green thing in their paths.

## ORDER ISOPTERA

Many of us shudder at the very mention of the word "termite." We may have heard of the towering structures they build in some parts of the world and how, unseen, they destroy wood by eating the inside of beams, supports, and legs of furniture, leaving only hollow shells. The termite is most destructive in the tropics and progressively less so as one moves northward or southward into cooler climes. So long as no wooden part of our house is in near contact with the ground, we are likely to have little trouble from these primitive insects. Always looking for something good to say about insects held in disfavor, Dr. Lutz reminds us that termites perform an important service in clearing away stumps and fallen timber. If this dead material were allowed to accumulate, there would be no room for new growth.

If we can stop worrying about termites long enough to look at their habits, we will find them fully as fascinating as the other social insects. Not even distantly related to the bees, wasps, and ants, the termites have a more highly developed caste system. Reproductive males and females with fully developed wings leave the colony in swarms at certain seasons and found new colonies. Another caste consists of sterile workers that perform the many duties required by colonies containing thousands, even millions of individuals. Making up still another caste are sterile soldiers with huge heads and mouthparts. There is also a caste of nasute warriors, soldiers with nozzlelike structures on their heads which are used to spray repellent on ants and other invaders. The king has no duties other than to inseminate the queen from time to time. She is a monstrously large individual, compared to the others, and little more than an egg-laying machine. During her lifetime, which may last as long as five or more years, she may become the mother of millions of individuals. Even the workers may live for three years or longer, which is quite a lifetime compared to the few weeks that worker honeybees live during the summer. To catch a glimpse of the strange world of the termites, we need only break open an infested stump or log and begin searching for the various castes and the royal couple.

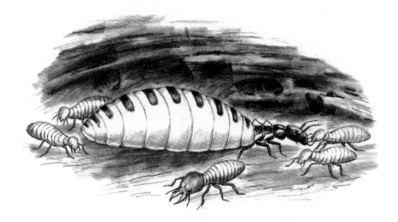

*Termite queen surrounded by attendants*

# ORDER HEMIPTERA

The insects making up this order are known as true bugs. As with other large groups of insects, some are beneficial to our interests, some are harmful, and others fall into the neutral category. Among the beneficial species, the wheel bug, belonging to a group known as the assassin bugs, preys upon such enemies of the gardener as hornworms, Japanese beetle larvae, and cutworms. A close relative, the masked bedbug hunter, enters houses and searches for one of its chief prey species, the bedbug. Where these biting insects are a problem, this is a valuable service indeed. Still another member of the group, the spined assassin bug, preys upon both the larval and adult stages of the Mexican bean beetle and other injurious insects as well. Although the stink bugs, for the most part, are not in our good graces, the two-spotted stink bug feeds upon cutworms and is such an effective predator generally that this stink bug and another, known as the spined soldier bug, have been used in the biological control of the Colorado potato beetle. The big-eyed bugs (*Geocoris* spp.) prey upon enemies of cotton, alfalfa, and sugar beets, including aphids and leafhoppers.

If the story ended here and the true bugs used their sucking mouthparts only to prey upon harmful insects, we might be tempted to call them some of our most valuable insect friends. Unfortunately, many species use their mouthparts to drain sap from plants. Thus the true bugs are also represented by some of the most destructive enemies of garden plants and agricultural crops. We meet them on our roses, zinnias, chrysanthemums, asters, dahlias, phlox, sunflowers, and snapdragons; also on fruits and vegetables. Moreover, the ambush bug kills bees as they come to flowers, thereby depriving the plants of one of their most important pollinating agents.

The squash bug feeds on the foliage of squash, pumpkins, melons, and gourds, causing the leaves to droop and turn black. Luckily, as is so often the case, this insect is held in check by other insects. According to Lester A. Swan and Charles S. Papp in *The Common Insects of North America*, larvae of tachina flies attack and parasitize squash bugs, destroying as much as 90 percent of the population. The same flies are equally effective in controlling stink bugs. Certain of the stink bugs, known for the ill-smelling fluid they discharge when disturbed, are serious garden and crop pests. But few bugs can compete with the chinch bugs when it comes to destroying crops and harming lawn grasses. According to Edwin Way Teale in his *Strange Lives of Familiar Insects,* the chinch bug drains away fifty million dollars' worth of sap from American cornfields and grainfields each year. Teale, who loved statistics, estimated that the number of chinch bugs in a single acre of infested wheat may be greater than the combined human populations of New York City and Chicago. Helping to hold down the enormous chinch bug populations are ground beetles, parasitic wasps, and various fungi. Birds also contribute to the slaughter.

## ORDER HOMOPTERA

This group of insects probably is no more popular with us than the preceding one. The Homoptera also have sucking mouthparts, but the beak, which they use for sucking, is located farther back on the head than in the Hemiptera. To varying degrees, groups belonging to this order, including cicadas, leafhoppers, froghoppers, treehoppers, aphids, scale insects, and mealybugs, are harmful to the interests of man. The sucking mouthparts, as in the true bugs, are used to drain sap from plants. We are certain to have some of these insects in our yard. Dr. Lutz's count for his 75-by-200-foot lot was seventy-five species compared to sixty-two species of Hemiptera.

Spending nearly all of their lives underground feeding on the sap of tree roots, the cicadas emerge en masse in summer to begin a noisy serenade that lasts only a few weeks. Two species found in eastern North America have the longest immature stages of any insects. The thirteen-year cicada appears as an adult only once every thirteen years, while the even longer-lived seventeen-year cicada appears only once every seventeen years. This does not mean that we necessarily have to wait thirteen or seventeen years, respectively, for the appearances of these two cicadas. Every few years another brood of one or the other of these two species is likely to hatch out in the area where we live. Although there are other cicadas with much shorter life cycles, the periodical cicadas, as they are called, are far more exciting. We recognize them by their stout black to brownish bodies, dark red eyes, and membranous wings with orange edging.

One of the most dramatic events in the insect world is the emergence of the periodical cicadas from their long stay underground. The full-grown nymphs at once begin climbing the nearest bushes and trees. After reaching a spot high enough, the nymph digs in with its claws and commences to molt for the last time. After a period of drying and hardening, the adult is ready to fly away to begin a short, merry life in which the male will spend its time playing the role of a musician. It makes a high-pitched whir or drone, which Edwin Way Teale calls a wail. He says the sound produces a feeling of melancholy and loneliness in him.

If there has been a large hatch, trees in the neighborhood will be decorated with thousands of shiny brown freshly shed skins. Still sticking to the bark, these objects will be sure to catch the attention of children. Another sign of a large hatch is trees with wilted foliage. To secure a place in which to deposit her eggs, the female cuts a slit in a twig. Wherever many females are engaged in this activity, trees are likely to be harmed. After the eggs hatch, the young drop to the ground. They at once burrow in to begin another long cycle that won't end until a lapse of thirteen or seventeen years. The thirteen-year cicada is found from Virginia southward, while the seventeen-year cicada ranges throughout much of the East.

Small insects only a few millimeters long, in contrast to the cicadas' length of an inch or more, the froghoppers, treehoppers, leafhoppers, and psyllids make up for their size by appearing in such numbers that they often cause serious harm to garden plants and agricultural crops. The damage to plants is inflicted by sucking their juices and, in a number of cases, by females making slits in stems or twigs for egg laying. Among the more serious pests in these groups are the potato leafhopper, damaging to potatoes, beans, eggplants, dahlias, and other plants, and the pear psylla, damaging to pear trees. The latter insect, like several other psyllids, injects a poison into leaves, causing them to turn yellow.

If we can look beyond the damage they do, the froghoppers and their close relatives are almost as interesting as the cicadas. The diamond-backed froghopper looks like a miniature frog and, like other froghoppers, surrounds itself during the nymphal stage with a frothy mass of tiny bubbles. We often see the bubbles on stems of plants and wonder what made them. If we remove some of the froth, we may uncover one or more tiny froglike objects. Usually only one young froghopper is found among the bubbles—sometimes as many as four or five. The small insects expel the bubbles apparently for the purpose of providing themselves with a relatively safe retreat from enemies. Once the adult stage has been reached, the froghopper leaves its bubbles and begins hopping about among grasses and other plants. These insects are also called spittlebugs in recognition of their spittle- or bubble-forming habit.

To escape detection by enemies, the treehoppers are masters of camouflage. Some, including the locust treehopper and thorn-mimic treehopper, look like thorns, while the buffalo treehopper has a hunched profile, reminding us of a miniature bison. The treehoppers are good flyers and jumpers. They are likely to be well represented among the small insects we scare up when cutting the grass.

Of great concern to gardeners and farmers are the leafhoppers. These often brightly colored, jumping insects injure plants by sucking their juices and are vectors for several plant diseases. Each species has a single plant or group of plants that it singles out for attack; therefore we have such names as beet leafhopper, potato leafhopper, apple leafhopper, rose leafhopper, grape leafhopper, and clover leafhopper. Judging from their names, these insects and others among the froghoppers, treehoppers, and related groups probably sound more damaging than they really are. Although they are harmful at times, it must be remembered that these insects are so minute that only through sheer weight of numbers can they inflict much damage. Helping prevent populations from reaching dangerous proportions are adverse weather factors and such natural control agents as birds and other insects.

What has been said of the leafhoppers and related groups applies almost equally well to the aphids. But the aphids, with twenty or more generations a year, are so prolific that even with innumerable enemies they somehow manage to hold their own and even flourish. Although seemingly defenseless, the aphids are not entirely without ways of protecting themselves. Their best-known defense is the sweet, sticky liquid, known as honeydew, which is secreted from the anus. This substance is so well liked by ants that some species tend aphids in much the same way that we tend cattle. The aphids, in many cases, are provided with shelters by the befriending ants, and the corn-root aphid is actually housed through the winter during its egg and larval stages in the underground nests of the cornfield ant. In the spring, the newly hatched aphids are carried by the ants to roots of smartweeds and other weeds where they can feed until the corn has sprouted. After the corn roots are at a proper stage for the aphids, the ants transfer their charges to this second location. Supplementing the help and protection they get from ants, many species of aphids exude a waxy substance when attacked which helps ward off predators.

Even Dr. Lutz, who can find something good to say about most insects, says he admires aphids but does not like them. He gives credit to small wasps, called chalcids, for being one of the most important insect agents in controlling aphids. The female of this wasp plants her egg with her ovipositor inside a living aphid. When the egg hatches, the larva eats its way through the aphid, soon killing it. The dried shells of aphids that have been parasitized by this wasp are a common sight on rose bushes and other plants favored by aphids. If it were not for such natural controls, we would be almost defenseless against the inroads of these overwhelmingly abundant insects.

As if we didn't already have enough small insects sucking juices of

*Ant obtaining honeydew from aphids*

our plants, the aphids have their counterpart in a group known as coccids, made up of small armored or unarmored scale insects and mealybugs. Gathering in large aggregations, in the same way as aphids, these insects feed upon juices of certain plants and can be very damaging. Although not as prolific as the aphids, they are better protected, having waxy coverings which range from powdery tufts to a scale under which the insect lives. While scale insects, during their adult life, remain anchored to their places of attachment, the mealybugs move about freely for most of their lives. We encounter these insects on many of our trees and garden shrubs.

The oystershell scale infests maples, elms, fruit trees, lilacs, and other woody plants. Each insect, only about one-eighth of an inch long, has the look and shape of an oyster shell. The San Jose scale infests fruit trees, often causing serious damage. The female lives under a circular scale only one-sixteenth of an inch in diameter and the male under a smaller, somewhat elongated scale. The cottony maple scale is found not only on maples but on many other trees, including fruit trees. For a while the cottony-cushion scale, from Australia, was on the point of destroying the citrus industry in California. But thanks to introductions in 1888 and 1889 of an Australian ladybird beetle, one of its natural enemies, the outbreaks were brought under control.

# ORDER NEUROPTERA

The net-veined insects, as they are sometimes called, or Neuroptera, help restore our confidence in the ability of insects to control their own numbers. Most members of this order prey upon other insects during their larval stage, and usually ones harmful to our interests. But one wouldn't expect services of this kind from larvae that look like the harmful bugs they prey upon. In lacewings and ant lions, the larvae are louselike creatures, mostly body and with well-developed mandibles for catching prey. Yet larval lacewings make significant inroads upon the aphid population and prey upon other harmful homopterans as well. Depending upon the family to which they belong, the larvae have earned the name "aphid lion" or "aphid wolf." California green lacewings are raised indoors by the thousands for release in greenhouses and vineyards. They prey upon mealybugs.

A complete metamorphosis changes the ugly larva into a frail-looking insect with transparent net-veined wings and long antennae. The adults in some species feed upon aphids and thereby continue the good work begun by the larvae.

The ant lions are best known for the conical pits they make in dry soil. Secreted at the bottom of a pit, the larval ant lion waits for any unwary insect or other small creature to stumble into its trap. To help it on its way downward, the ant lion may shower its victim with particles of dirt. We may find the pits made by ant lions in dry soil under the eaves of our house or any overhanging structure. The adult ant lion is a handsome insect with membranous wings and in appearance very much like a damselfly. We may find these insects outside our lighted windows at night.

## ORDER COLEOPTERA

Chances are that we will have more beetles in our yard than any other group of insects except for the Lepidoptera. During his survey, Dr. Lutz recorded 259 kinds of beetles in his yard and 477 kinds of moths and butterflies. The Coleoptera represent a third of all known insects. North America has about 30,000 species. But it will take some searching to find even a small sample of the ones that inhabit our yard. By turning over stones and pieces of wood and digging into the soil, we will uncover quite a number. If we look behind pieces of loose bark or open up a rotting log, we will find still others. Species known as May beetles and June beetles are attracted to bright lights at night and, much to our annoyance, enter our houses, if they can find an opening, and fly against walls and furniture. Also active at night are the so-called fireflies or lightning bugs. Really beetles, these insects fly about, intermittently flashing their luminescent signals.

As we might anticipate in a group this large, the beetles contain a number of pests among their ranks, including some notorious ones. The rose chafer, a long-legged reddish-brown beetle, feeds on flowers, leaves, and fruits of many of our prized garden plants during its adult stage. Infestations of these beetles occur in June and by early July are about over. But while they are with us, the beetles can do a lot of damage to roses, peonies, irises, and other flowers as well as fruits and vegetables. Fortunately, the rose chafer does not flourish in closely built suburbs and will cause little damage in this kind of environment.

Accidentally introduced in 1916, the Japanese beetle is a serious garden pest in parts of the East. It is bad enough when the larvae ruin our lawns by feeding upon roots of grasses, but the adults add to our woes by collecting in large numbers on favorite flowers, fruits, and leaves. Where they have been feeding they leave little but badly damaged plant tissue. In many areas the Japanese beetle is on the wane because of bird and insect predators and also a commercially available "milky disease" caused by a bacteria.

The long-horned beetles are wood borers during the larval stage and as adults may continue to feed on wood or, in many cases, on leaves, flowers, or even pollen. Some species are large with smooth, shiny exteriors and many are brightly colored. If these beetles were not so destructive, we could be more admiring of them. Among the enemies of long-horned beetles are woodpeckers, braconid wasps, ichneumon wasps, ambush bugs, and wheel bugs. Woodpeckers, such as the pileated, drill into dead wood to prey upon the larvae, while ichneumon and braconid wasps reach the larvae with their ovipositors. Whether the larvae are eaten by woodpeckers or parasitized by wasps, the beetle population is held in check. Ambush bugs and wheel bugs prey upon adult beetles that come to flowers to eat either the flower or the pollen.

Among the other beetles that damage trees, shrubs, and garden plants we find two enemies of the potato and related plants in the three-lined potato beetle and Colorado potato beetle. Beans also have their beetle enemies. One comes from an unexpected group. The Mexican bean beetle, known for the damage it does to leaves and green pods of bean plants, is a member of the ladybird beetle family. Instead of preying upon aphids and other harmful insects, this yellowish-brown insect with sixteen small black dots on the wing covers became a vegetarian. The same evolutionary path led the squash beetle, another member of the ladybird beetle family, to feed upon the leaves of squash plants. This beetle is yellow with fourteen black dots.

Making up for these two "black sheep" in the family, the ladybird or ladybug beetles, as they are also called, are among our most valuable allies in controlling aphids. The alligator-shaped larvae can often be found among the aphids, ravenously consuming them. Unlike many other insects, which change to other foods during the adult stage in their life cycle, the ladybird beetles keep right on eating aphids. The diets of these friends of the gardener also include scale insects, mealybugs, and plant-eating mites.

We recognize the adult ladybird beetle by its round, brightly colored body with spots and its small size (between one-sixteenth and three-eighths of an inch). Depending upon the species, the adults fall into two basic color combinations—red or yellow body with black spots or black body with white, red, or yellow spots. The bright colors are to warn predators that food in the form of a ladybird beetle is not advisable. Brightly colored insects are, as a rule, ill-tasting.

Dr. Lutz recorded eleven species of ladybird beetles in his garden and valued their services so much that he brought in additional individuals to help keep the aphid population under control. We can do the same. Also, when, as sometimes happens, adult ladybird beetles seek out our house as a warm place to hibernate for the winter, we can be welcoming and let them in. They will disappear into crevices and crannies and we'll see no more of them until spring and then we can let them out again. On a vastly larger scale, ladybird beetles in parts of the West seek out secure retreats in the mountains as places to spend the winter. There is a thriving business involved in collecting the hibernating beetles and supplying them for later use in orchards and on farmlands. Two species from Australia, the mealybug destroyer and the vedalia, were introduced during the last century to control the cottony-cushion scale. As mentioned earlier, the timely arrival of the ladybirds saved the California citrus industry.

Much less appreciated because they are seldom seen, the ground beetles also provide useful services. Long-legged, for the most part, black, and active at night, members of this family scurry through the grass attacking any small prey that meet their food requirements. The slower-moving larvae are also predaceous. In New England a ground beetle imported from Europe, *Calosoma sycophanta*, preys upon caterpillars, including those of the highly destructive gypsy moth. These beetles seek their prey both on the ground and in trees. The fiery hunter preys upon cutworms and armyworms, while the fiery searcher, a close relative, preys upon a long list of injurious caterpillars and through this activity has earned the name "caterpillar hunter." Adult beetles climb trees. Still another ground beetle, the eastern snail-eater, preys upon snails and slugs.

While most ground beetles defend themselves from enemies by releasing foul-smelling secretions, the bombardier beetle goes a step further and releases an odoriferous fluid from anal glands which volatilizes explosively, making a noise like a tiny popgun. The spray looms up like a small cloud of smoke. No wonder a predator will back away when confronted not only with a nauseous odor and a noisy "pop" but also a smoke screen! Since bombardier beetles, represented by a number of species, are found throughout the United States and southern Canada, there is always a chance of turning up one in our garden.

Dr. Lutz recorded forty species of ground beetles in his yard during the course of his survey. He was particularly grateful for the ones that ate cutworms and gypsy moth caterpillars.

## ORDER LEPIDOPTERA

Having already discussed butterflies and moths in previous chapters, I will add only a few comments about their roles in relation to garden plants. Few butterflies during their larval stage and none in the adult stage harm plants. The one butterfly in our garden that we need have any serious concern about is the European cabbage butterfly. The larvae are destructive to cabbages, radishes, and nasturtiums. Since this butterfly's accidental introduction in 1860, it has spread throughout much of North America and is one of the most common butterflies in thickly populated districts and agricultural regions.

Reminding us of the lacewings during their larval stage, the harvester butterfly during this stage in its life cycle also feeds upon aphids. This is a unique adaptation for a butterfly. Nearly all the others are vegetarians during the larval stage. Even the adult harvester is attracted to aphids. It does not eat them but subsists on the sweet liquid that is excreted by aphids and drips down onto leaves and other surfaces. This is the same honeydew that is so eagerly taken by bees, wasps, and ants. Preying upon aphids at an early stage in the life cycle and living on their produce at another hardly seems consistent. But what can we expect from a butterfly that, contrary to all the rules, has a carnivorous diet during its early stages!

In contrast to butterflies, moths can be extremely damaging. We probably lose more foliage to moths than to any other group of insects.

*Praying mantis about to attack*

Again, as in butterflies, it is only the larvae that do the damage. The adult moth is completely harmless. It is the immature stage, whether we call the moth at this point a larva, caterpillar, or worm, where the trouble begins. Equipped with short projections on the underside, which serve as legs, and powerful jaws, the larvae in most species are quite mobile and move about in search of plants that meet their food needs. Each species feeds exclusively on a particular plant or group of plants. After going through several molts and eating almost steadily, the larva is ready to spin a cocoon.

As an adult, the moth may not eat at all or may subsist upon flower nectar, plant juices, and liquids from fermenting fruit. During this final stage of the life cycle, many moths redeem themselves in our eyes by pollinating flowers. But we may forget services of this kind when we think of the harm that so many of them cause. The list of destructive species is long indeed and includes such familiar names as European corn borer, lima-bean pod borer, corn earworm, spruce budworm, tomato hornworm, tent caterpillar, codling moth, gypsy moth, browntail moth, and clothes moth. Among moths, as among insects generally, about half the destructive species are of foreign origin. For the most part, these immigrants arrived accidentally. They came with imported nursery stock, seeds, and grain or as stowaways on ships and planes. Fortunately, especially during the egg and larval stages, moths are vulnerable to a wide variety of foes as well as the weather. Among their enemies are reptiles, small mammals, birds, and other insects.

Living completely in the open, except for species like the tent caterpillar, which return to their "tents" after feeding, these soft, slow-moving insects make tempting prey. To be sure, many have established defenses such as emitting irritating fluids or protecting themselves with stinging hairs. Nevertheless, there are always enemies that can penetrate a defense no matter how skillful it may be. Parasitic wasps are among the implacable foes of caterpillars. Groups known as braconid, ichneumon, and chalcid wasps prey upon caterpillars by sucking their juices or by laying their eggs either inside them or on the surface. If the eggs are laid externally on the caterpillar, the wasp usually takes the precaution of paralyzing the host by injecting a poison. In many cases, the wasp, using her ovipositor, places her eggs deep within the tissues of the living caterpillar. As the eggs hatch, tiny larvae begin feeding upon the internal organs of the caterpillar. Sometimes it is a long-drawn-out affair with the parasitic larvae overwintering in the host. Whatever the case, the caterpillar is doomed to eventual destruction. Of the three groups of parasitic wasps, the chalcids are the most helpful in exerting control over moths during their larval stage. We have also seen the importance of these wasps in helping control aphids.

## ORDER DIPTERA

The flies are the familiar two-winged insects that so often bother us with their bites and buzzing. The group contains not only the house fly, midges, black flies, deer flies, horse flies, and bot flies, but the even more obnoxious mosquitoes. Members of this order are easily recognized by their one pair of membranous wings, large compound eyes, and sucking mouthparts. The second pair of wings, seen in other flying insects, is represented in the Diptera by small knobbed structures called halteres. It is believed that these serve as stabilizers when the insect is in flight.

Whatever our feelings may be about the Diptera, this large order that contains over 16,000 North American species performs many useful services. Dr. Lutz recorded no less than 258 species in his small yard and we will probably have a sizable number in our yard. Most of the flies that reside in our yard or appear as visitors are helpful species. Flies provide food for other wildlife and some of them pollinate flowers, some act as scavengers, and some are parasitic or predaceous on other insects, including many that are among our most serious insect pests.

As mentioned in the chapter on bees, the hover flies (family Syrphidae) are important pollinators of garden flowers. Some of them look so much like bees that we have difficulty in knowing whether we are looking at a fly or a bee. Among the flesh flies (family Sarcophagidae) are useful scavengers as well as species that parasitize other insects. But the tachinid flies (family Tachinidae) are the real joy of the gardener or should be. Parasitizing the larvae of other insects, they help control a long list of pests, including armyworms, brown-tail moth, gypsy moth, cutworms, May beetles, squash bug, and stink bugs. Tachinid flies commonly deposit eggs or larvae either internally or externally on the host species. Larvae of the variegated cutworm tachina fly are deposited by the female on plants, where they wait until the right caterpillar comes along. If it is a cutworm or armyworm, the larva attaches itself and bores in to commence living upon the host's internal tissues. By the time the host has been consumed until it is only a shell, the parasite has grown and fattened and is ready to pupate. The fly that emerges from this not uncommon cycle among the insects looks very much like a house fly. Some of the tachinid flies are the same size as house flies and many are larger. Although, to our way of thinking, parasitic insects, like the tachinid flies, seem cruel in the way they get their start in life, we benefit from having many fewer insect pests in our garden.

Much the same process is seen in other families of the Diptera. Big-headed flies (family Pipunculidae) feed as larvae upon various Homoptera, especially leafhoppers. Certain of the flesh flies owe their early nutrition to such insect pests as grasshoppers, gypsy moths, and spruce budworms. Bee flies (family Bombyliidae) look like small bumblebees and visit flowers for nectar; as larvae they are parasites of grasshoppers, beetle larvae, solitary wasps, and bees. Robber flies (family Asilidae) are useful predators during both the larval and adult

*Hummingbird pursuing insect*

stages. Among the insects that fall victim to these fierce-looking flies are May beetles, grasshoppers, leafhoppers, and other flies, including horse flies. For their help in checking harmful insects, we can forgive the robber flies for their occasional destruction of honeybees.

Besides being pollinators, many of the hover flies are highly destructive to aphids when the fly is in its larval stage. If we were to examine an aphid colony, chances are that we would find maggotlike green insects among them and it would be easy to conclude that these were aphids in some stage of their life cycle. However, these small grubs are larval hover flies and each one during its two to three weeks of larval existence is said to consume about a thousand aphids.

Not all flies are protectors of garden plants. The narcissus bulb fly (family Syrphidae) eats a cavity in the center of various bulbs during its larval stage. Another member of this family harms carrots, celery, and parsnips. The apple maggot is a fruit fly (family Tephritidae) that during its larval stage tunnels its way through apples and other fruits. Fortunately, the Mediterranean fruit fly, a scourge of the citrus grower, is now not known to be permanently established north of Nicaragua. Leaf miners (family Chloropidae) damage grasses, chrysanthemums, hollies, and other plants. However, we can't add sawflies to the list of flies destructive to plants. Although called flies, these foliage eaters belong to the next group, the Hymenoptera.

# ORDER HYMENOPTERA

Parasitism, seen so widely in the Diptera, reaches its highest level of development in certain of the Hymenoptera. This large order contains the bees, ants, wasps, sawflies, and horntails. Since the bees were discussed in a previous chapter and ants are largely neutral so far as garden plants are concerned, this section will be devoted mainly to the remaining three groups. At the same time, I can't completely ignore the ants. They are everywhere and considered by many to be the most successful of all insects. In common with termites, social bees, and social wasps, they live in colonies and divide duties among various castes. The workers lead much the same kind of busy life seen in the bees but live much longer. Worker ants may live three or four years and a queen may live twelve to seventeen years. The queen (there may be more than one in a colony) is essential for egg laying and keeping the colony intact. Reproductive males die soon after the mating flight.

The life styles and foods of some of the ants are reflected in such names as army ant, harvester ant, honey ant, carpenter ant, leaf-cutting ant, and garden ant. Garden ants (*Lasius* spp.) are among the most common species found in yards and gardens. So long as these small brown ants do not enter the house and get into the sugar, lard, and other foods, we have little reason to complain about them. But indirectly they do contribute to injury to garden plants. These ants and several others go to great lengths to protect aphids, by sheltering them and driving off or killing their enemies. But, on the whole, the garden ants are beneficial. They aerate the soil, break down organic matter, aid in the pollination of flowers, and prey upon injurious forms of life.

It is much harder to summarize our feelings about the wasps. We regard them with suspicion because many of them can inflict painful stings. At the same time, we are not likely to be aware of the good they do by parasitizing far more harmful insects. The damage they do to other insects largely goes unseen.

During the course of his survey, Dr. Lutz recorded about thirty species of wasps in his yard. These included the yellow jacket, bald-faced hornet, velvet ant, giant ichneumon, spider wasps, paper wasps, potter wasps, and gall wasps. Along with wasps, he played host to ants, bees, and sawflies—a total of 167 species belonging to the Hymenoptera. The only ones he complained about were the sawflies for damaging his currants and leaves on his pear trees. His wife, however, objected to carpenter ants coming into the kitchen. He finally cut down the cherry tree where the ants made their nest and eventually the ants departed. If he was ever stung by any of the Hymenoptera that frequented his yard, he doesn't say so.

We may have as many Hymenoptera near us as did Dr. Lutz and scarcely be aware of it. Absorbed as we are with our business and they with theirs, we are not likely to have many contacts with these insects. Only a few showy or ill-tempered members of this order will ever go out of their way to sting us. Like many others, I learned the hard way that the velvet ant is not an ant and not to be trusted. Small, usually black and red wasps with a vicious sting, they should not be provoked. Only the wingless female has a sting.

Also to be treated with caution are the yellow jackets. Placing their nests in underground burrows, stumps, or decaying logs, the yellow jackets are the black-and-yellow or black-and-white wasps that often gather as soon as food is spread out on a picnic table. Besides sampling our food, they may sting us if we are not careful. The same may be said of the bald-faced hornet, whose large paper nests are often seen attached to limbs of trees. Smaller paper nests without an outside covering are made by the paper wasps (family Vespidae). Instead of manufacturing paper for their nests, the mud daubers (family Sphecidae) use mud gathered from the edges of streams and ponds to build tubular nests arranged in rows under the eaves of outbuildings and other protected places. The nests are provisioned with spiders. We need to be careful around these wasps, as they have a painful sting. Members of the same family, the sand-loving wasps nest in the ground and provision their nests with grasshoppers or crickets. If looks could terrify, the ichneumon wasps with their extremely long ovipositors would be the most frightening species of all. But the ovipositor is used solely for boring into wood and depositing an egg on an insect larva. The giant ichneumons with ovipositors up to four and a half inches long seek out horntail larvae hidden within the trunks of trees. The ovipositor can pierce through several inches of wood. Along with two other families of wasps—the braconids and chalcids—the ichneumons, as we saw earlier, are among our most important allies in holding down populations of harmful insects.

Sometimes a high degree of artistry goes into the nests built by wasps for holding the larva and its food supply. The potter wasps build a perfectly shaped nest of clay which looks like a miniature pottery jug; this is attached to a twig and provisioned with larvae of beetles and moths that have first been paralyzed with a poison. The eggs of the potter wasps are attached to the sides or top of the interior of the pot by slender threads.

After the accidental introduction of the Japanese beetle in 1916, efforts were made to find a form of biological control. One of the best candidates was a wasp called the spring tiphia, which was imported from Korea in 1926. The female of this wasp burrows into the ground to reach the Japanese beetle grub. She paralyzes the grub by stinging and then deposits her egg. A close relative, the five-banded tiphiid wasp, seeks grubs of May beetles for the same purpose.

Sawflies and horntails differ from bees, ants, and wasps in not having a slender pedicel, or stalk, between the abdomen and thorax. Instead these two portions of the body are broadly connected. Although they look like wasps, we cannot credit these members of the Hymenoptera with performing useful services. In fact, they do considerable damage to trees and other plants.

*Dragonfly catching insects in midair*

The caterpillars of sawflies, often yellow with black spots, are foliage eaters, frequently damaging oaks, birches, alders, larches, and other trees. Some species form galls on plants and others mine leaves. The female horntail has a long ovipositor which she uses to drill deep into plants or dead and dying trees. Unlike the ichneumons, she does not parasitize other insects but leaves her eggs inside a plant that will supply nourishment for the larvae. Her efforts are to no avail if one of the ichneumon wasps discovers her nest site.

## WHAT IS THE SOLUTION?

In reacting to the damage that some insects cause in our garden or to our trees, we can take one of two approaches. We can rush to the nearest garden store and buy a powder or spray that will supposedly kill whatever it is that is doing the damage or we can let nature take its course. The biological assistance that is ever at hand may be slower and less thorough, but we should ask ourselves if we really need to exterminate the species that is doing the damage. Perhaps simply curtailing its excesses is all that is required. Many times a modest amount of pruning by an insect species is more helpful to the gardener than harmful. Beatrice Hunter explains this in her *Gardening without Poisons* and includes root pruning by insects if it is not carried too far. A lack of insect pruning, she states, could lead to an excessive harvest of weakened fruit or vegetables. Admittedly pruning by insects is apt to make plants look unsightly for a period of time. But, as in the case of damage by the rose chafer, all one has to do is wait. The infestation will disappear of its own accord and the plants will grow new foliage.

If we wait, there is also a good chance that natural controls will come to our aid. This is the slower but safer method. Sometimes we can assist by releasing predators, such as ladybird beetles, in our yard. And we shouldn't forget the good help we receive from birds. Chickadees, for example, find and eat tiny insect eggs that most of us never see. The list of wildlife allies that will help us if we would but let them would fill pages. To harm these allies by taking away their food is a high price to pay for sudden and frequently unsure eradication of an insect foe. As Dr. Lutz states: "Wholesale, indiscriminate slaughter of insects does much more harm than good."

In the list that follows I have given the name of an insect pest in the first column, and in the second, insects that through either predation or parasitism help in the control of the pest species. This list is only a small sample of pests and their insect control agents, but it includes some of our most damaging foes and best friends.

| | |
|---|---|
| Aphid | Big-eyed bug |
| | Braconid wasp |
| | Chalcid wasp |
| | Fire beetle |
| | Harvester butterfly |
| | Hover fly |
| | Lacewing |
| | Ladybird beetle |
| | Tree cricket |
| Armyworm | Chalcid wasp |
| | Fiery hunter (ground beetle) |
| | Tachinid fly |
| Brown-tail moth | Braconid wasp |
| | Tachinid wasp |
| Cankerworm | Potter wasp |
| Chinch bug | Chalcid wasp |
| | Ground beetle |
| Cicada | Giant cicada killer (wasp) |
| Colorado potato beetle | Murky ground beetle |
| | Spined soldier bug |
| | Two-spotted stink bug |
| Cutworm | European ground beetle |
| | Fiery hunter (ground beetle) |
| | Fire ant |
| | Mason wasp |
| | Tachina fly |
| | Two-spotted stink bug |
| | Wheel bug |
| European corn borer | Chalcid wasp |

|  |  |
|---|---|
|  | Ichneumon wasp |
|  | Tachina fly |
| Fall armyworm | Ground beetle |
|  | Spined soldier bug |
| Grasshopper | Bee fly |
|  | Blister beetle |
|  | Checkered beetle |
|  | Grasshopper maggot (fly) |
|  | Robber fly |
|  | Sand-loving wasp |
| Gypsy moth | Braconid wasp |
|  | Chalcid wasp |
|  | European caterpillar hunter (beetle) |
|  | Fiery searcher (beetle) |
|  | Sarcophagid fly |
|  | Tachina fly |
| Horntail | Ichneumon wasp |
| Hornworm | Braconid wasp |
|  | Wheel bug |
| Japanese beetle | Spring tiphia (wasp) |
|  | Wheel bug |
| Leafhopper | Big-eyed bug |
|  | Big-headed fly |
|  | Dryinid (wasp) |
|  | Ladybird beetle |
|  | Robber fly |
| Long-horned beetle | Ambush bug |
|  | Braconid wasp |
|  | Ichneumon wasp |
|  | Wheel bug |
| May beetle | Five-banded tiphiid (wasp) |
|  | Pelecinid (wasp) |
|  | Robber fly |
|  | Tachina fly |
| Mealybug | Chalcid wasp |
|  | Lacewing |
|  | Ladybird beetle |

| | |
|---|---|
| Mexican bean beetle | Spined assassin bug |
| Sawfly | Chalcid wasp |
| | Ichneumon wasp |
| | Tachina fly |
| Scale insect | Chalcid wasp |
| | Ladybird beetle |
| Squash bug | Tachina fly |
| Stink bug | Tachina fly |
| Tent caterpillar | Fiery searcher (beetle) |
| | Sarcophagid fly |
| Termite | Ant |
| Treehopper | Dryinid (wasp) |

# 11 / *Earthworms— Enrichers of the Soil*

Up until now I have
neglected perhaps the
most important consid-
erations of all when it
comes to turning our
yard into a better
habitat for wildlife
—the soil and the
organisms in it.
If we think of the
soil at all, it is usually
in terms of its geological
makeup. The color and tex-
ture of the soil tell us whether
it is sand, clay, or a rich loam
good for growing plants. Rocks
and pebbles also reveal something
about the soil. A stony soil may be hard
to till but it is likely to contain minerals needed by
plants. Our visual examination will also tell us if the soil is
well drained or not. If there are standing pools of water long after a
rainstorm, we know that water is not running off or percolating through
the soil and we will have to improve the drainage.

*Woodcock probing for worms*

But the soil is more than particles of inert material. To varying
degrees it is a zoological garden filled with small forms of life that many
of us never see or give thought to. It takes a strong microscope to see

the teeming bacteria that live in well-composted soils. Among the more visible forms of life in a shovelful of earth are earthworms, ants, beetles, insect larvae, spiders, springtails, mites, centipedes, millipedes, and wood lice. The roles played by these organisms in enriching and aerating the soil are so important that life on earth would be difficult without their assistance.

The soil organisms go about their tasks without any conscious help or encouragement from us. For this we can be thankful. But if we knowingly or unknowingly provide help, their numbers increase and we benefit through greater productivity in our soil and consequently better, more vigorous plants and a better life for everything that feeds upon plants. Many of our gardening and agricultural practices do improve conditions for soil organisms. Others have an opposite effect. By applying practices that are helpful to soil organisms and eliminating those that do not, we work with nature to improve the soil.

The web of life that exists in the soil is so complex that we may lose our way if we try to meet the needs of each and every organism. Therefore, it is best to single out one group—a group that we know something about—and use this as our model. The earthworms come to mind as one of the most important and numerous of soil organisms. They have been extolled as indispensable enrichers of the soil since the time of Gilbert White, the eighteenth-century British naturalist and curate. No less a figure than Charles Darwin devoted forty years of research to earthworms. His writings on the earthworm filled a great void in man's knowledge of them. In spite of Darwin and many others who have pointed out the importance of earthworms, soil scientists often ignore the existence of earthworms and sometimes advocate practices that are harmful to them.

In *The Earthworm Book,* Jerry Minnich writes that there may be as many as 2,200,000 earthworms in a single acre of soil. By weight, earthworms may make up from 20 to 80 percent of the soil fauna. But of over 1,800 known species, only a few are of importance to gardens and agriculture. The two species that are most helpful to North American gardeners are the night crawler (*Lumbricus terrestris*) and the field worm (*Allolobophora caliginosa*). These two species, like other earthworms, are hermaphrodites with complicated reproductive systems. A single earthworm contains male and female reproductive organs, which are confined to a few segments in the anterior portion of the body. At mating time, two earthworms lie side by side, with the male organs of one worm inseminating the female organs of the other, while at the same time the male organs of the second worm are inseminating the female organs of the first. The night crawler comes to the surface to copulate, whereas in other species copulation takes place underground. After fertilization has taken place, the next stage is egg laying. The eggs are released in a cocoon which, depending upon the species, contains from one to twenty eggs. The pea-shaped cocoon is deposited near the surface of the soil. The tiny earthworms that eventually hatch out grow into adults without going through any further stages in the life cycle.

Burrowing deep into our soils, the earthworms are normally seldom seen. But the night crawlers, as their name implies, appear at the surface during the night and actively engage in harvesting dead leaves and other organic matter. This material passes through their bodies and is returned to the soil. Earthworms also come to the surface during wet weather but no one knows why. Those that remain at the surface after the sun comes up are likely to be killed by ultraviolet rays or by birds and other predators. Other clues to the presence of earthworms are the casts they leave at the surface. After a mixture of earth and vegetable matter has passed through the worm's digestive system, it is voided in the form of spiral-shaped pellets known as casts. Minnich tells us that castings left by earthworms contain one-third more bacteria than surrounding soil and five to eleven times as much nitrogen, phosphorus, and potassium. As impressive as these figures are, they do not tell the whole story. As earthworms burrow deep into the soil, they create "runways" for other organisms and open up the soil for air and water movement. Gilbert White recognized this function when over two hundred years ago he wrote: "Without worms, the earth would soon become cold, hard-bound, and void of fermentation, and consequently sterile." Minnich writes that soils with earthworms drain four to ten times faster than soils without them. He goes on to say that they neutralize the soil, keeping it neither too acid nor too alkaline.

Surely services such as these deserve a reward! We are already offering a reward if we return humus to the soil and apply other organic methods. But to be more scientific about it, we should examine each of several steps that we can take. All are accepted practices and ones that

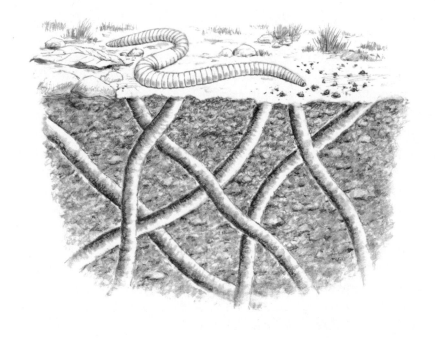

*Earthworm and its tunnels*

most of us would undertake anyway. The only drawback to several of these measures will be a slight untidiness—something we have met before when catering to wildlife.

Our goal of helping earthworms and improving the soil should begin with soil samples to find out if our soil is too acid or too alkaline. Earthworms help in correcting an imbalance in our soil but they cannot normally do it all without some assistance on our part. From soil samples sent to an appropriate government or private agency, we will find out what the $p$H rating of our soil is. This is a designation on a scale from 0.0 to 14.0 to tell us if our soil needs treatment. Readings below 5.9 indicate too acid a soil; this calls for an application of lime. Readings above 7.0 indicate too alkaline a condition; this can be corrected with the use of sulphur. As a rule, soils east of the Mississippi tend to be on the acid side; soils west of the Mississippi tend to be on the alkaline side. A $p$H near the neutral point on the scale (7.0), where acid and alkaline elements are in balance, is about right for most garden and agricultural plants. But, if anything, plants thrive best with a slight degree of acidity. A number of plants, including hollies, blueberries, mountain laurel, rhododendrons, camellias, and azaleas, require an acid soil.

If we have an unfavorable *p*H reading, there are several steps we can take. An application of ground limestone, using 50 pounds to every 1,000 square feet of lawn or garden space, will do much to correct an overly acid soil condition. Liming should be conducted in the fall and may have to be repeated at three-year intervals where there is a severe deficiency. Lime is not a fertilizer. It corrects a *p*H deficiency, unlocks minerals and other nutrients in the soil, and serves to loosen soil particles.

If the *p*H reading shows that our soil is too alkaline, we can apply sulphur as a corrective. Dusting sulphur, used at a rate of 15 pounds per 1,000 square feet, will give us a good start at lowering the *p*H. Although not the miracle worker that lime is, sulphur is a basic element in the manufacture of protein by plants. According to R. Milton Carleton in *Your Garden Soil,* sulphur is especially important for good growth in cabbages and such garden plants as sweet alyssum, stock, candytuft, nasturtium, and dame's rocket. Fortunately, compost is a good source of sulphur. If we have been diligent about applying compost to our soil, we may have all the sulphur that our garden needs.

The next question is whether our soil needs additional help from fertilizers. Almost certainly there will be deficiencies in our soil that can be corrected by a well-balanced fertilizer or liberal composting. Some gardeners prefer chemical fertilizers; others rely solely on organic methods. Since organic methods are safer, less costly, and, in contrast to chemicals, favor the presence of earthworms, many gardeners, myself included, rely upon them exclusively. I am willing to concede, however, that chemical fertilizers, like 10-10-10,* when used in modest amounts are unlikely to harm soil organisms or "burn" plants. But there is nothing like well-rotted compost to restore the soil and make a home for beneficial soil organisms. James Crockett, in his *Crockett's Victory Garden,* calls compost a magic elixir and the gardener's best friend. He points out that among its chief benefits are enrichment of the soil and an increase in its ability to hold moisture.

---

*The numbers given to a particular fertilizer stand for the percentages of nitrogen, phosphorus, and potassium contained in the product. In 10-10-10, each of these basic nutrients required by plants is present in equal proportions.

The building of a compost heap calls for a certain amount of skill and a bit of hard work from time to time. But if approached as a challenge, it can be a lot of fun and not just another gardening chore. You begin by clearing a spot in a shady corner of the yard. The compost will be heaped upon bare ground so as to provide easy access to it by soil organisms. It is these all-important organisms that turn organic matter into the rich humus that is so easy to spread on lawns, garden beds, and the like. We can either stack the compost without enclosing it or use boards or wire to hold it in place and keep out marauding animals. A stack about four feet square, topped off layer after layer (each layer from five to ten inches in thickness) with rich earth mixed with some lime, manure, and chemical fertilizer, is what most gardening books call for. If we have placed our faith in earthworms and other soil organisms, we may decide that we can do without chemicals of any kind. Jerry Minnich, our authority on the earthworm, states that most chemical fertilizers, with the exception of ammonium sulphate, are relatively benign to earthworm populations. But the long-term effects of using chemical fertilizers, he warns, are apt to be harmful. He also warns that high-nitrogen chemical lawn fertilizers should be avoided because they create highly acid conditions unfavorable to the survival of earthworms.

Whatever our position may be in regard to chemical fertilizers, the next step, after we have our compost heap in a neat pile, is to turn it. This is done after the pile has been in position for about one month. Using a pitchfork, we thoroughly stir up the compost we have so neatly laid down. This is to let in air so that soil organisms will not be smothered. It is also helpful to apply water to the pile from time to time. We should sprinkle each layer as it is placed and sprinkle again whenever the pile is turned. The pile should be turned again three to four weeks after the first turning. Under summer conditions and with plenty of moisture, the material in our compost heap will have become thoroughly decomposed and ready for use in about six months.

Today, when so many of us live long distances from farming districts, it is not always easy to obtain the organic matter that goes into the building of a compost heap. Instead of being able to include liberal amounts of chicken, cow, horse, or pig manure, we are obliged to rely on whatever vegetable material our yard supplies and leftovers from the kitchen. First of all, we have obvious sources of organic matter in the form of leaves, grass clippings, weeds pulled from flower beds, the wilted stalks of garden vegetables, fallen fruits and nuts, hedge clippings, and sawdust. Less appealing but making excellent compost are the contents of our garbage can. Everything from chicken eggshell and coffee grounds to leftover bread and meat scraps can go into the compost heap if we have fenced it off from scavengers. Exceptions are bones, tinfoil, and other non-degradable objects that might turn up later in flower beds. For the same reason, we should avoid putting large sticks and pieces of wood in the compost heap. But we should not overlook fallen seeds, hulls, and droppings that have accumulated in the vicinity of our bird feeders. Any weevil-ridden or spoiled bird seed should also be relegated to the compost heap. Refuse from the woodpile and ashes from a wood stove are not to be overlooked. Wood ashes should first be mixed with earth and allowed to set for a day or two before being added, to prevent the formation of lye, a substance harmful to soil organisms. Large quantities of oak leaves and pine needles, because of their high acid content, can also be harmful to soil organisms and therefore should not be placed upon the compost heap.

If the compost heap and all it entails seems like too much work, we have an easier way proposed by Joan Lee Faust in *The New York*

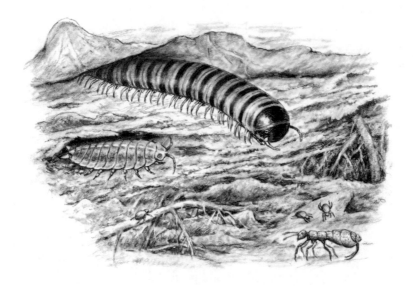

*Common inhabitants of a compost heap—*
*millipede, sowbug, mites, and springtail*

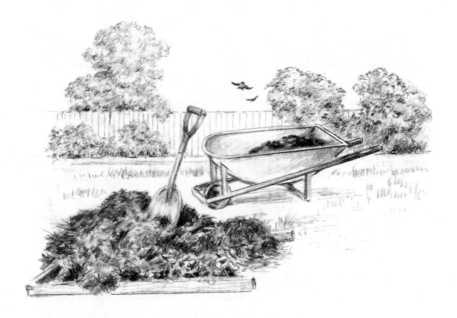

*Compost pile*

*Times Garden Book.* She uses her whole garden as a compost heap. Whatever organic matter she can find, whether kitchen scraps, leaves, grass cuttings, or cow manure, she deposits in her garden. This material builds up her soil and gives her some of the finest fruits and vegetables nature can provide. In much the same way, farmers for centuries, before the advent of chemical fertilizers, spread manure and other organic matter over their fields and pastures. The same practice is conducted today by dairy farmers and others who have access to sources of animal manure. Although most of us are too fastidious to apply these methods to our front yard or flower beds, we should not overlook direct composting as a means of enriching less visible parts of our yard.

The real benefits to our garden and earthworms come when the compost (now turned to a fine humus) is spread onto flower beds, vegetable beds, and lawns or is heaped around shrubbery. Humus-rich soils are ideal for growing plants and perfect for earthworms. The more humus we can apply to our soil, the better all around for plants, earthworms, and animals, such as robins, that feed on earthworms.

We can see, touch, and taste the benefits earthworms confer upon garden plants. Our flowers are healthier and larger in the fertile soil. Our lawn is greener and better able to withstand dry weather. The harvest from our vegetable garden is more bountiful and tastier. Even though we may not give the earthworm credit for all this, it has done its share and more with some assistance from us. Our composting and liming will have greatly improved food and soil conditions for the earthworm.

There is another side to having earthworms besides that of benefiting the soil—one that is even less appreciated by us. Earthworms are at the bottom of a food chain that supports some of the most common and best-known forms of wildlife. As is the case with most food chains, the lowest link is a herbivore. Earthworms, through their diet of half-decayed leaves, grasses, and the like, qualify as herbivores even though they feed upon dead rather than green vegetable matter. In this sense we could call them scavengers. However this may be, their food habits are wholly beneficial; they turn waste matter into the humus that makes our soil bloom.

Judging from the eager way fish take to an earthworm dangling at the end of a fishing line, these wiggly creatures are tasty morsels for a great many forms of wildlife. In our yard, there is no more ardent consumer of earthworms than the robin. Running a short distance, stopping, cocking its head, the robin visually detects the presence of an earthworm and with a carefully aimed jab of its bill pulls it out of the ground. Not many birds are this skillful in taking earthworms from their burrows, but an astute house sparrow knows just when to rush up to a surprised robin and steal its earthworm. Other members of the thrush family, including the wood thrush and hermit thrush, use the same techniques as the robin in procuring earthworms. Still another technique is used by woodcock and gulls. Aware of the fact that rapid vibrations will bring earthworms to the surface, these birds have a special way of patting the soil with one of their feet so as to produce enough of a vibration to lure earthworms. About two-thirds of the diet of our American woodcock consists of earthworms. When we see a woodcock on our lawn, we can be sure that it is searching for earthworms. Shrews and moles, however we may view their presence just below the surface of our lawns and gardens, are also avid earthworm eaters.

Among reptiles and amphibians, toads feast happily upon earthworms. They become active after dark, when night crawlers come to the surface. Garter snakes when young feast upon earthworms. The box turtle, as it ambles through the vegetable garden sampling our ripe tomatoes, is also on the lookout for earthworms. When a rainstorm washes earthworms into streets and gutters and eventually into sizable bodies of water, fish, frogs, and turtles finally have their opportunity.

The next level in the food chain is made up of animals that feed upon consumers of earthworms. We are as much a part of this chain as are foxes, skunks, weasels, and hawks. The next time we help ourselves to fish served with fresh vegetables, we might ask ourselves what role earthworms played in supplying us with these foods.

# 12 / *Misunderstood Reptiles and Amphibians*

*Green anole (American chameleon)*

While most people readily accept the idea of attracting birds, butter-flies, and other colorful or harmless forms of wildlife to their yards, there is a drastic change in attitude when it comes to animals that crawl, sting, bite, or in any way look dangerous. The biters are regard-ed with special disfavor if they happen to belong to the class Reptilia and, in particular, the suborder Serpentes (snakes). Regardless of how small or harmless they may be, the snakes, because of a few dangerous biters among them, have a curse upon their heads. A snake can scarcely show itself in the open in daylight without someone coming after it with the intent to take its life.

In his book on rattlesnakes, Laurence M. Klauber laments the fact that our fear of snakes has had results quite the opposite of those desired. "It causes people to become so paralyzed upon encountering a rattler in the field," he writes, "that they cannot take the most elementary safety precautions. If bitten by a snake, they are in no condition to judge whether it was venomous or harmless. This is a matter of importance in deciding whether painful or even dangerous remedial measures are necessary . . ." He goes on to say that destroying harmless snakes removes competition from the poisonous ones and may eliminate certain destroyers of rattlesnakes among the other snakes. Indiscriminate killing of snakes, according to Klauber, can lead to the protection and increase of dangerous poisonous snakes. He advises that children should be taught to avoid snakes, *not to be terrified of them.* He calls our fear of snakes cultivated, not instinctive.

The chances of dying of snakebite are so infinitesimal these days that the fear of snakes is out of all proportion to the danger. According to statistics in *Urban Entomology* by Walter Eberling, during the ten-year period 1950–59 there were 229 human deaths from bees, wasps, ants, spiders, and scorpions and 138 from snakes. Rattlesnakes were the chief offenders among the snakes, causing 94 deaths. Bees and wasps were each responsible for causing more deaths in the ten-year period than rattlesnakes.

In the Great Lakes region and more northern parts of New York State and New England, there are no poisonous snakes. The cottonmouth, a poisonous snake of southern swamplands, is found no farther north than southeastern Virginia and southern Illinois. The coral snake, responsible for only two fatalities during the ten-year period, is a southern species not found north of the Carolinas. It can be seen that the risk of snakebite by a poisonous species is extremely small or nonexistent in many parts of the country. In cities and most suburbs, the chances are equally slim. The few snakes surviving in densely populated districts are, for the most part, small, retiring, and harmless.

On the other hand, one should be careful about poisonous snakes in newly established housing developments that have encroached upon wildlife habitat in arid parts of the West. The sidewinder, a western rattlesnake, is to be reckoned with wherever it is found in its range in desert areas of western Arizona and nearby Nevada and California. Fortunately, this rattlesnake does not have very toxic venom.

The snakes are only one group of reptiles. Along with the crocodilians, turtles, and lizards, they have a representation of 283 species in North America north of Mexico. The amphibians, which include the salamanders, frogs, and toads, are represented by 194 species within the same geographical limits. These two groups are known collectively as the herpetozoans, or herps for short. While normally not a very conspicuous or numerous part of our yard and garden fauna, the herps play an important role that is, for the most part, helpful to our interests. It will pay us to become better acquainted with this frequently abused and overlooked group of animals.

The South and Southwest have the richest herp faunas, with numbers and species tending to progressively decline as one moves northward. Not many people are even aware that they have a herp fauna within the confines of their property. The problems of identification make this group a difficult choice for the nature hobbyist. Moreover, most herps are so well hidden and are so well camouflaged that we have to go to some lengths to learn of their presence.

Reminiscent of Dr. Lutz's list of all the insects he found in his suburban yard is a project of Mrs. Olive Goin in Florida. Wife of a well-known herpetologist and an expert in herpetology herself, Mrs. Goin set out to count reptiles and amphibians on a residential lot. Four and a half years after she had embarked upon this project, she had compiled an astonishing total of forty species—all of them within the half-acre lot where she and her husband lived near Gainesville in northern Florida. Most of us, living in similar surroundings, would probably have recorded fewer than ten species in the same length of time.

Mrs. Goin describes her project in a book called *World Outside My Door*. That her yard was different from most yards and probably better suited for herps is seen in the kind of yard upkeep practiced by the Goins. The yard, with its grove of oak trees and partly overgrown field, was allowed to remain wild. Except for some removal of underbrush, there was no cutting or clearing. The Goins did not maintain a garden or a formal lawn. Leaving things pretty much as they were and providing a water-filled cement basin, four feet long, three feet wide, and four inches deep, were all the enticements needed to produce suitable conditions for a thriving herp fauna. The basin turned out to be a good breeding place for toads and frogs. Clumps of Spanish moss, dead leaves, logs, and branches left on the ground provided good hiding places.

By doing the exact opposite of what most homeowners do—namely, almost nothing—the Goins had achieved the proper sort of habitat for a sizable number of reptiles and amphibians to be found in that part of Florida. The final species totals after the four and a half years were fourteen toads and frogs, four salamanders, six lizards, twelve snakes, and four turtles.

For those having qualms about snakes, Mrs. Goin is reassuring. She states that they were only a minor element in the herp fauna and did not approach the frogs and lizards in abundance. She saw only about two snakes a month and considered only one, the coral snake, at all dangerous. Many of the snakes and other forms recorded in the Goin yard were wanderers. Some appeared seasonally, others only during wet weather, still others only during dry weather. Mrs. Goin concludes that, like rabbits and lemmings, her guests had cycles of scarcity and abundance. During periods of scarcity, Mrs. Goin had difficulty finding the secretive animals that were the objects of her search.

About the time Mrs. Goin was conducting her study, my wife and I were living near Gainesville. I was a graduate student in biology at the University of Florida and Dr. Goin was one of my professors. One day, when spading my garden, I turned up a pinkish wormlike creature about ten inches long. Not having any idea what it was, I took it to Dr. Goin. He told me that it was a worm lizard (*Rhineura floridana*)—something of a rarity and worth getting excited about. Blind, without legs or ear openings, this small lizard is found only in Florida and may often live its entire life underground. Finding this lizard whetted my curiosity about the unseen forms of life that may abound at our doorsteps but which we normally become aware of only by accident.

During more recent years, I shared many excursions with a herpetologist friend named Gary Williamson. He searches for herps in order to learn more about them, including their range limits. Most of his finds are under pieces of tin roofing, in ruins of old buildings, or under logs or loose bark of trees. He finds a surprising variety of snakes in probing through the debris of fallen houses. A good conservationist, he keeps only the specimens he needs for talks to nature groups. After turning over logs or pieces of tin, he always carefully returns these objects to their former positions. In this way, there is a minimum of disturbance to the animals that live underneath.

My friend is fascinated by poisonous snakes. Aware of their diminishing numbers in many areas, he lends them a helping hand by sometimes transferring rattlesnakes and others to habitats where he feels they will be safer from human persecution. On a number of occasions, I've driven long distances with one of Gary's rattlesnakes tied up in a bag on the back seat. I have found the nearby presence of one of these snakes a bit unnerving. My boyhood was spent in snake-infested country and the admonitions of parents and grandparents about the dangers of snakes have tended to influence my attitude toward them. I am happy to see others engaged in conservation efforts, such as Gary's, but I would rather not handle snakes myself. As for the occasional hitchhiker who innocently accepted a ride with us, I won't describe his or her reactions when it was discovered that there was another "passenger" on the backseat.

## HARMLESS SNAKES

The poisonous snakes are the first to retreat before the advance of civilization. Left behind are small innocuous species that rarely make themselves known. Two of the most secretive of the small snakes are the worm snake and northern brown or DeKay's snake. John Kieran, in his *Natural History of New York City,* reported the presence of both living under rocks and boards in Central Park. As seen in a recent census of park wildlife, there are eight species of herps within the limits of this much-used park in the heart of one of the world's largest cities. Besides the two species of snakes, Central Park plays host to two species of frogs, one species of toad, and three species of turtles.

The northern brown snake, whose diet consists largely of worms and slugs, is known for its ability to survive in odd plots of land in the middle of large cities. This is equally true of the several subspecies found from the Great Plains eastward. The earth snakes, about the same size as the brown snakes, also feed upon earthworms and are capable of adapting to suburban yards and empty lots in cities. Still another small snake that shows similar adaptability is the ringneck. For years I played host to a small population that lived in my cellar and took refuge in leaves that sometimes blew in when the door was open. With a bright light-colored ring encircling the neck, yellow, orange, or red below and dark above, the ringneck is one of our more handsome snakes. Its appearance and docile ways help it win over friends among people that, on the whole, are opposed to snakes.

The garter snakes are frequently seen out in the open. Able to adapt to a wide variety of habitats, these yellowish and brown striped snakes are often seen in vacant lots and in yards and gardens. When disturbed, this snake retreats to whatever cover happens to be most handy—a rock pile, stone wall, or grassy margins of wetlands. On the whole rather trusting in nature, garter snakes are not quite so subject to unthinking slaughter as many other snakes. They help control some garden pests but the largest share of their diet consists of useful species like toads, frogs, and earthworms.

We sometimes play host to a clownlike snake that is all bluff and fury but completely harmless. This is the hognose snake, which tries its best to repel us by looking and acting like a deadly cobra. If the cobra part of the act fails to achieve its end, the hognose begins to thrash about realistically and then rolls over, looking for all the world as if it had just been killed. So convincing are its death agonies that we could easily be taken in if we hadn't already heard about this trick. Feeding chiefly upon toads, the hognosed snake, represented by several species and subspecies, provides little in the way of economic benefit but is such a clown that we can't help but enjoy its antics.

If the term "dainty" suits any snake, I would reserve it for the green snakes. Slender and as green as the leafy foliage they keep to, the green snakes are occasional visitors to yards and gardens. We should welcome them. They prey upon such enemies of the gardener as grasshoppers, crickets, and hornworms. The rough green snake is found from Pennsylvania and central Illinois southward, while the smooth green snake appears just to the north of the range of its close relative. The smooth snake also has scattered populations in parts of the West.

A number of the larger snakes are killed on sight simply because they look dangerous. The rat snakes, which make themselves at home in barns, outhouses, and sometimes even the house itself, are excellent mouse and rat hunters but too fearsome-looking for many homeowners. The corn snake, in its never-ceasing pursuit of rats, sometimes enters homes in cities. Wilfred T. Neill, in a 1950 issue of *Herpetologica*, stated that the corn snake was astonishingly abundant in many southern cities and that each autumn the young turned up in parlors, kitchens, and pantries. Neither the young nor the adults are likely to receive a warm welcome. John L. Behler tells us in *The Audubon Society Field Guide to North American Reptiles and Amphibians* that the name "corn snake" probably did not originate from any association this snake may have with corn; rather it seems to have its origin in the similarity of the belly markings to the checkered patterns of kernels of Indian corn. Considered by many to be a beautiful snake, this frequent inhabitant of barns and outbuildings is chiefly southern in distribution.

According to Neill, the red-bellied watersnake is a visitor to parts of Augusta, Georgia, and other southern cities. Making their way from reservoirs by way of water pipes, the snakes appear in all kinds of places, including goldfish ponds. One resident of Augusta blamed the disappearance of his goldfish on stray cats when the actual culprit was a red-bellied watersnake.

The common kingsnake, whose habitat, as described by Behler, may include dry rocky wooded hillsides, river swamps, coastal marshes, prairie, desert, and chaparral, is at home nearly everywhere except in the North. Neither this kingsnake nor several others are found much north of the southern and central states. Those who fear snakes should think twice before killing a kingsnake. Constrictors, these snakes eat other snakes, including rattlesnakes, copperheads, and coral snakes. One member of the group, known as the mole snake, spends much of its life in mole tunnels preying upon mice and moles. If only we had a better understanding of the food habits of our more common snakes, we might feel better disposed toward them and more willing to tolerate their presence in the vicinity of our homes.

# LIZARDS

Most of us living in the East are not overly aware of the presence of lizards. We have few species and most of them are accomplished at staying out of sight. In arid parts of the West, lizards are a more visible feature of the landscape. This group of reptiles seems to adapt best to hot, dry conditions. But at least those of us in the Southeast do have the green anole, a small lizard that thrives in well-watered gardens and is

*Texas horned toad*

friendly enough to appear at windows and even to come into the house if offered the opportunity. In pursuing flies, beetles, moths, and spiders, the green anole easily makes its way up sides of houses or along tree trunks. This anole seems to have a preference for flower boxes filled with petunias or garden balsam, and it also makes itself at home on the stems and leaves of the amaryllis lily. But it may be that the flowers in question happen to be growing in sunny places where this small lizard likes to rest or indulge in its courtship performances. The green anole has the chameleonlike ability to change color—from green to brown and back to green—in response to variations in temperature, light, humidity, and even its own emotional state. These changes have nothing to do with camouflage.

Sharing some of the same habitats as the green anole are other eastern lizards, including the skinks. Mrs. Goin had the green anole and five other species in her yard. Living under Spanish moss or in the crevices of fallen timber, her other lizards were far less visible. The five-lined skink is a terrestrial species that forages about among rock piles and rotting logs. Found from Florida and Texas to the Great Lakes, this lizard has the widest range of any strictly eastern species. Somewhat more confined to the South, the broad-headed skink is an arboreal species living on trunks and branches of trees; it may also be found in empty lots in urban areas. A third member of the genus, the southeastern five-lined skink, is partial to drier habitats and can be found both in yards and gardens and in sandy wastes on coastal islands.

The fence lizard, with representatives in both the East and the West, is partial to old ruins, deserted houses, cabins in the woods, and other sites where man is not busy with his clipping and cutting. The fence lizard blends in so well with its chosen background that we often fail to notice it. But once it is disturbed, it scurries away with its tail slightly elevated and scoots around a tree trunk or wall to get out of our line of vision. If we follow it, there is another dash as the lizard repeats the same performance. Feeding largely upon insects, the fence lizard picks its prey off the ground or out of the air with a lightning flick of its tongue. One was seen to catch an insect every time the tongue went out. There are reports of fence lizards eating vegetable matter, including fallen rose petals.

In rocky, arid parts of the West, lizards are apt to be much more plentiful than in wooded sections of the East, but not necessarily more visible. The horned lizards offer an example of how well an animal can blend into its surroundings. Having the appearance of a toad, but not as puffed up, and with spiny projections on its body, the Texas horned toad is a formidable-looking animal. It shows itself to be a lizard by scampering away when we approach it too closely. Other western horned lizards, relying upon their camouflage, will almost allow themselves to be stepped on. We may meet the horned lizards almost anywhere in Texas and in the Rocky Mountain region from Canada to Mexico. They are likely to be encountered where housing developments spread into desertlike country.

Luckily, the chuckwalla, another western lizard, is a denizen of boulder-strewn desert country and not an inhabitant of yards and gardens. Strictly a vegetarian, this large, chunky lizard lives on a diet of green leaves, buds, flowers, and fruit. It seems to have a special liking for yellow flowers. The chuckwalla is found in western Arizona and adjacent parts of Utah, Nevada, and California.

## TURTLES

The most avid vegetarian among the herps that visit our yards is the box turtle. Young box turtles are primarily carnivorous, but upon becoming adults, they take increasing amounts of vegetable food, including a number of garden vegetables. One year box turtles made such inroads upon our ripe tomatoes that we took to transferring the turtles to distant points. Apples, watermelon, cantaloupe, mulberries, and strawberries are included in the vegetable part of their diets. We benefit from their liking for slugs, snails, centipedes, and caterpillars. The statement that box turtles may live over one hundred years is based upon dates and initials carved on shells. We can't be sure of the accuracy of these data. But one at Boyertown, Pennsylvania, was reported to have come in suitable weather almost daily for more than thirty years to a back door for a breakfast of bread soaked in milk. The automobile is the box turtle's worst enemy and the reason why this turtle is absent from most heavily populated districts. Dogs also take a toll. But take a walk in wooded country almost anywhere in the East, except more northern sections, and chances are good that you will find either the shell of a dead box turtle or a living one. As the name of this turtle suggests, the animal can close itself up in its boxlike shell when danger threatens. The best time to find box turtles is after a heavy summer shower.

Unless there is a stream or some other body of water near us, we are unlikely to be visited by other kinds of turtles. But turtles do come ashore to lay their eggs and sometimes wander quite far inland. If we should see a turtle the size of a dinner plate with a disproportionately large head lumbering along, stopping to gaze about, and then moving on again, it may very well be a snapping turtle. This is one turtle to treat with respect. Its powerful jaws can snap off a broomstick as quick as a flash!

The snapping turtle and also the painted turtle have demonstrated an ability to survive under the pressure of expanding urbanization. The basic requirement for these turtles is water in the form of ponds or streams. With so many farm ponds and other ponds being constructed these days, the outlook for these two turtles, and others as well, is favorable. But the snapping turtle is not a welcome addition if the pond is for ducks and other waterfowl. This turtle takes a heavy toll of young ducks. A balance in numbers is sometimes achieved if skunks are present in the area. No other animal seems quite so accomplished at finding and eating the buried eggs of snapping turtles.

*Box turtle sampling strawberry*

## TOADS AND FROGS

The toads are the one herp representative that nearly everyone knows and frequently sees. Unlike the frogs, which must spend their lives in or near water, toads leave the water once they have completed the egg and larval stages in their metamorphosis. The early stages are completed much more rapidly than in frogs. The eggs hatch in three or four days, producing tiny tadpoles. These swim about eating microscopic plants and animals. After somewhere between forty and sixty days (twelve to thirteen days for spadefoot toads), the tadpoles change into miniature toads whose immediate purpose is to reach high ground. Thanks to short egg and larval stages, toads often hatch out in temporary rain pools and therefore are not dependent upon permanent bodies of water.

Although a female toad may lay somewhere between 5,000 and 25,000 eggs, first the tadpoles and then the newly hatched small toads are preyed upon so heavily by animals of many kinds that only a few will reach protected places where they will establish their abodes. If it is our yard, toads taking up residence will seek damp places under loose bricks or boards or perhaps a cranny somewhere under the house. To aid these friends of the gardener, we can dig a few small pits about two or three inches deep and partially cover them with boards. Equally important will be a source of water where the toad can sit and absorb moisture through its skin. Toads do not drink water but absorb it. A ground-level birdbath is an ideal place for a toad in need of water.

Among the many enemies of toads are crows, hawks, skunks, garter snakes, and hognose snakes. Thanks to poison glands in the skin, toads are protected to some extent from a number of predators, including dogs. A dog, after getting a taste of the toad's skin, will promptly release its hold.

The toad that has taken up residence in our yard may, with some luck, live to a ripe old age. Mary C. Dickerson, in *The Frog Book*, tells of one that lived to be thirty-six years old. Whatever age our toad does live to, one thing is certain: it will dispose of a lot of insect pests during its lifetime. According to Dickerson, 88 percent of its food consists of insects and other small creatures considered to be pests in the garden.

*Toad catching insect*

Among its prey are cutworms, armyworms, tent caterpillars, injurious beetles, slugs, snails, and sow bugs. Only 1 percent of the food of this toad consists of earthworms.

The toad does its hunting at night and takes only objects that move. It captures some of its prey while quietly sitting in one place. With a sudden flick of its sticky tongue, it may pick a mosquito out of the air or snap up a cricket. After a while, our toad hops about in the darkness finding still other small prey that may bring its nightly total to somewhere between fifty and a hundred bugs and insects of various kinds. If our yard has a good toad population, we will have little need to wage a war on harmful insects.

The two common toads in the East are Fowler's toad and the American toad. They look almost alike and sometimes hybridize. Both are friends of the gardener. Southward from Virginia, the southern toad takes over. This toad is also a valuable ally of man. It lives in yards and gardens and is as indefatigable as any of the toads in taking small pests as it makes its nightly rounds.

All eighteen species of toads found in this country have feeding habits that are of value to the gardener or agriculturist. John L. Behler, in his guide to reptiles and amphibians, gives some idea of the habits of toads not mentioned so far. The Gulf coast toad of Louisiana and Texas is frequently seen catching insects under streetlights and even turns up in city storm sewers. The Great Plains toad of the Great Plains region and Southwest is called "a voracious predator of cutworms." On the other hand, if we are pet owners living in southern Florida or extreme southern Texas, we wouldn't want to have the giant toad (*Bufo marinus*) living anywhere near us. This toad, introduced to this country because of its value as a destroyer of harmful insects, releases a poison through its skin that may cause illness or death in any dog or cat that bites one.

Under the pressure of urbanization, toads have, for the most part, fared better than other herps. So long as there are lawns and gardens, hiding places, and water in which to deposit eggs, toads not only survive but often fare very nicely. Among the toads that seem to do best under urbanization are Fowler's toad, the American toad, and the spadefoot toads, burrowing species found in both the East and the West.

With closer ties to water, frogs are much less in evidence around homes and gardens than toads, except perhaps where the yard contains a permanent pool or borders a body of water. It should be remembered that an artificial pond must have gently sloping sides if tiny toads or frogs, changing from the tadpole stage, are to reach high ground. If unable to leave the water, they drown.

Some frogs do wander quite far from water. The pickerel frog is said to spend more time away from water than in it. Much the same can be said of the closely related leopard frog, with representatives throughout most of North America. Both of these frogs obtain a sizable portion of their diet in grassy fields where there is good hunting for spiders, beetles, crickets, and grasshoppers. In contrast, the bullfrog, our largest North American frog, obtains all of its food in or at the edge of the body of water where it makes its home. Bullfrogs eat aquatic insects, small fish, snails, and whatever they can catch around the rim of their pond. In contrast to leopard and pickerel frogs, whose tadpoles develop into frogs in one season, bullfrog tadpoles take two or three seasons to develop. Therefore these frogs must have permanent bodies of water in which to live. Yet the bullfrog is capable of taking advantage of small ponds within the limits of large cities. Wilfred T. Neill, in his account of reptiles and amphibians in urban areas of Georgia, states that bullfrogs are surprisingly abundant in residential sections of Augusta. They live in goldfish ponds and make their way from place to place through underground drains. Bullfrog tadpoles, as well as those of southern toads, frequented a large swimming pool on the outskirts of Augusta.

Treefrogs, tiny creatures ranging in size from half an inch to two and one-half inches, are seldom seen, but their voices are one of the characteristic sounds of spring and summer. The spring peeper's chorus on the first warm evenings of early spring is one of the sounds we most eagerly listen for after a cold winter. This small treefrog is found from quite far north in eastern Canada all the way to northern Florida and the Gulf coast.

The squirrel treefrog (*Hyla squirella*) is the one most often heard in urban areas in the South. Called the "rain frog" because of its greater vocal activity during rain showers, this treefrog is said to literally drop from the sky as it loosens its hold and falls from trees in pursuit of insects. It is found in habitats of all kinds, including gardens and trees lining city streets. Mrs. Goin, in her Florida study, said these small treefrogs would sometimes get on the roof and fall down the chimney. It was not uncommon to find squirrel treefrogs inside the house.

*Bullfrog*

## SALAMANDERS

Sometimes mistaken for lizards, salamanders are poorly represented in our garden fauna and, with few exceptions, are hard to find even in their preferred woodland or aquatic habitats. Unlike lizards, which have scales on their bodies and toes with claws, salamanders have smooth or warty skins and are without claws. Some species spend their entire lives in water, whereas others are partly or wholly terrestrial. All require a moist habitat. The species that is best adapted to suburban yards is the red-backed salamander (*Plethodon cinereus*), the common salamander of glaciated areas of the northeastern United States and southeastern Canada. Although normally found under boards, logs, stones, and trash of various kinds, this salamander, like other members of this genus, wanders about at night in damp weather. Part of the success of the red-backed salamander seems to lie in the fact that it does not require water for the egg or larval stage. The female lays her eggs in a small underground cavity or within a rotten log and stays with the eggs until they hatch within two months' time. This species can be recognized by its red back and mottled black and white undersurface.

Sometimes during or after a summer shower, residents of wooded areas in the East will see dozens, or perhaps hundreds, of bright-colored, very small salamanders moving about as though looking for food. The small creatures—only one and a half to three or four inches long—sometimes wander into yards and gardens. Known as efts, they delight us with their beauty and give aid to makers of crossword puzzles. Actually an eft is the land stage of aquatic salamanders known as newts. Hatching out in quiet streams, lakes, ponds, and ditches, newts pass through an aquatic larval stage and then, in some species, there is a terrestrial stage lasting from one to three years, followed by a return to the water. The eft stage, as it is called, may be skipped altogether even in species where it does occur. Whether it passed through the eft stage or not, the adult newt always lives in water and breathes with the help of gills.

The common species east of the Great Plains is the eastern newt (*Notophthalmus viridescens*). We recognize the eft stage in this salamander by the bright red or orange coloring of the efts and their red spots. Adults are normally olive green but can also be yellowish brown or dark greenish brown. This species owes its success, in large part, to skin glands which secrete a poison that is highly irritating to the mucous membranes in a predator's mouth. Toads are similarly endowed with poison glands. Predators, such as dogs, cats, and predaceous wild mammals, soon learn to avoid species that have poison glands in their skin.

Newts eat insects of various kinds, leeches, worms, small crustaceans, and eggs and larvae of other amphibians. Other salamanders have similar food tastes. The marbled salamander, for example, during its larval stage eats the larvae of spotted salamanders. As we have seen in the chapter on water, competition between various species of aquatic organisms is unusually keen and cannibalism is not uncommon. The salamanders can be as ruthless as any of the others when it comes to obtaining food.

# APPENDIX
# BIBLIOGRAPHY
# INDEX

# *Appendix*

ABELIA. Popular hedge plants, the abelias bloom profusely through the summer. The small tubular white flowers are patronized by hummingbirds, hummingbird moths, bees, and butterflies. The common species is glossy abelia (*A. grandiflora*).

ABUTILON, flowering maple. Tender shrubs with large bell-shaped flowers, the flowering maples are chiefly far western. Their nectar-rich flowers attract hummingbirds, bushtits, orange-crowned warblers, and orioles.

ACHILLEA, yarrow. Both the weed known as yarrow (*A. millefolium*) and cultivated garden yarrows are well patronized by butterflies.

ACONITUM, monkshood. The blue hooded flowers of monkshood (*A. napellus*) are visited by honeybees and bumblebees.

AESCULUS, buckeye. Ruby-throated hummingbirds may be seen seeking out the blossoms of red buckeye (*A. pavia*) when they first arrive in spring in the Deep South.

AGAPANTHUS. Sometimes called lily of the Nile, plants in this genus have blue or white tubular flowers which attract hummingbirds. Popular plants in California.

AGAVE, century plant. The agaves or century plants are among the most popular hummingbird plants in the Southwest. The greenish-yellow bell-shaped flowers often drip with nectar. Other visitors that come for the sweet liquid include orioles, white-winged doves, and bats.

AGERATUM. Butterflies visit the blue flowers of ageratum (*A. houstonianum*), and the seeds are readily taken by a number of birds, including juncos and goldfinches.

ALBIZIA, silk tree. Sometimes called mimosa, the silk tree (*A. julibrissin*) is covered with fuzzy pink and white blossoms in July and August. Hummingbirds throng to the flowers and an occasional butterfly is attracted.

ALCEA (ALTHAEA), hollyhock. The well-known hollyhock (*A. rosea*) with its mallowlike blossoms is well patronized by hummingbirds, orioles, honeybees, and bumblebees. The northern oriole eats the seeds. If the foliage is somewhat damaged, the caterpillar of the painted lady butterfly may be to blame. This is a minor price to pay for having these beautiful butterflies.

ALLAMANDA. A tropical vine with huge yellow flowers, the common allamanda (*A. cathartica*) supplies hummingbirds with nectar. In the West Indies, the birds pierce the flower base in order to tap the supply.

ALOE. Succulent herbs with spiny, toothed leaves, the aloes have flowers full of nectar, and consequently are much visited in the Southwest by hummingbirds and orioles.

AMARANTHUS. Not to be confused with weeds belonging to the same genus are two garden annuals whose seeds are sought after by members of the finch family. The plants in question are love-lies-bleeding (*A. caudatus*) and Joseph's coat (*A. tricolor*).

AMARYLLIS. The summer flowers of amaryllis or belladonna lily (*A. belladonna*) are much visited by hummingbirds.

AMELANCHIER, shadbush or serviceberry. Shrubs or small trees, the shadbushes have early summer fruits which are greatly relished by birds and small mammals. Two species commonly grown for ornament are downy serviceberry (*A. canadensis*) and Allegany serviceberry (*A. laevis*).

AMPELOPSIS, pepper vine, porcelain vine. Relatives of the grapes, the pepper vines supply fruits that are well liked by birds. The fruits, which may be lilac, porcelain blue, or whitish, ripen in the fall and are rather ornamental.

ANTIGONON, coral vine. Suitable only for warmest sections, coral vine (*A. leptopus*) has pink heart-shaped flowers which are well favored by bees. A long blooming season and high nectar yield make this plant a favorite among beekeepers. Hummingbirds also visit the flowers.

ANTIRRHINUM, snapdragon. The common snapdragon (*A. majus*) is highly selective in dispensing nectar. Only bumblebees and rarely honeybees can push their way past the blossom's tight outer lips. Hummingbirds occasionally probe the blossoms with their long bills.

Apocynum, dogbane. The dogbanes are rarely grown in gardens. But the small greenish white or pinkish flowers are exceptionally inviting to butterflies and other nectar-loving insects. The writer has listed thirty-eight species of butterflies coming to the flowers.

Aquilegia, columbine. The dainty flowers of the columbines, with their long, nectar-filled spurs, are ideal hummingbird and bumblebee drinking fountains. The hummingbirds reach the nectar legitimately by probing with their bills. But the bumblebees generally gain access by biting holes in the spurs. Honeybees obtain nectar at the holes made by the larger, stronger bumblebees. Both our native American columbine (*A. canadensis*) and the European columbine (*A. vulgaris*) are grown in gardens and contribute nectar to visitors such as those mentioned.

Arabis, rock cress. These small rock-garden plants, with white or pink flowers, provide food for the larvae of a number of butterflies, including whites, falcate orange tips, and marblewings.

Aralia, devil's-walking-stick or Hercules'-club. In spite of prickly stems and leaves, our native walking-stick (*A. spinosa*) is coming into its own as an ornamental shrub. The closely similar Japanese angelica tree (*A. elata*) has long been planted for ornament. Both plants produce black fruits that are popular with birds in the fall.

Arborvitae (see *Thuja*)

Aristolochia, Dutchman's-pipe. A twining vine, with large leaves and flowers shaped like pipes, Dutchman's-pipe (*A. durior*) is used to screen porches or cover sides of houses. The plants furnish food for the larvae of pipevine and polydamas swallowtails. The pipevine swallowtail also lays its eggs on the foliage of Virginia snakeroot (*A. serpentaria*).

Aronia, chokeberry. Although their fruits are sometimes eaten by birds, especially in late winter, the chokeberries are not widely utilized by wildlife as food plants. The two common species are red chokeberry (*A. arbutifolia*) with red fruit and black chokeberry (*A. melanocarpa*) with black fruit.

Artemisia, dusty miller. Well suited to seacoast gardens, dusty miller (*A. stellerana*) has spikelike clusters of yellow flowers which lure bees and other nectar-feeding insects.

Asclepias, milkweed. Aside from the tropical bloodflower (*A. curassavica*), the only other garden milkweed is our native butterfly weed (*A. tuberosa*). Its orange-yellow flowers are highly attractive to butterflies.

But other milkweeds, including common milkweed (*A. syriaca*) and swamp or red milkweed (*A. incarnata*), have about equal butterfly appeal. The monarch and its close relatives not only visit the milkweeds for nectar but use the plants almost exclusively for their eggs and larvae. Honeybees and bumblebees are apt to be even more plentiful at milkweed blossoms than butterflies.

ASPARAGUS. The pleasures of eating asparagus are well known to us. Birds benefit in the fall when small fruits amid the lacy foliage ripen and turn red. Mockingbirds are fond of them. Asparagus (*A. officinalis*), like the marigolds, has nematocidal properties and helps rid the soil of these tiny pests (see *Tagetes*).

ASTER. Also called Michaelmas daisies, the asters lend their beauty to both the garden and the countryside. As the flowers come into bloom in late summer and fall, they begin receiving attention from bees and butterflies. The plants act as hosts to the larvae of crescent spot butterflies and birds sometimes take the seeds.

AUCUBA, Japanese aucuba. Not enough is known about Japanese aucuba (*A. japonica*) to comment upon its wildlife value. A handsome shrub with variegated leaves and red fruits that persist all winter, this is a plant worth watching for possible wildlife use.

AUTUMN CROCUS (see *Colchicum*)

AUTUMN OLIVE (see *Elaeagnus*)

AZALEA (see *Rhododendron*)

BACHELOR'S BUTTON (see *Centaurea*)

BANANA (see *Musa*)

BARBERRY (see *Berberis*)

BAYBERRY (see *Myrica*)

BEAUTY-BERRY (see *Callicarpa*)

BEAUTY BUSH (see *Kolkwitzia*)

BEE BALM (see *Monarda*)

BEGONIA. Popular as house plants and, when the weather is warm enough, appearing in flower beds, the begonias might seem to confuse nectarfeeders with their endless shapes and colors. Nevertheless, hummingbirds are eager patrons and seem to choose scarlet begonia (*B. coccinea*) over most of the others.

BELLFLOWER (see *Campanula*)

BERBERIS, barberry. Better for nesting sites and shelter than for food, the barberries do serve us well and should continue to be a part of the wildlife garden. Japanese barberry (*B. thunbergii*) is the common species and is often used as a hedge plant. Its greenish-yellow flowers in spring attract bees and rare visits by hummingbirds. The red fruits that follow cling to bushes through the winter and provide emergency fare for birds during times of food shortage. Much the same wildlife advantages can be found in European barberry (*B. vulgaris*), which also has persistent red fruits. Darwin barberry (*B. darwinii*) is less often planted than the other two, but its persistent purple fruits seem somewhat more popular with birds.

BERGAMOT (see *Monarda*)

BITTERSWEET (see *Celastrus*)

BLAZING STAR (see *Liatris*)

BLEEDING HEART (see *Dicentra*)

BORAGE (see *Borago*)

BORAGO. Often grown in the herb garden, borage (*B. officinalis*) is known for its honey-producing qualities. The nectar-rich blue flowers appear through a large part of the summer and fall and are eagerly patronized by bees.

BOSTON IVY (see *Parthenocissus*)

BOTTLEBRUSH (see *Callistemon*)

BOUGAINVILLEA. In southern Florida and other frost-free sections, the reds and purples of bougainvillea blossoms decorate walls, sides of houses, and any other site where this shrubby vine is grown. Adding to the color are the many hummingbirds and butterflies that come freely to the blossoms.

BOUNCING BET (see *Saponaria*)

BOUVARDIA. The tubular red, pink, or white flowers of bouvardia seem made for hummingbirds. Where grown in Texas and other parts of the Southwest, hummingbirds are frequent visitors. Sweet bouvardia (*B. longiflora*) is a bush, two to four feet high, with fragrant white flowers. *B. ternifolia* is a larger bush with red flowers.

BRAZIL PEPPER TREE (see *Schinus*)

BUCKTHORN (see *Rhamnus*)

BUDDLEIA, butterfly bush. Shrubs belonging to this genus, with their honey-scented clusters of small tubular flowers, are overwhelming favorites of many butterflies. The highly fragrant flowers also attract hummingbird moths and bees. There is a butterfly bush for every warmer part of the year. Fountain buddleia (*B. alternifolia*), with lilac-purple flowers, begins blooming in May and is followed in June by the bright yellow flowers of globe butterfly bush (*B. globosa*).

Through August and early September, we can depend upon various varieties of orange-eyed butterfly bush (*B. davidii*), which may display white, red, pink, or purple flowers.

BUTTERFLY BUSH (see *Buddleia*)

BUTTERFLY WEED (see *Asclepias*)

CALIFORNIA FUCHSIA (see *Zauschneria*)

CALIFORNIA PEPPER TREE (see *Schinus*)

CALIFORNIA POPPY (see *Eschscholtzia*)

CALLIANDRA, powder puff. Shrubs with fuzzy, long-stamened blossoms (or powder puffs), these plants are mostly tropical and are found in the United States only in warmer parts of Florida and the Southwest. Their contribution lies in blossoms that are designed for pollination by birds. With us, hummingbirds perform this function.

CALLICARPA, beauty-berry. Our native beauty-berry (*C. americana*) has such attractive purple berries that gardeners living in the South will see little need for planting any of the several exotic species belonging to this genus. But the hardier Japanese beauty-berry (*C. japonica*) is required for more northern gardens. The beauty-berries furnish birds with food in fall and early winter and are particularly popular with mockingbirds. Bees visit the blossoms.

CALLISTEMON, bottlebrush. Well named, the flowers of these subtropical shrubs do look like bottlebrushes. In many of the bottlebrushes, the flowers are a bright red, a color that serves to attract hummingbirds. Other bird visitors include the cardinal and house finch.

CALLISTEPHUS, China aster. More like chrysanthemums than asters in appearance, the China aster (*C. chinensis*) becomes useful to wildlife when the seeds ripen. The small seeds are taken by a number of birds.

CALLUNA, heather. Grown partly for beauty and partly for sentiment, heather (*C. vulgaris*) has the added advantage of being a good bee plant.

CAMELLIA. The camellias, ornamental shrubs with dark evergreen leaves and waxy white, pink, or red flowers, offer a special favor to hummingbirds. The blooming period is from October to April, when little else is available to hummingbirds attempting to overwinter in the Southeast or along the Pacific coast.

CAMPANULA, bellflower. Easily recognized by bell-shaped blue or white flowers, the bellflowers are a common sight in gardens. The flowers are visited by bees and the seeds taken by seed-eating birds. Canterbury bells (*C. medium*) is sometimes rated as one of the best of garden honey plants.

CAMPSIS, trumpet creeper. This woody vine becomes a mecca for hummingbirds when its orange-red tubular flowers are in bloom in late summer. The ruby-throated hummingbird, unable to reach the nectar by hovering in its usual manner, plunges into the long funnel. Orioles and sphinx moths also come to the blossoms, and chickadees and goldfinches gather seeds from the pods in winter.

CANDYTUFT (see *Iberis*)

CANNA. In parts of the Southwest, the canna is in bloom almost the year round. The flowers, with their bright orange, reds, and other colors, supply nectar so freely that hummingbirds are ever nearby.

CAPE HONEYSUCKLE (see *Tecomaria*)

CARAGANA, Siberian pea tree. In Canada and more northern states the yellow pealike flowers of the pea tree (*C. arborescens*) offer sustenance in May when not many other sources of nectar are available for bees and hummingbirds.

CARDINAL FLOWER (see *Lobelia*)

CASTOR BEAN (see *Ricinus*)

CATNIP or CATMINT (see *Nepeta*)

CEANOTHUS, wild lilac. Chiefly western in distribution but with an eastern representative in New Jersey tea (*C. americanus*), wild lilacs rate fair to good when it comes to bees and hummingbirds. Several species are host plants to spring azure and brown elfin butterflies.

CELASTRUS, bittersweet. A minor source of bird food, the fruits of American bittersweet (*C. scandens*), as well as those of introduced species, are normally left clinging to vines through early winter. When other foods begin to be in short supply, birds may begin taking them.

CELOSIA, cockscomb. A gaudy plant from the tropics with strangely shaped flower heads, cockscomb (*C. argentea cristata*) sheds seeds that are taken by a number of seed-eating birds.

CENTAUREA. Close relatives of the thistles, the centaureas or knapweeds, as they are sometimes called, fill an important wildlife niche in the garden. They take the place of thistles without having the objectionable qualities that are associated with thistles. Excellent butterfly and bee plants, the knapweeds also supply goldfinches, house finches, and other birds with seeds in late summer. The most important garden species is cornflower or bachelor's button (*C. cyanus*).

CENTURY PLANT (see *Agave*)

CERCIS, redbud. Early spring blossoming, at about the time the flowering dogwood comes into bloom, makes the eastern redbud (*C. canadensis*) one of the charming sights of spring gardens and woodlands. The abundant early blossoms are the delight of bees which have recently emerged from their hives. The flowers are also visited by hummingbirds.

CHAENOMELES, quince. Early-blooming shrubs, like the redbuds, the quinces offer a treat to bees and hummingbirds when few other sources of nectar are available. Orioles also visit the flowers. Red is the most common floral color in this group.

CHASTE TREE (see *Vitex*)

CHEIRANTHUS, wallflower. In England, where wallflowers are much more commonly seen than on our side, they are considered to be among the best spring plants for bees and butterflies. With us, the common wallflower (*C. cheiri*) is patronized by both bees and butterflies.

CHELONE, turtlehead. A lovely wildflower, our native turtlehead (*C. glabra*) deserves a place in the garden but is hard to grow. The flowers are visited by bees and hummingbirds and the plants are one of the few larval food plants of the highly localized Baltimore butterfly. Another native turtlehead (*C. lyonii*) offers the same advantages to wildlife and is better adapted to garden use.

CHERRY (see *Prunus*)

CHICORY (see *Cichorium*)

CHINA ASTER (see *Callistephus*)

CHINESE PHOTINIA (see *Photinia*)

CHOKEBERRY (see *Aronia*)

CHRISTMASBERRY (see *Heteromeles*)

CHRYSANTHEMUM. On the whole, the chrysanthemums rate rather poorly from the standpoint of wildlife usage. This is particularly true of the more highly cultivated varieties, especially those with double blossoms. But the oxeye daisy (*C. leucanthemum*) is a wildflower that is patronized by bees and eagerly by butterflies. Some butterfly use occurs with the others, and birds, including house finches, take the seeds of chrysanthemums.

CHUPAROSA (see *Justicia*)

CICHORIUM, chicory. One of those plants that has all the characteristics of a weed but enough beauty to allow it a place in the garden, chicory (*C. intybus*) has a long blooming season with seed pods and blue flowers present at the same time. A good bee plant, chicory offers a second treat in the form of seeds that are eagerly taken by goldfinches.

CITRUS, orange. The blossoms of the orange, with their delicious fragrance, are reason enough to have the trees. Bees are frequent visitors to the flowers and supply the orange blossom honey that is so much in demand. Still other nectar-feeders, including the hummingbirds and butterflies, come to the blossoms. Known as orange dogs, caterpillars of the giant swallowtail do some damage to the foliage of the trees. But this can be excused to a large degree when the adult butterflies begin feeding at the orange blossoms.

CLEMATIS. As a general rule, the horticultural varieties of clematis are lacking in nectar and therefore receive few visits from insects. But *C. paniculata*, with fragrant blossoms in late summer, is heavily patronized by bees and is sometimes visited by butterflies.

CLEOME, spiderflower. Receiving its common name from its spidery seed pods, spiderflower (*C. spinosa*) has a long flowering season through the summer and early fall. The flowers are immensely popular with bees. Visits are chiefly in early morning and toward nightfall—times when the flowers freely secrete nectar. Hummingbirds are likely to appear at the appropriate times to get their share. The seeds are taken by mourning doves.

CLOVER (see *Trifolium*)

COCKSCOMB (see *Celosia*)

COLCHICUM, autumn crocus. Colorful lilies, whose blossoms appear on stems only six or so inches high, the autumn crocus (*C. autumnale*) is one of the late-season flowers patronized by butterflies.

COLUMBINE (see *Aquilegia*)

CONEFLOWER (see *Rudbeckia*)

CORAL-BELLS (see *Heuchera*)

CORALBERRY (see *Symphoricarpos*)

CORAL VINE (see *Antigonon*)

COREOPSIS. Goldfinches have a special fondness for the small seeds of members of the composite family, including those of coreopsis.

CORNFLOWER (see *Centaurea*)

CORNUS, dogwood. The value of the dogwoods, both as nesting sites for birds and as bird food plants, has been discussed in previous chapters. Of minor interest is the fact that dogwoods are host plants for the spring azure, one of the daintiest of butterflies. While our native flowering dogwood (*C. florida*) has everything one could ask for in the way of spring blossoms and fall color and food for birds, there are several others, native and exotic, worth considering. Japanese dogwood (*C. kousa*), cornelian cherry (*C. mas*), and Siberian dogwood (*C. alba*) are exotics that offer beauty and food for birds. Much the same can be said of several other natives, including red osier dogwood (*C. sericea*), gray dogwood (*C. racemosa*), and alternate-leaved dogwood (*C. alternifolia*).

COSMOS. With a long flowering season through the summer and early fall, cosmos sooner or later receives attention from bees and butterflies. But the chief popularity of these daisylike members of the composite family comes when the seeds ripen. They are taken avidly from the flower heads by goldfinches, white-throated sparrows, house finches, and juncos.

COTONEASTER. There are so many cotoneasters planted for ornament that one hardly knows where to begin in choosing the best kinds for wildlife. It is safe to say that nearly all with red fruits have bird appeal. One of the best for all-around use is the popular rock spray (*C. horizontalis*) with its semi-evergreen leaves and bright red berries in the fall. Birds, usually after a long wait, take the berries, and the small pink flowers that appear in June invite bees and now and then a hummingbird looking for a few small sips of nectar.

CRAB APPLE (see *Malus*)

CRAPE MYRTLE (see *Lagerstroemia*)

CRATAEGUS, hawthorn. The major wildlife uses of the hawthorns, as mentioned in previous chapters, are as nesting sites for birds in summer and a source of food for them in fall and winter. The best hawthorn for winter food is the Washington thorn (*C. phaenopyrum*), whose small scarlet fruits sometimes cling to the tree until April. The glossy hawthorn (*C. nitida*) and cockspur thorn (*C. crus-galli*) can sometimes be counted upon to provide food for birds in winter. Cedar waxwings often vary their diets by eating both the fruits and the flower petals of hawthorns in spring. Bees come to the blossoms and so do hummingbirds.

CROCUS. In Britain the early spring blossoms of crocus (especially yellow blossoms) are often attacked by house sparrows and other birds. One theory is that the birds are seeking nectar. Bees, conferring their services as pollinators, are more legitimate visitors. The common crocus (*C. vernus*) is the one seen most often in gardens.

CURRANT (see *Ribes*)

DAFFODIL (see *Narcissus*)

DAHLIA. So long as dahlias are not overly large and double-flowered, they receive good patronage from nectar-feeders. Bees are the common visitors, while occasional appearances of butterflies and hummingbirds can be expected.

DAME'S ROCKET (see *Hesperis*)

DANDELION (see *Taraxacum*)

DAPHNE. A small ornamental shrub with early blossoms followed in June by bright scarlet berries, February daphne (*D. mezereum*) serves wildlife by providing very early nectar for bees and early fruit for birds. In Britain greenfinches take the fruit of this plant even before it has ripened.

DAUCUS, Queen Anne's lace. Usually the lacy white flowers of Queen Anne's lace (*D. carota*) seem devoid of insect life. But occasionally bumblebees can be seen tumbling all over the flower heads gathering nectar and pollen, and butterflies also come to the blossoms. The flowers are very erratic in offering their sustenance and for long periods give almost nothing. The handsome black swallowtail lays its eggs on the plants and the larvae soon emerge to begin eating the leaves.

DAYLILY (see *Hemerocallis*)

DEAD NETTLE (see *Lamium*)

DELPHINIUM. Whether one grows delphiniums, which are perennials, or larkspurs, which are annuals, makes no difference to nectar-feeders. Both are members of the same genus and retain nectar in long spurs. Hummingbirds are among the chief pollinators. Although their preference is for red-flowered species, like *D. cardinale* and *D. nudicaule*, they are almost equally attentive to the blue flowers that are so dominant in this group. Bumblebees are the other common visitor.

DEUTZIA. Easily mistaken for mock orange, the deutzias are one of our very common garden shrubs. The flowers in late May and June are patronized by bumblebees.

DEVIL'S-WALKING-STICK (see *Aralia*)

DIANTHUS, pinks. The pinks, including sweet william (*D. barbatus*), qualify chiefly as moth flowers. The sphinx moths, for the most part, come at night, but the clearwings, including the hummingbird moth, are exceptions. Other visitors to the pinks, with their fragrant pink, rose-colored, or white flowers, include butterflies and hummingbirds. The seeds are of minor value as bird food.

DICENTRA, bleeding heart. Bleeding heart (*D. spectabilis*), with its pink heart-shaped flowers that hang like pendants, is mainly a bee plant. Butterflies are sometimes seen at the flowers and also an occasional hummingbird. In the West, the butterfly clodius parnassian uses the bleeding heart and others as a host plant.

DICTAMNUS, gas plant. By serving as a host, the gas plant (*D. albus*), an old favorite in gardens, assists the giant swallowtail in maintaining a more northern population.

DIGITALIS, foxglove. In British Columbia and other parts of the Northwest, foxglove (*D. purpurea*) is held in favor by beekeepers. The blossoms are good providers of nectar for about five weeks, beginning in mid-June. The flowers are much visited by bumblebees and occasionally by hummingbirds.

DOGBANE (see *Apocynum*)

DOGWOOD (see *Cornus*)

DUSTY MILLER (see *Artemisia*)

DUTCHMAN'S-PIPE (see *Aristolochia*)

ELAEAGNUS. It is safe to say that, with the possible exception of dogwoods and viburnums, no other group of garden ornamentals offers so many wildlife advantages as members of this genus. Wildlife benefits range from nectar for bees to nesting sites and food for birds. There is an elaeagnus for every yard and every climate zone. One can pick shrub-sized smaller ones or the Russian olive, which can grow into a small tree. All have varying degrees of silvery foliage and reddish fruits well liked by birds. There is almost an elaeagnus for every season. Thorny elaeagnus (*E. pungens*) produces blossoms in late fall. These are highly fragrant and provide bees with one of their last sources of nectar before they retire to their hives for the winter. By May, thorny elaeagnus is ready with a crop of ripe fruit—a welcome offering to birds that are starting to nest. By midsummer, cherry elaeagnus (*E. multiflora*), with its silvery foliage, has begun to offer birds its cherry-like fruits. In the fall, we have a wider choice of plantings belonging to this group. Autumn elaeagnus (*E. umbellata*) is one of the most widely planted of all and highly recommended for wildlife use. Its red and silver-colored fruits are eagerly taken by a wide variety of birds. The even more silver-colored foliage and fruits of silverberry (*E. commutata*) are highly ornamental; the fruit, like that of other species, is readily taken by birds. Russian olive (*E. angustifolia*) also produces fall fruit well liked by birds, but this elaeagnus is somewhat too large and ungainly for most yards.

ELDERBERRY (see *Sambucus*)

ENGLISH IVY (see *Hedera*)

EPILOBIUM, fireweed. Also known as willow herb, fireweed (*E. angustifolium*) is not only a wildflower that appears most abundantly after fire but also an acceptable garden flower. A long flowering period from July until frost gives bees, hummingbirds, and hummingbird moths a long season to visit for nectar.

ESCHSCHOLTZIA, California poppy. While whole fields of these plants, with their yellow to orange blossoms, can be found in the West, we in the East have only those that are planted in gardens. The flowers attract bees and the seeds that come later are favored by birds.

EUONYMUS. An important group of shrubs and vines—many with evergreen leaves and pink, orange, or red fruits in the fall—the euonymus genus has much to offer from an ornamental standpoint but is lacking in contributions to wildlife. There are exceptions in good bee patronage to the flowers and some bird use of the fruits. Winged euonymus (*E. alata*) is probably the best in the group when it comes to supplying bird food.

EUPATORIUM, thoroughwort. Meadow plants belonging to this genus are rarely seen in the garden. But the purple or white flowers of these tall herbs are decorative and attract butterflies and bees. For wildlife purposes, joe-pye weed (*E. maculatum*), boneset (*E. perfoliatum*), and mistflower (*E. coelestinum*) are well worth having in a corner of the garden.

EUPHORBIA. Two quite different plants in this group are noted for their rich supplies of nectar. Poinsettia (*E. pulcherima*), so much in evidence around Christmastime, has blossoms that fairly drip with nectar. Plants left in the open in summer are likely to be visited by hummingbirds, bees, and butterflies. Snow-on-the-mountain (*E. marginata*), at home in northern yards and gardens, has flowers that yield a honey so peppery that it is said to burn the mouth.

EVENING PRIMROSE (see *Oenothera*)

EVENING STOCK (see *Matthiola*)

FEBRUARY DAPHNE (see *Daphne*)

FIRECRACKER PLANT (see *Russelia*)

FIRE THORN (see *Pyracantha*)

FIREWEED (see *Epilobium*)

FLOWERING MAPLE (see *Abutilon*)

FLOWERING QUINCE (see *Chaenomeles*)

FORGET-ME-NOT (see *Myosotis*)

FORSYTHIA. Before forsythia puts on its display of bright yellow blossoms in early spring, birds may have found the flower buds. House finches and a sizably long list of other birds pluck the buds and early flowers of forsythia. The birds may find this green food a tonic after subsisting upon seeds all winter. Seldom are enough flowers taken to impair the massed yellow that greets us each year.

FOUR-O'CLOCK (see *Mirabilis*)

FOXGLOVE (see *Digitalis*)

FUCHSIA. Thanks to the fact that fuchsias thrive out of doors in more southern sections, hummingbirds have an opportunity to visit the nectar-rich flowers that seem especially made for them. Farther north plants in hanging baskets are available to hummingbirds during the summer. Although primarily hummingbird plants, fuchsias receive some patronage from bees and butterflies.

GAILLARDIA. The flowers of the gaillardias, with their combinations of red and yellow, are at times irresistible to bees. The great spangled fritillary and other butterflies pay visits while the seeds are of minor benefit to birds.

GARDEN BALSAM (see *Impatiens*)

GARDENIA. The well-known gardenia of southern gardens (*G. jasminoides*) has only a few wildlife patrons. Among these are the sphinx or hawk moths that, as darkness falls, come to the waxy white flowers noted for their fragrance.

GAS PLANT (see *Dictamnus*)

GENTIAN (see *Gentiana*)

GENTIANA. The gentians are like the snapdragon in having flowers that block easy access by most pollinators. This is particularly true of the closed or bottle gentian (*G. andrewsii*), whose tubular blue flowers are more or less permanently closed. Nevertheless the sphinx or hawk moths, with their long tongues, are successful in reaching the nectar. Many of the gentians are visited by hummingbirds.

GERANIUM (see *Pelargonium*)

GILIA. With blue or blue-violet flowers and related to phlox, the gilias are native to our West. The flowers are pollinated primarily by hawk moths and hummingbirds. Butterflies are occasional visitors. For close relatives of gilias and once included in the genus, one must turn to another genus, *Ipomopsis* (which see).

GLADIOLUS. The wildlife advantages of growing gladioli are many. They are popular hummingbird plants and visited by honeybees and bumblebees. Beekeepers report that the flowers are among those having the highest nectar yields. Since hummingbirds show a decided preference for plants with red flowers, *Gladiolus cardinalis*, with its large crimson flowers, might be the best choice.

GLOBE AMARANTH (see *Gomphrena*)

GLOSSY ABELIA (see *Abelia*)

GOLDENROD (see *Solidago*)

GOMPHRENA, globe amaranth. One of the everlastings, globe amaranth (*G. globosa*) has flowers that may be pink, purple, violet, or white. The flowers have modest butterfly appeal with a visitor list that includes the common checkered skipper.

GRAPE HYACINTH (see *Muscari*)

HAMELIA, scarlet bush. A native of south Florida, scarlet bush (*H. patens*) has been widely introduced into cultivation and can now be seen in many semitropical yards and gardens. Growing to about ten feet, scarlet bush offers a year-round profusion of tubular red flowers. The nectar-rich flowers are visited by bees, hummingbirds, and numerous species of butterflies. A single bush may have a dozen butterflies feeding at one time. Among the more common visitors are zebras, gulf fritillaries, and long-tailed skippers. As if the bushes and their flowers hadn't already offered enough advantages to wildlife, there are periods when the fruit is ripe and eagerly taken by birds. At first red and then turning black, the fruit is eaten by numerous species, including mockingbirds and cardinals. It is unfortunate that this bush isn't hardy enough to be grown farther north.

HARDY ORANGE (see *Poncirus*)

HAWTHORN (see *Crataegus*)

HEATHER (see *Calluna*)

HEBE (VERONICA). Formerly under the more euphonious genus name of *Veronica*, the hebes are tender shrubs from New Zealand whose brightly colored flowers are much visited by bees. For equally good wildlife advantages one should grow the true veronicas or speedwells (which see).

HEDERA, ivy. The English ivy (*H. helix*) that climbs so vigorously over trees and up sides of walls has a good friend in the beekeeper. The small greenish-yellow flowers that appear in late fall provide hard-pressed honeybees with their last good harvest of the season. Wasps, bumblebees, butterflies, and a variety of small flies are as eager for this final treat as are the honeybees. The flowers are soon followed by green fruits that slowly ripen and turn black during the winter. The fruit is a major source of food for birds in winter and early spring.

HELIANTHUS, sunflower. The common sunflower (*H. annuus*), grown widely for bird food, has good ornamental value as well. Like many other plants, this one combines beauty with food benefits to wildlife. But normally there is less wastage and more wildlife use if we gather the large seed heads after the seeds are ripe and store them for later use at the bird feeder. A variety called "black oil sunflower seed" is now replacing the striped seeds that were formerly the only kind offered at feed stores. It has been pointed out that the black oil seed consists of 70 percent kernel and 30 percent hull, whereas the striped seed consists of 57 percent kernel and 43 percent hull. These "meatier" oil seeds, therefore, offer birds comparatively more food value per seed. Moreover, birds can open the oil seeds more easily, which is of advantage to smaller birds, such as sparrows, juncos, and pine siskins.

HELIOTROPE (see *Heliotropium*)

HELIOTROPIUM, heliotrope. The flowers of the common heliotrope (*H. arborescens*) open more fully at night and exude a strong fragrance that attracts the night-flying sphinx moths. The flowers of these old-fashioned shrubby perennials range from dark violet to white in color and have a vanillalike fragrance which is also present during the day. The aroma has also been compared to that of cherries in a baked pie. Butterflies, as well as moths, come to the flowers.

HEMEROCALLIS, daylily. The daylily that is seen more commonly than others in gardens and, as an escape, in the wild is the tawny daylily (*H. fulva*). Its large orange or sometimes red or yellow blossoms are rich in nectar and therefore much visited by nectar-feeders. Hummingbirds practically disappear in the blossoms as they feed. Orioles, too eager to wait until the blossoms open, have a habit of tearing them apart to get at the nectar. The flowers are also patronized by the tiger swallowtail.

HERCULES'-CLUB (see *Aralia*)

HESPERIS, dame's rocket. One of the more ornamental members of the mustard family, dame's rocket (*H. matronalis*) produces fragrant white or purple blossoms that appear through the summer. The flowers are visited both by night-flying sphinx moths and by day-flying hummingbird moths. The seeds are taken by goldfinches.

HETEROMELES, Christmasberry or toyon. An evergreen shrub, much planted as an ornamental in California, with red fruits in winter. The fruits are eagerly taken by birds, and the flowers are visited by bees. Formerly this plant was in the genus *Photinia*.

HEUCHERA, coral-bells. A small garden plant with pendulous, bell-shaped flowers that are pink or red, coral-bells (*H. sanguinea*) has all the attributes needed to attract hummingbirds. The birds respond by paying visits beginning in late May when the flowers open.

HIBISCUS. The best-known member of this genus and a plant found throughout the tropics is Chinese hibiscus (*H. rosa-sinensis*). In warmer parts of this country the gaudy red, white, pink, or yellow flowers are visited not only by hummingbirds and orioles but occasionally by blue jays, painted buntings, cardinals, and house finches. More northern sections have a good substitute in shrub althea or rose of Sharon (*H. syriacus*). Also planted in southern yards, shrub althea comes into bloom in late summer and lures bumblebees, hummingbirds, and orioles with its large colorful blossoms. The white-lined sphinx, a hawk moth that flies by day, also visits the flowers.

HIGHBUSH CRANBERRY (see *Viburnum*)

HOLLY (see *Ilex*)

HOLLYHOCK (see *Alcea*)

HONEYSUCKLE (see *Lonicera*)

HOSTA, plantain lily. The plantain lilies, with their white, blue, or purple flowers in spikes and often variegated leaves, are a familiar part of our garden scene. The flowers are sometimes visited by hummingbirds.

HUMMINGBIRD'S TRUMPET (see *Zauschneria*)

HYDRANGEA. Most hydrangeas have little to offer wildlife. Many have flowers that are sterile, which rules out seeds or nectar. But the few that have useful flowers receive visits from flies, wasps, honeybees, and bumblebees.

HYPERICUM, St.-John's-wort. The bright yellow flowers of members of this group are followed by capsules filled with seeds. The seeds are taken by juncos and several other finches.

HYSSOP (see *Hyssopus*)

HYSSOPUS. As with other mints, hyssop (*H. officinalis*), with small blue flowers, is a rich source of nectar for bees and butterflies.

IBERIS, candytuft. Well suited for rock gardens, the candytufts belong to the mustard family and bear red, white, or purple flowers. Besides offering nectar to bees and butterflies, the plants produce seeds that attract seed-eating birds.

ILEX, holly. All hollies offer fruits that are acceptable to birds. Some, perhaps because they have astringent fruits, are not favored by birds, as a rule, until after winter sets in. American holly (*I. opaca*), English holly (*I. aquifolium*), possum haw (*I. decidua*), yaupon (*I. vomitoria*), and Chinese holly (*I. cornuta*)—all with red fruits—usually hold their crop well into winter. Winterberry (*I. verticillata*), with red fruits, may have its fruits taken by birds anywhere from mid-fall until late winter. Black-fruited hollies, like inkberry (*I. glabra*) and Japanese holly (*I. crenata*), hold their fruits well but ravenous flocks of robins may suddenly clean out the supply in January or February.

IMPATIENS, jewelweed, garden balsam. The best members of the genus in terms of wildlife usage are the jewelweeds, which grow in wet woodlands. The spotted orange flowers of *I. capensis* or the yellow flowers of *I. pallida* furnish some of the most likely feeding places for hummingbirds in late summer. The blossoms are also visited by honeybees and bumblebees. A number of birds scratch beneath the plants in winter to retrieve the seeds. The ever so common garden balsam (*I. balsamina*) is the garden counterpart of the wild plants. It, too, furnishes food for wildlife. Although visited by bees, hummingbirds, and butterflies, this plant is not nearly as bountiful as its wild cousins.

IPOMOEA, morning glory. Besides the common morning glory (*I. purpurea*), with its blue or white blossoms, there are a number of others with names like cypress vine, cardinal climber, and starglory. These have red blossoms and are popular with hummingbirds. Although all morning glories receive attention from hummingbirds, the flowers are not open long enough through the day for them to obtain adequate amounts of nectar.

IPOMOPSIS, standing cypress. Formerly belonging to *Gilia*, plants in this genus are so popular with hummingbirds that they deserve notice. Standing cypress (*I. rubra*), with its brilliant rose-scarlet tubular flowers, is a plant of the southern United States and Mexico. Skyrocket (*I. aggregata*) has equally brilliant scarlet flowers and is a plant of the Far West.

IRIS. Of all the many irises that grow in gardens or in the wild, only a few seem to attract nectar-feeders. Those that do are visited by humming-birds, hummingbird moths, and butterflies.

JAPANESE AUCUBA (see *Aucuba*)

JASMINE (see *Jasminum*)

JASMINUM. The jasmines are noted for fragrant blossoms that, for the most part, appear quite early. The earliest of all is winter jasmine (*J. nudi-florum*), whose blossoms are a lifesaver for hummingbirds attempting to spend the winter in the North. Common white jasmine (*J. offici-nale*) lends its fragrance to the warm night air of summer and, like most jasmines, is visited by sphinx or hawk moths.

JEWELWEED (see *Impatiens*)

JONQUIL (see *Narcissus*)

JOSEPH'S COAT (see *Amaranthus*)

JUNIPER (see *Juniperus*)

JUNIPERUS. With their stiff evergreen foliage, compact habit, and blue waxy fruits in winter, the junipers are widely used for foundation plantings. The ones most often seen are Chinese juniper (*J. chinensis*) and common juniper (*J. communis*) and their many horticultural varieties. Their popularity extends to birds. The junipers, which include low-growing evergreens as well as the red cedar (*J. virginiana*), which becomes a tree, provide nesting sites for birds and supply fruits that help see bluebirds, robins, cedar waxwings, and yellow-rumped warblers through the winter.

JUSTICIA (BELOPERONE). The shrimp plant (*J. brandegeana*) and chuparosa (*J. californica*) are now in this genus rather than *Beloperone*. Both plants, suited only for warmer sections, have tubular flowers that attract hummingbirds. Along the Texas coast, the shrimp plant offers one of the few flowers available for wintering hummingbirds. The chuparosa fulfills the same function in providing for hummingbirds in warmer parts of the Southwest. Moreover, the nectar-filled bases of the flower are snipped off and eaten by such birds as the mocking-bird, house finch, and white-crowned sparrow. Bees are attracted to the blossoms.

KNAPWEED (see *Centaurea*)

KNIPHOFIA, red-hot poker, torch-lily. For a truly exotic-looking plant, those living in more southern sections have the red-hot poker, or torch-lily (*K. uvaria*), to fall back on. Although from Africa, the pokerlike clusters of orange, red, or yellow flowers on long stalks seem made for our hummingbirds. Both hummingbirds and orioles readily come to the flowers for nectar.

KOLKWITZIA, beauty bush. A flowering shrub that reminds one of weigela, the beauty bush (*K. amabilis*) comes into bloom in late spring or early summer. The pink flowers are bell-shaped and have yellow throats. Immensely popular with bumblebees, the flowers also attract honeybees, butterflies, and hummingbirds.

LAGERSTROEMIA, crape myrtle. One of the most colorful flowering plants of mid to late summer, crape myrtle (*L. indica*) offers a riot of color with its white, pink, red, or purple blossoms. Moderately suitable as a hummingbird and butterfly plant, crape myrtle provides seeds later on that are taken by a number of seed-eating birds.

LAMIUM, dead nettle. A little too weedlike for most gardeners, the dead nettles are members of the mint family and have pink, purple, or lavender flowers. The name "mint" is enough to suggest that these plants are well patronized by bees and this is very true indeed.

LANTANA. One of those plants that some consider to be a weed and others a garden flower, lantana (*L. camara*) does well throughout warmer parts of the world. Even though each flower in the clusters that blanket these shrubs is tiny and holds minute amounts of nectar, hummingbirds, butterflies, and bees are not deterred from making visits. Lantana is the larval food plant of the lantana butterfly, a species imported by Hawaii to help control the spread of this plant.

LARKSPUR (see *Delphinium*)

LATHYRUS, pea. Most members of the pea family are adapted to pollination by honeybees. Sweet pea (*L. odoratus*), however, is an exception in that honeybees cannot ordinarily depress the keel which shields the entrance to the nectary. But bumblebees are sometimes successful and so is an occasional hummingbird. The sweet pea and other peas are larval food plants of the marine blue, a western butterfly, and several of its close relatives.

LAVANDULA. The ever popular lavender (*L. angustifolia*), with its aromatic foliage, is one of the best of the herb garden plants for bees and butterflies. The honey from lavender is of a superior grade with a slight tinge of the plant's fragrance.

LEMON BALM (see *Melissa*)

LEVISTICUM, lovage. Grown in the herb garden for its celery-flavored seeds, lovage (*L. officinale*) has small greenish-yellow flowers which are much visited by honeybees.

LIATRIS, blazing star. The purple, blue, or white flowers of plants in this genus are borne in tall terminal spikes and are rich in nectar and pollen. The flowers attract butterflies, including the tiger swallowtail, and hummingbirds. Later on finches visit the plants to gather seeds.

LIGUSTRUM, privet. If privet bushes are not too severely clipped, they produce flowers in midsummer that entice bees and butterflies. The honey from privet, however, tastes so disagreeable that it is fit only for the bees themselves. Among butterfly visitors are the painted lady, American painted lady, red admiral, and monarch. Birds are slow to take the small black fruits that hang in clusters on the bushes in fall and winter. But as winter sets in, this gradually changes and the privet fruits become an important source of food for many birds until well into spring. California privet (*L. ovalifolium*) is a good hedge plant and, along with border privet (*L. obtusifolium*), common privet (*L. vulgare*), and ibota privet (*L. ibota*), is much planted in the North. All four are good providers of winter bird food. In warmer sections two evergreen privets with glossy leaves—Japanese privet (*L. japonicum*) and glossy privet (*L. lucidum*)—are commonly grown as ornamentals or hedge plants. In addition, Chinese privet (*L. sinense*), a deciduous species, is highly popular. Although all privets have wild-life value, it must be remembered that this usefulness ends if flower buds are lost through clipping.

LILAC (see *Syringa*)

LILIUM. Thanks to generous offerings of nectar, the flowers of lilies are freely visited by all the expected forms of wildlife. Among the bird visitors are hummingbirds and orioles. Overly eager to reach the nectar, orchard orioles sometimes attack the buds and blossoms and tear them to pieces. Hooded orioles in the West obtain nectar by piercing the base of the corolla. The more mannerly hummingbirds hover before the blossoms and even disappear inside when obtaining nectar. Both the tiger lily (*L. tigrinum*) and the Turk's-cap lily (*L. superbum*) are especially favored by hummingbirds. Day- and night-flying sphinx moths are frequent visitors to lilies with white blossoms. Those of the Madonna lily (*L. candidum*) are favored after darkness sets in.

LILY (see *Lilium*)

LIMNANTHES, meadow-foam. Not a well-known flower, meadow-foam (*L. douglasii*) deserves mention only because it has been extolled by bee-keepers.

LINDERA, spicebush. For those wishing to make more use of native plants, spicebush (*L. benzoin*) is a good choice. Found in moist woods from Maine and Michigan to Florida and Texas, spicebush has small yellow flowers in early spring and bright red fruits in the fall. The plants are best known for their aromatic twigs and leaves. If anything, birds strip the plants of their fruit all too quickly. Another wildlife use of spicebush is that of insects laying their eggs on the foliage. Spicebush is a larval food plant of the spicebush swallowtail and promethea moth.

LOBELIA, cardinal flower. A wildflower of moist, shady habitats, the cardinal flower (*L. cardinalis*) nevertheless can be grown successfully in the garden. The tubular red flowers seem made for hummingbirds. Other visitors include bumblebees and sphinx moths.

LOBULARIA, sweet alyssum. Carpeting flower beds with mounds of fragrant white, pink, or violet flowers, sweet alyssum (*L. maritima*) has a long flowering season and is of some value to nectar-feeders. But the tiny flowers do not offer enough substance to detain visitors for very long.

LONICERA, honeysuckle. Well represented in the garden by shrubs and twining vines, the honeysuckles rate highly as suppliers of wildlife food. If it were not for its invasive tactics, Japanese honeysuckle (*L. japonica*) would be an ideal choice. But our native trumpet honeysuckle (*L. sempervirens*) is a good substitute. It has good ornamental value, and the orange or scarlet blossoms continue to appear from late spring until almost the end of summer. Hummingbirds are the most frequent visitors to the blossoms, whereas orioles sometimes tear them apart to get at the nectar. Woodbine (*L. periclymenum*) is a somewhat similar vine introduced from Europe. Its flowers are often visited by night-flying sphinx moths. The bush honeysuckles have as much, if not more, to offer wildlife as the vines. Tatarian (*L. tatarica*) and Morrow (*L. morrowii*) bush honeysuckle furnish robins and other birds with large crops of red fruit during the summer. The tart red fruit of Amur bush honeysuckle (*L. maackii*) is ordinarily not taken by birds until late fall or winter. Winter bush honeysuckle (*L. fragrantissima*) surprises us by suddenly showing blossoms on warm days in winter. Blossoming continues throughout the spring. The highly fragrant white blossoms serve as a kind of salad for cardinals, house finches, and other birds. They eat the blossoms greedily but usually enough are left to supply us with a share of their beauty. American fly honeysuckle (*L. canadensis*) is occasionally a larval food plant of the rare Baltimore, a butterfly belonging to the checkerspots.

LOVAGE (see *Levisticum*)

LOVE-LIES-BLEEDING (see *Amaranthus*)

LUPINE (see *Lupinus*)

LUPINUS. Popular with many western hummingbirds, the lupines come into bloom in early summer and may cover whole fields as well as sections of the garden. The native Texas bluebonnet (*L. subcarnosus*) is visited freely in early spring by bees that come for the pollen. The lupines are important as larval food plants of a number of butterflies, including the eastern tailed blue.

LYTHRUM, purple loosestrife. Taking hold in thousands of acres of bogland and freshwater marshes, purple loosestrife (*L. salicaria*) is in disrepute because of its invasive tactics. Better behaved in the garden, its panicles of red-purple flowers attract hummingbirds, bees, butterflies, and hummingbird moths in late summer. The flowers are a particularly good source of honey.

MAHONIA, Oregon grape. A close relative of the barberries, Oregon grape (*M. aquifolium*) is a semi-evergreen with purple-black fruits that ripen in early summer. The fruit is mildly popular with the mockingbird, cardinal, and several others. The very early yellow blossoms are sometimes killed by frost. If they survive, they provide some of the first nectar available to bees in spring.

MALUS, crab apple, apple. A member of the same genus as the crab apples, the common apple tree offers a long list of advantages to wildlife. Not far behind are the crab apples or flowering crabs. Much tidier in appearance and with striking floral displays in late spring, the crab apples possess most of the wildlife advantages of the apple and their smaller fruits are far easier for birds, such as waxwings, robins, and evening grosbeaks, to handle. Bees and hummingbirds visit the blossoms. Sargent crab apple (*M. sargentii*) and Japanese flowering crab apple (*M. floribunda*) offer beautiful floral displays in spring and colorful red fruit in fall that is well liked by birds. If we are looking for crab apples that hold their fruit well into winter, two of the best are Zumi crab apple (*M. zumi calocarpa*) and Siberian crab apple (*M. baccata* var. 'Bob White').

MARIGOLD (see *Tagetes*)

MARJORAM (see *Origanum*)

MATTHIOLA, evening stock. It is almost safe to say that plants with very fragrant flowers opening only at night are meant to be pollinated by sphinx moths. This is true of evening stock (*M. bicornis*), a member of the mustard family with fragrant purple blossoms.

MEADOW-FOAM (see *Limnanthes*)

MELILOTUS, sweet clover. Although not sufficiently ornamental to be admitted to the garden, the sweet clovers rate highly as bee plants and soil builders and are one of the best honey plants in this country. White sweet clover (*M. alba*) has a number of butterfly visitors, including the eastern tailed blue.

MELISSA, lemon balm. Of the many plants in the herb garden that bees visit for nectar, this is one of the best. Lemon balm (*M. officinalis*) has lemon-scented foliage and small white flowers.

MENTHA, mint. Useful additions to the herb garden, the mints have small purplish, lilac, or white flowers that are much visited by bees and also by wasps, small flies, and some of the smaller butterflies. Spearmint (*M. spicata*) and peppermint (*M. piperita*) are well regarded by beekeepers.

MERTENSIA, Virginia bluebells. The spring and early summer flowers of Virginia blues (*M. virginica*) are pink when they first open and later become lavender or blue. Primarily bee plants, the flowers also sometimes attract hummingbirds.

MIGNONETTE (see *Reseda*)

MILKWEED (see *Asclepias*)

MIMULUS, monkey flower. Found chiefly in the West, the monkey flowers have blossoms that resemble those of the snapdragon. Bees are the main pollinators, while red-flowered species, like *M. cardinalis*, are well patronized by hummingbirds.

MINT (see *Mentha*)

MIRABILIS, four-o'clock. Also known as marvel-of-Peru, four-o'clock (*M. jalapa*) invites pollinators after about 4 p.m., when the flowers open, and from then until about 9 a.m. This timing permits visits by day- and night-flying sphinx moths and hummingbirds. The flowers' rich fragrance toward nightfall serves to lure the moths. Flowers are red, yellow, or white, with often a single plant bearing all three colors. The seeds are taken by several birds, including the cardinal.

MOCK ORANGE (see *Philadelphus*)

MONARDA, bee balm, bergamot. True to its name, bee balm (*M. didyma*) is one of the best of the bee plants. Hidden in pink, red, or scarlet flowers, the rich nectar supplies also entice hummingbirds, hummingbird moths, and butterflies. Wild bergamot (*M. fistulosa*) has lavender blossoms and receives much the same patronage. Among the butterfly visitors to the monardas are the great spangled fritillary, black swallowtail, and monarch. Where several monardas are present, hummingbirds tend to visit those with red blossoms and bees those with lavender ones. From late June until early August, there is scarcely a dull moment in flower beds where monardas are grown.

MONKEY FLOWER (see *Mimulus*)

MONKSHOOD (see *Aconitum*)

MORNING GLORY (see *Ipomoea*)

MORUS, mulberry. The popularity of mulberries as a source of food for birds in summer is well known. But the enthusiasm of gardeners for these small trees can be dampened because of the litter that falls during the fruiting season as well as that left behind by birds that have been feasting. Red mulberry (*M. rubra*), with fruit that ripens in midsummer, has a long fruiting season. White mulberry (*M. alba*) is early-ripening and furnishes food for only a week or two. Russian mulberry (*M. alba tatarica*) is a good compromise if one is looking for a small mulberry that won't leave as much mess and yet is highly popular with birds for a short period in early summer.

MOUNTAIN ASH (see *Sorbus*)

MULBERRY (see *Morus*)

MUSA, banana. A plant of the tropics, the common banana (*M. paradisiaca*) does quite well in southern Florida and southern California. Hummingbirds visit the blossoms.

MUSCARI, grape hyacinth. A bulb plant whose small bell-shaped blue flowers give bees a boost in early spring when they urgently need nectar.

MYOSOTIS, forget-me-not. Of minor value to bees and butterflies, the forget-me-nots do make a small contribution. Their seeds are sometimes taken by birds.

MYRICA, bayberry. Plants belonging to this genus are sometimes called bayberries and sometimes wax myrtles. All are evergreen or semi-evergreen, have aromatic foliage, and bear waxy gray fruits that cling to the branches all winter. The fruits are a mainstay in the diets of many wintering birds, including the tree swallow, catbird, bluebird, and yellow-rumped warbler. The plants are confined chiefly to coastal areas but are being widely used elsewhere as ornamental shrubs.

NANDINA. Colorful autumn foliage and clusters of bright red fruit make nandina (*N. domestica*) almost as popular as pyracantha in the warmer sections where it is grown. Since birds are often slow to take the fruit, the plants are likely to remain decked with color through the winter.

NARCISSUS, jonquil, daffodil. A joyful sight in early spring, the opening of the blossoms of the jonquil on one of the first warm days also sees bees streaming from their hives. Jonquils are one of the first flowers they go to. However, they usually have to rely upon bumblebees to first bite through at the base of the blossoms. These punctures allow honeybees to gain a share of the nectar for themselves.

NASTURTIUM (see *Tropaeolum*)

NEPETA, catnip, catmint. A plant that sends cats into a frenzy of pleasure, catnip (*N. cataria*) is also a good bee plant and goldfinches eat the seeds.

NICOTIANA, flowering tobacco. Garden plants, as well as the tobacco of commerce, belong to the genus *Nicotiana*. The garden plants can be divided into those with fragrant blossoms (usually white) that open only at night, and colorful day-blooming plants that are lacking in fragrance. Flowering tobacco (*N. alata*) is a night-flowering species whose fragrant white flowers lure sphinx moths. Colorful day-flowering varieties of this plant have been developed by nurserymen. Sander tobacco (*N. sanderae*) is a hybrid that opens during the day and bears crimson or rose-colored flowers. The day-flowering species are excellent hummingbird plants. Tree tobacco (*N. glauca*), an introduced plant from South America, is one of the flowering shrubs most sought after by hummingbirds in southern Texas and California. With yellow or greenish-yellow flowers about one and one-half inches long, tubular, rich in nectar, and present on plants almost the year round, it is no wonder that tree tobacco rates highly as a hummingbird plant. Orioles also visit the flowers for nectar and the seeds are eaten by golden-crowned sparrows and lesser goldfinches.

NIGHT-FLOWERING CATCHFLY (see *Silene*)

OENOTHERA, evening primrose. Like the flowering tobaccos, the evening primroses have both day- and night-flowering representatives. The common evening primrose (*O. biennis*), whose yellow blossoms open late in the day, is night-flowering and pollinated by sphinx moths. The showy evening primrose (*O. speciosa*), with pink or white flowers, stays open all day. The flowers are well patronized by bees, hummingbirds, and hummingbird moths. Seeds of many of the evening primroses remain in pods through the winter and provide food for goldfinches.

ORANGE (see *Citrus*)

OREGON GRAPE (see *Mahonia*)

ORIGANUM, marjoram. Occupying an important place in the herb garden, the marjorams are used for seasoning and medicinal purposes. The pink, purplish, or white flowers are so attractive to honeybees and bumblebees that they will often desert other nearby flowers to feed exclusively at those of the marjorams. Three species in a herb garden, including sweet marjoram (*O. marjorana*), wild marjoram (*O. vulgare*), and Cretan dittany (*O. dictamnus*), were receiving equal attention from bees and diverting them from the many other honey plants also growing there. Honey obtained from marjorams is said to be as tasty as that from clover. Butterflies also visit the blossoms.

OXEYE DAISY (see *Chrysanthemum*)

PAEONIA, peony. It is no wonder that peonies are popular. Even when neglected they produce beautiful rose, red, or white blossoms year after year. Bees not only come to the flowers for pollen but sample a nectar-like substance that oozes from newly opening buds. Ants are also very fond of this substance. Single flowers offer much more pollen than double ones and therefore are much more attractive to bees.

PAPAVER, poppy. The Oriental poppy (*P. orientale*) is the common species seen in gardens. The flowers offer little if any nectar but are eagerly visited by bees for pollen. Plants with red flowers sometimes receive attention from hummingbirds. Whether the birds are deceived by the color or are looking for insects is not known. This poppy displays other colors besides red.

PARTHENOCISSUS, Virginia creeper, Boston ivy. If only for their brilliant fall foliage, the two vines in question would be used to cover walls and sides of buildings. When the leaves turn scarlet in early fall, the fruits of the two vines turn blue. The fruit of Boston ivy (*P. tricuspidata*) is, as a rule, consumed more quickly by birds than that of Virginia creeper (*P. quinquefolia*). Fruits of the latter are sometimes still clinging to the vine as late as March.

PASSIFLORA. Vines that grow only in warmer sections, the passionflowers have one special wildlife use: furnishing food for the larvae and adults of several butterflies. During the larval stage, the Gulf fritillary, variegated fritillary, and close relatives feed upon one or more species of passionflower. The adults may remain to sip nectar from the flowers.

PASSIONFLOWER (see *Passiflora*)

PEA (see *Lathyrus*)

PEAR (see *Pyrus*)

PELARGONIUM, geranium. The garden geranium (*P. hortorum*), seen so often in flower beds, in window boxes, and as house plants, is subject to occasional visits by hummingbirds when in the open. Red-flowered plants are more likely to receive attention than those of other colors.

PENSTEMON. A large genus of western flowers, with some adapted to pollination by bees and others by hummingbirds. Penstemons are larval food plants of several small western butterflies known as checkerspots. The seeds of penstemons are eaten freely by finches.

PENTAS. The pentas are small flowering shrubs from tropical Africa that closely resemble the bouvardias (which see). Like the latter, they are good hummingbird plants and can be grown only in the warmest sections of the country. *P. lanceolata* has tubular star-shaped flowers that come in a wide range of colors. Best known as a butterfly plant, this pentas is regarded as second only to lantana, among tropical plants, in the ability to lure butterflies. The giant swallowtail is one of the butterfly visitors in southern Florida.

PEONY (see *Paeonia*)

PEPPER VINE (see *Ampelopsis*)

PETUNIA. Overwhelming abundance and a long blooming season conspire to make the petunia (*P. hybrida*) one of the most visited nectar plants in our yard. The colorful, funnel-shaped flowers offer opportunities, but limited ones, for hummingbirds, hummingbird moths, night-flying sphinx moths, bees, and butterflies. The flowers scarcely contain enough nectar to make visits by nectar-feeders profitable. The seeds of petunias are taken by juncos, fox sparrows, and several of the small finches.

PHASEOLUS, scarlet runner bean. A climber with brilliant red flowers and long pods, scarlet runner bean (*P. coccineus*) is grown as much for ornament as for food. The flowers are well patronized by hummingbirds. Bumblebees successfully obtain nectar from the pealike flowers but the feat is usually too difficult for honeybees.

PHILADELPHUS, mock orange. Of the many mock oranges planted for ornament, sweet mock orange (*P. coronarius*) is perhaps the best one for wildlife. When the bushes come into bloom in May, their sweet-scented flowers attract bumblebees, honeybees, wasps, flies, hummingbird moths, and butterflies. Mock orange species lacking in fragrance are far less attractive to insects and do not bring these many visitors.

PHLOX. Garden phlox (*P. paniculata*), sweet william phlox (*P. divaricata*), and annual phlox (*P. drummondii*) are among the species that seem to receive the most attention from wildlife. Their long flowering periods and wide range of colors attract hummingbirds, hummingbird moths, night-flying sphinx moths, bees, and butterflies. A number of birds take the seeds.

PHOTINIA. Shrubs or small trees with red fruits that persist well into winter, the photinias would seem to be ideal suppliers of winter bird food. However, with the exception of cedar waxwings, birds seem little attracted to the fruits. Chinese photinia (*P. serrulata*) is much planted in more southern sections.

PHYTOLACCA, pokeweed. Almost handsome enough, with its red stalks and black juicy fruits, to be considered a garden plant, pokeweed (*P. americana*) finds its way into the yard anyway. Birds devour the fruits and leave the seeds behind in their droppings. If allowed to grow, seedlings turn into robust plants that by autumn support heavy crops of fruit. As long as the supply lasts, birds come in almost a steady stream to get their share of the harvest.

PONCIRUS, hardy orange. A shrub belonging to the citrus family (Rutaceae), hardy orange (*P. trifoliata*) has long, sharp thorns, citruslike flowers, and small, extremely bitter, orangelike fruit. The plants provide impenetrable nesting cover for birds and are used as larval food plants by the giant swallowtail. This thorny shrub can safely be grown as far north as Maryland and in protected sites all the way to New England.

POPPY (see *Papaver*)

PORTULACA. The common portulaca (*P. grandiflora*) is a low, sprawling herbaceous plant with bright-colored flowers and fleshy leaves and stems. The flowers have such an appeal for bees that they are sometimes seen reveling among the stamens before flying off with their burdens of nectar and pollen.

POWDER PUFF (see *Calliandra*)

PRIMROSE (see *Primula*)

PRIMULA. The early spring flowers of the primroses are visited by night-flying sphinx moths, bees, and butterflies. In Europe, house sparrows and other birds are in the habit of tearing apart buds and flowers with the likely intent of procuring nectar. Yellow flowers are particularly susceptible to damage of this kind.

PRIVET (see *Ligustrum*)

PRUNELLA, self-heal. It is surprising how many butterflies find the purple flowers of self-heal (*P. vulgaris*), a lowly weedlike plant of lawns and flower beds belonging to the mint family. The writer has a list of twenty-one butterfly species coming to the flowers.

PRUNUS, cherry. Not only the cherries but cherry laurel, plum, peach, flowering almond, and apricot belong to this genus that is so important to us from an economic standpoint. During the spring the blossoms of most species are busily visited by bees. Petals of the same blossoms are sometimes eaten by cedar waxwings, and still other bird visitors, the orioles, may come for nectar. When the fruit ripens in summer, birds are again back in the trees. Robins are the most likely visitors to cherry laurel (*P. laurocerasus*), an evergreen often used as a hedge plant in the South. Of the flowering cherries, two are well suited to supplying birds with fruits in summer: Higan cherry (*P. subhirtella*), which has small black cherries that ripen in early summer, and Nanking cherry (*P. tomentosa*), which has pea-sized red fruits that may ripen as early as late May.

PURPLE LOOSESTRIFE (see *Lythrum*)

PUSSY WILLOW (see *Salix*)

PYRACANTHA. Few flowering shrubs offer more beauty in winter than the fire thorns or pyracanthas with their large clusters of red or orange fruits. Birds, for reasons that are hard to decipher, are tempted by the fruits of some bushes and not those of others. One of the best plants in the group for birds is scarlet fire thorn (*P. coccinea* 'Lalandei'). It is also one of the hardiest. The flowers of the pyracanthas are much visited by bees.

PYRUS, pear. The common pear tree of commerce has been superseded in the garden and along streets by the Callery pear (*P. calleryana*). With good ornamental properties and fruit only half an inch in length, this tree is quite different from the pear trees (*P. communis*) we are all familiar with. Although the small fruits are of no use to us, they are taken in the fall by blue jays, mockingbirds, and others.

QUEEN ANNE'S LACE (see *Daucus*)

QUINCE (see *Chaenomeles*)

REDBUD (see *Cercis*)

RED-HOT POKER (see *Kniphofia*)

Reseda, mignonette. Grown primarily for the fragrance of its flowers, mignonette (*R. Odorata*) has long interested beekeepers because of large honey yields in some instances.

Rhamnus, buckthorn. Shrubs or small trees, the buckthorns have a long fruiting season, beginning in July and sometimes lasting until late fall. Flowers and green, red, and black (fully ripe) fruits can often be seen on the same plant. Birds generally wait until the fruit turns black. Alder buckthorn (*R. frangula*) is one of the best from the standpoint of ornament and birds. Used widely for landscaping, this buckthorn has a columnar form which goes well with modern architecture. Coffeeberry (*R. californica*) is a native species in the Far West with much the same uses as alder buckthorn. Common buckthorn (*R. cathartica*) is not as ornamental as the other two species and has escaped into the wild in the Northeast. Its fruits, however, are much used by birds. The flowers of the buckthorns are well visited by bees, with coffeeberry being noted for the good honey bees make from its blossoms.

Rhododendron. Distinguished from the azaleas on the basis of their flowers having ten or more stamens to only five in azaleas, the rhododendrons have about the same wildlife value. The flowers are visited by bees and hummingbirds. However, the larger rhododendrons, like tree rhododendron (*R. arboreum*), take up so much room in the yard and offer so little to wildlife that the gardener might think in terms of removing these oversized plants and replacing them with more useful species. The azaleas, the other large group belonging to this genus, are consistently small plants suitable for nearly every garden but rarely hardy enough for northern winters. But sweet azalea (*R. arborescens*) can be grown quite far north and has fragrant early summer flowers that are much patronized by hummingbirds. Pinxter flower (*R. periclymenoides*) has the same qualities except that its blossoms appear somewhat earlier. Butterflies are attracted to the early blossoms of azaleas, particularly to those of wild plants. Among the visitors to a wild azalea in swampland were tiger swallowtails, pipevine swallowtails, pearl crescents, silver-spotted skippers, and hummingbird moths.

Rhus, sumac. Regarded with some suspicion because of such toxic members of the genus as poison ivy and poison sumac, the sumacs have been slow to gain popularity as garden plants. Yet the non-poisonous sumacs, such as fragrant sumac (*R. aromatica*), shining sumac (*R.*

*copallina*), and staghorn sumac (*R. typhina*), are highly ornamental with their fall color and good suppliers of winter bird food. Although birds are sometimes slow to take the fuzzy, hard, reddish fruits, by early winter they begin turning more and more to the sumacs. Along with poison ivy (*R. radicans*), the sumacs become a mainstay of wintering birds, including many game birds. The cottontail may harm plants by gnawing the bark.

RIBES, currant. Alternate hosts to the white pine blister rust, currants shouldn't be grown in areas where this pine is present. It is unfortunate that the currants have this drawback and also that some species are susceptible to black stem wheat rust. However, under some conditions the currants can be welcomed to the garden for their ornamental value and usefulness to wildlife. The early spring flowers attract both bees and hummingbirds. Two of the best currants for early use by hummingbirds are winter currant (*R. sanguineum*) with red blossoms and clove currant (*R. odoratum*) with yellow blossoms. Golden currant (*R. aureum*) with yellow blossoms is one of the best for bees and honey production. The currants provide another benefit to wildlife by yielding crops of red, black, or blue-black fruit in the fall that is eagerly taken by birds.

RICINUS, castor bean. Often grown as an ornamental in warmer sections, the castor bean (*R. communis*) should be regarded with suspicion because of its highly poisonous seeds. But the flowers are much visited by bees and offer a honey that is as safe for us as it is for the bees.

ROCK CRESS (see *Arabis*)

ROSA. As a group the roses offer comparatively little to wildlife. However, some species make up for the poor performance of others by offering hips that are consumed by birds and flowers that are visited by bees. Japanese or multiflora rose (*R. multiflora*) is by far the best from the standpoint of supplying bird food. Abundant crops of small red hips in the fall remain on the bushes and keep catbirds, mockingbirds, robins, and many other birds supplied with food. This rose also provides excellent nesting cover for birds. Unfortunately, Japanese rose is too invasive to be planted almost anywhere. A better garden plant, rugosa rose (*R. rugosa*) has large red hips that are within the capacity of cardinals and other strong-billed birds. Although most roses offer little if any nectar, honeybees and bumblebees frequently visit the flowers for pollen. If hummingbirds visit roses, as they sometimes do, chances are that they are looking for insects. Intensively cultivated garden varieties of roses have far less to offer wildlife than plants closer to the wild stock.

ROSE (see *Rosa*)

ROSE OF SHARON (see *Hibiscus*)

ROSEMARY (see *Rosmarinus*)

ROSMARINUS, rosemary. Thanks to aromatic foliage and culinary uses, rosemary (*R. officinalis*) occupies an important place in the herb garden. Excellent honey from the violet-blue blossoms is another reason for growing rosemary. Hummingbirds, as well as bees, visit the flowers and the seeds are taken by goldfinches.

RUDBECKIA, coneflower. The coneflowers are daisylike members of the composite family and are known chiefly as wildflowers. But several, including the black-eyed Susan (*R. hirta*) and golden glow (*R. laciniata* var. 'Hortensia'), are used in the garden. The flowers of coneflowers attract a wide variety of butterflies. The plants provide larval food for the silvery crescentspot butterfly.

RUSSELIA, firecracker plant. The tubular red flowers of the firecracker plant (*R. equisetiformis*) look like small firecrackers and adorn the small tropical shrubs on which they grow. A popular ornamental in southern Florida, the firecracker plant is well utilized by hummingbirds. The flowers are present the year round.

SAGE (see *Salvia*)

ST.-JOHN'S-WORT (see *Hypericum*)

SALIX, pussy willow. Offering almost the first flowers of spring, pussy willow (*Salix* spp.) not only gladdens our hearts with their fuzzy gray blossoms but helps restore the depleted larders of honeybees.

SALVIA, sage. The sages, with their aromatic leaves and attractive typically mint flowers, are suitable for both the herb garden and the flower border. The much-planted scarlet sage (*S. splendens*) adds its bright scarlet hue to the garden and provides an ideal drinking fountain for hummingbirds. The seeds are eaten by goldfinches and house finches. Although other sages are visited by hummingbirds, the plants are chiefly known for the eager way they are patronized by bees and the good honey that is the end product. One of the best sages for honey production is garden sage (*S. officinalis*), grown primarily in eastern gardens. Autumn sage (*S. greggii*) is a good bee plant in the Southwest, and in the West bees can choose between black sage (*S. mellifera*) and purple sage (*S. leucophylla*). Pineapple sage (*S. elegans*), with scarlet flowers in the fall, is a good bee plant for warmer sections.

SAMBUCUS, elderberry. Weedlike shrubs, almost handsome enough for the garden, the elderberries produce heavy crops of fruit that are in demand in late summer for jelly and wine-making. Birds find the fruit before we do and seriously compete with us for the harvest. Scarlet elder (*S. pubens*), with bright red fruit in midsummer, deserves a place in the garden. The more sober black fruits of American elder (*S. canadensis*) adorn the bushes in late summer and early fall. Bees are early-season patrons of elderberries and freely visit the flowers for nectar.

SAPONARIA, bouncing bet, soapwort. The pale pink flowers of bouncing bet (*S. officinalis*) increase in fragrance toward dusk, a clear invitation to night-flying sphinx moths.

SASSAFRAS. A good bird food plant, sassafras (*S. albidum*) has mitten-shaped leaves and an aromatic odor when leaves or twigs are crushed. Birds are attracted to the blue fruits in the fall. As many as forty species were recorded eating fruit one autumn at a tree in Kentucky. Sassafras is a larval food plant of the spicebush swallowtail and promethea moth.

SATUREJA, winter savory. A member of the mint family, winter savory (*S. montana*) is one of the many herb garden plants that are well patronized by bees.

SCABIOSA. The several garden flowers in this genus are visited to some extent by bees and butterflies, and the seeds are sometimes taken by birds.

SCARLET BUSH (see *Hamelia*)

SCARLET RUNNER BEAN (see *Phaseolus*)

SCHINUS, pepper tree. Two small evergreen trees belonging to this genus are well known as ornamentals in Florida and California. Unfortunately, Florida's Brazil pepper tree (*S. terebinthifolius*) has far more bad qualities than good. It has become a weed tree, spreading far and wide over southern Florida. Moreover, birds not infrequently become intoxicated after eating the small red fruits. Cedar waxwings and robins are the main victims and fall prey to cats or collide with moving vehicles when partially paralyzed after eating the fruit. The California pepper tree (*S. molle*) seems to be safely patronized by birds. The red fruits are taken in fall and winter. The trees are highly ornamental with their gnarled trunks and lacy, pendant foliage.

SEDUM. The sedums are larval food plants of the buckeye and variegated fritillary butterflies. Showy sedum (*S. spectabile*) is a good bee plant.

SELF-HEAL (see *Prunella*)

SERVICEBERRY or SHADBUSH (see *Amelanchier*)

SHRIMP PLANT (see *Justicia*)

SHRUB ALTHEA (see *Hibiscus*)

SIBERIAN PEA TREE (see *Caragana*)

SILENE, night-flowering catchfly. Although regarded as a weed, night-flowering catchfly (*S. noctiflora*) has some ornamental value, and the pink or white flowers attract night-flying sphinx moths.

SILK TREE (see *Albizia*)

SKIMMIA. With bright red berries that persist well into winter and ever-green foliage, Japanese skimmia (*S. japonica*) qualifies as a good ornamental. Not enough is known about the plant to say whether the fruits are taken to any extent by birds. Most evidence suggests that they are not.

SNAPDRAGON (see *Antirrhinum*)

SNOWBERRY (see *Symphoricarpos*)

SNOW-ON-THE-MOUNTAIN (see *Euphorbia*)

SOLIDAGO, goldenrod. When the golden, sometimes white, blossoms of the goldenrods appear in late summer and fall, they quickly lure honey-bees, bumblebees, butterflies, wasps, flies, and other nectar-feeding insects. Two of the best species for honey production are lance-leaved goldenrod (*S. graminifolia*) and rough-stemmed goldenrod (*S. rugosa*). Among the many butterfly visitors, the regal fritillary, monarch, red admiral, American painted lady, and buckeye are apt to be particularly conspicuous. Goldenrods become useful to birds when the seeds ripen. Goldfinches and redpolls sometimes swarm over the flower heads of plants that have gone to seed. In this country the goldenrods are not often tolerated in the garden. But in Britain, where the plants have been introduced from America, they are popular garden flowers.

SORBUS, mountain ash. Small trees with colorful clusters of red, orange, pink, or white fruits, the mountain ashes combine beauty with good bird-attracting properties. The only complaint is that birds devour the fruit so quickly and thoroughly in the fall that seldom is any left for decoration. Our most commonly planted species is European mountain ash (*S. aucuparia*), one of the best for birds and also very decorative.

SPEEDWELL (see *Veronica*)

SPICEBUSH (see *Lindera*)

SPIDERFLOWER (see *Cleome*)

SUMAC (see *Rhus*)

SUNFLOWER (see *Helianthus*)

SWEET ALYSSUM (see *Lobularia*)

SWEET CLOVER (see *Melilotus*)

SWEET PEA (see *Lathyrus*)

SWEET WILLIAM (see *Dianthus*)

SYMPHORICARPOS, coralberry and snowberry. Two of a kind, these small shrubs are useful for covering slopes and providing shelter for wildlife. The small flowers are a valuable source of nectar and they are much visited by bees and occasionally by hummingbirds. It is mainly in the fruit that the two plants show their differences. Coralberry (*S. orbiculatus*), which does not blossom until late summer, has coral-red fruit that clings to the bushes through early winter. Snowberry (*S. albus*), on the other hand, blossoms much earlier and by midsummer the snow-white fruits, about the size of marbles, are in evidence. Birds are not overly fond of the fruits of either plant. But as emergency food for birds in winter—especially pheasants and other upland game birds—both snowberry and coralberry supply an important need. Both are used as larval food plants by hummingbird moths.

SYRINGA, lilac. Lilacs come into bloom at a time when good sources of nectar are badly needed. This is why the spring blossoms are often alive with bees, butterflies, and sometimes hummingbirds. Among the butterflies seen at lilacs are the American painted lady, red admiral, and various of the swallowtails. Evening grosbeaks occasionally come to lilac bushes in winter to harvest the seeds. The Japanese tree lilac (*S. reticulata*), in bloom in late June and July, successfully competes with privets for patronage by bees.

TAGETES, marigold. Besides being one of the annuals most commonly planted for ornament, marigolds have a wide range of other uses. They are good bee and butterfly plants and are occasionally visited by hummingbirds. Clive Farrell, writing of England, calls the French marigold (*T. patula*) and the African marigold (*T. erecta*) among the best of the daisy family for butterflies. Both butterflies and bees seem to visit marigolds more in late summer—a period of the year when nectar-rich flowers are likely to be in short supply. Marigolds are a larval food plant of the dwarf yellow butterfly, a species found in the West and Midwest. In contrast to uses of this kind is the marigold's ability to repel certain pests of other garden plants. The leaves have oil glands which give off a scent that drives away some insects. The scent is said to be effective in warding off flies, aphids, and cucumber beetles. Apparently even rabbits are offended by the scent and stay away from beds in which marigolds are grown. The Mexican marigold (*T. minuta*) has the strongest scent and is the species to grow where good repellency is needed. Even the root systems of marigolds come to our aid by giving off a sulphur-containing substance that is effective in discouraging nematodes. Microscopic, threadlike worms, nematodes suck plant juices and cause serious damage to plants of many kinds. The two best marigolds to use in controlling root nematodes are the same two recommended by Farrell as good butterfly plants—the French and African marigolds. Both are widely grown in gardens and have yellow or orange blossoms. It may be added that the nematocidal effects of marigold roots are paralleled to some extent by asparagus roots, which also give off toxic juices that kill nematodes.

TARAXACUM, dandelion. Whether gardeners like this lowly plant or not, the dandelion (*T. officinale*) takes hold anyway. Its virtues might as well be appreciated. The yellow flowers do offer a bit of color and bees have no prejudices about coming to them for nectar and pollen. When the fuzzy, winged seeds appear on flower heads, flocks of finches often descend to the lawn to reap a small harvest.

TAXUS, yew. With their evergreen foliage and bright red fruits the yews have a great deal to offer in the way of ornament and food and shelter for wildlife. The two yews commonly planted for ornament are English yew (*T. baccata*) and Japanese yew (*T. cuspidata*). The latter is more hardy and therefore suitable for more northern sections. A fleshy, cuplike cover that surrounds part of the seed is the fare that brings cardinals, blue jays, robins, and other birds to yew bushes during the fall.

TECOMARIA, Cape honeysuckle. A vine or shrub, depending upon how it is used, Cape honeysuckle (*T. capensis*) replaces trumpet creeper as *the* plant for hummingbirds in warmer parts of Florida and the Southwest. The flowers are tubular and a brilliant orange-red.

THOROUGHWORT (see *Eupatorium*)

THUJA, arborvitae. Handsome evergreens that serve the same landscaping needs as the yews, the arborvitaes are reasonably good wildlife plants. They provide cover and their seeds in fall and early winter are taken by birds. American arborvitae (*T. occidentalis*) is the one grown in the North; Oriental arborvitae (*T. orientalis*) is suitable for milder sections, including the Deep South.

THYME (see *Thymus*)

THYMUS. Used in the herb garden and rock garden and as ground cover, the thymes are notably good honey plants.

TORCH-LILY (see *Kniphofia*)

TREE TOBACCO (see *Nicotiana*)

TRIFOLIUM, clover. The clovers are generally regarded as good lawn plants. If the lawn, or a portion of it, is not kept too closely clipped, clover will have a chance to flower. The blossoms are so highly favored by bees and butterflies that nearby garden flowers are often deserted. Red clover (*T. pratense*) is primarily a bumblebee flower and is also visited by large showy butterflies as well as small ones. White clover (*T. repens*) primarily attracts honeybees; also small butterflies, such as the eastern tailed blue, spring azure, and pearl crescent.

TROPAEOLUM, nasturtium. The common nasturtium (*T. majus*), with its yellow, orange, or red flowers, is a standard garden favorite and has a very long blooming season. The nectar, which is contained in a long spur, is out of reach of honeybees but available to bumblebees and hummingbirds. Nasturtiums are among the most popular hummingbird plants and the flowers are visited by monarch butterflies. The foliage of nasturtiums has a pungent odor which is said to repel woodchucks and rabbits and reduce damage to nearby plants from aphids and other insects.

TRUMPET CREEPER (see *Campsis*)

TULIP (see *Tulipa*)

TULIPA. There are a bewildering variety of tulips to choose from. If the needs of wildlife are to be considered, single, not double, blossoms should be chosen, and red and orange are the best colors. Tulips are among the flowers most likely to be visited by hummingbirds returning from their winter sojourn in the tropics.

TURK'S-CAP LILY (see *Lilium*)

TURTLEHEAD (see *Chelone*)

VERBENA. Garden verbena (*V. hortensis*) affords a good example of how plants with small colorful flowers sometimes outdo the large showy blossoms when it comes to getting the attention of nectar-feeders. Throughout the summer and until the first killing frost, the flower

clusters of verbena receive a long list of visitors, including bumblebees, honeybees, butterflies, and occasionally hummingbirds.

VERONICA, speedwell. The blue flowers of the veronicas are especially
adapted for pollination by hover flies (Syrphidae). But they are also
freely visited by bumblebees and honeybees.

VIBURNUM. With names like snowball, nannyberry, arrowwood, withe rod,
black haw, and highbush cranberry, it is no wonder that many plants
in this genus are not clearly recognized as viburnums. But the native
and introduced shrubs that make up the genus do have a number of
features in common that make them good wildlife plants. The white
blossoms, which in some species are highly fragrant, draw bees,
while the fleshy berrylike fruits that appear later are well received by
birds. Laurustinus (*V. tinus*), which can be grown only in the warmest
sections, begins blooming in late autumn and in early spring produces
fruit on bushes that are still in flower. Somewhat later, fragrant viburnum (*V. carlesii*), with highly fragrant flowers, offers its harvest.
Its blue-black fruits are normally available to birds by early summer.
Among the many viburnums offering fruit from late summer until
the end of autumn are arrowwood (*V. dentatum*), withe rod (*V. cassi-
noides*), nannyberry (*V. lentago*), black haw (*V. prunifolium*), and Siebold viburnum (*V. sieboldii*). All are excellent bird food plants.
Linden viburnum (*V. dilatatum*), suited only for warmer sections,
holds its fruit well into winter and is also a popular bird plant. The
record for long-lasting fruits in this genus goes to the highbush cranberries. The fruits of the American cranberry bush (*V. trilobum*) begin turning red in late July and remain on the plant all winter and
into spring. Birds are slow to take the fruits and this is often to their
advantage. Robins, waxwings, and other birds that may be hard-
pressed for food in early spring sometimes have only the cranberry
bushes to fall back on. The European cranberry bush (*V. opulus*) has
the same characteristics as our cranberry bush and is widely planted.
The only viburnums to avoid, if wildlife is a consideration, are the
snowballs. Their showy white blossoms are apt to be sterile and therefore the plants provide no fruit.

VIOLA. The violets offer a small contribution to the butterfly fauna by having their leaves eaten by the larval forms of many of the fritillary
butterflies.

VIOLET (see *Viola*)

Virginia Bluebells (see *Mertensia*)

Virginia Creeper (see *Parthenocissus*)

Vitex, chaste tree. The chaste tree (*V. agnus-castus*), with its spikes of small lavender-blue flowers in late summer, is a good bumblebee and butterfly plant. But a lesser-known species, cut-leaved chaste tree (*V. negundo heterophylla*), should be considered if honeybees and their honey are the important factor.

Wallflower (see *Cheiranthus*)

Wax Myrtle (see *Myrica*)

Weigela. Of the several shrubs that bloom in early summer, none can quite compete with the weigelas for a variety of wildlife patrons. The pink or red funnel-shaped flowers, which appear in late May and June, are always well received by nectar-feeders. Patrons include hummingbirds, sphinx or hawk moths, bumblebees, honeybees, and nectar-sipping flies. The seeds supply winter food for juncos, tree sparrows, redpolls, and pine siskins. The weigela seen most often in gardens, *W. florida,* sometimes called old-fashioned weigela, has rosy-pink flowers.

Willow (see *Salix*)

Wisteria. During its blooming period from May through early summer, Chinese wisteria (*W. sinensis*), with its cascades of fragrant violet-blue flowers, dominates the part of the yard where it grows. The flowers attract bumblebees and honeybees and, to a lesser extent, hummingbirds and butterflies. Other wisterias, including native species, seem to have very much the same wildlife values. Wisteria is a larval food plant of several butterflies, including the silver-spotted skipper and marine blue.

Yarrow (see *Achillea*)

Yew (see *Taxus*)

Zauschneria, California fuchsia, hummingbird's trumpet. Growing to about two feet, hummingbird's trumpet (*Z. californica*) is a shrub with inch-long tubular flowers that are scarlet in color. The flowers are perfectly adapted to the feeding habits of hummingbirds. The blooming season in California, where the plant is well patronized by hummingbirds, is from early September until December.

Zinnia. Ranking with the marigold as one of our most popular garden annuals, the common zinnia (*Z. elegans*) offers a great deal in the way of ornament and wildlife values. During its long blooming season, butterflies are often seen hovering around its brightly colored flowers.

Among those that visit the flowers for nectar are the monarch, Gulf fritillary, red-spotted purple, and silver-spotted skipper. Although not a favorite hummingbird flower, it is not unusual to see a ruby-throat or some other hummingbird making the rounds of blossoms, stopping at each floret to obtain a small sip of nectar. Goldfinches are so fond of the seeds that they sometimes come to flower heads to take seeds while they are still green.

# Bibliography

The wildlife gardener's list of helpful literature sources.

ALLAN, P. B. M. 1948. *Moths and Memories*. London: Watkins and Doncaster.

ARBIB, R., AND SOPER, T. 1971. *The Hungry Bird Book*. New York: Taplinger.

BEHLER, J. L. 1979. *The Audubon Society Field Guide to North American Reptiles and Amphibians*. New York: Alfred A. Knopf.

BENT, A. C. 1932. *Life Histories of North American Gallinaceous Birds*. U.S. Natl. Mus. Bull. no. 162. Washington, D.C.

———. 1939. *Life Histories of North American Woodpeckers*. U.S. Natl. Mus. Bull. no. 174. Washington, D.C.

———. 1940. *Life Histories of North American Cuckoos, Goatsuckers, Hummingbirds, and Their Allies*. U.S. Natl. Mus. Bull. no. 176. Washington, D.C.

BISHOP, S. C. 1967. *Handbook of Salamanders*. Ithaca, N.Y.: Comstock Pub. Associates (first published 1943).

BORROR, D. J., AND WHITE, R. E. 1970. *A Field Guide to the Insects*. Boston: Houghton Mifflin.

BRIGGS, S. A., ED. 1973. *Landscaping for Birds*. Washington, D.C.: Audubon Naturalist Society.

BROOKLYN BOTANIC GARDEN. 1977. *Nursery Source Guide: A Handbook*. *Brooklyn Botanic Garden Record*, 33(2). Brooklyn, N.Y.: Brooklyn Botanic Garden.

CARLETON, R. M. 1961. *Your Garden Soil*. New York: Van Nostrand.

CARMODY, D. 1983. "From Trees to Reptiles: A Central Park Census." *New York Times*, April 25.

CLARK, A. H. 1932. *The Butterflies of the District of Columbia and Vicinity.* U.S. Natl. Mus. Bull. no. 157. Washington, D.C.

COMSTOCK, J. H. 1949. *An Introduction to Entomology.* Ithaca, N.Y.: Comstock Pub. Co.

CONANT, R. 1975. *A Field Guide to Reptiles and Amphibians of Eastern and Central North America.* Boston: Houghton Mifflin.

COVELL, C. V., JR. 1984. *A Field Guide to the Moths.* Boston: Houghton Mifflin.

CROCKETT, J. U. 1977. *Crockett's Victory Garden.* Boston: Little, Brown.

CROMPTON, J. 1958. *A Hive of Bees.* Garden City, N.Y.: Doubleday.

DAVISON, V. E. 1967. *Attracting Birds from the Prairies to the Atlantic.* New York: Thomas Y. Crowell.

DeGRAAF, R. M., AND WITMAN, G. M. 1979. *Trees, Shrubs and Vines for Attracting Birds: A Manual for the Northeast.* Amherst: University of Massachusetts Press.

DENNIS, J. V. 1975. *A Complete Guide to Bird Feeding.* New York: Alfred A. Knopf.

————. 1981. *Beyond the Bird Feeder.* New York: Alfred A. Knopf.

DICKERSON, M. C. 1969. *The Frog Book.* New York: Dover.

duPONT, E. N. 1978. *Landscaping with Native Plants.* Chadds Ford, Pa.: Brandywine Conservancy.

EBERLING, W. 1975. *Urban Entomology.* Berkeley: University of California Press.

FAUST, J. L. 1974. "Mulching and Repellent Plants." In *The New York Times Garden Book.* New York: Alfred A. Knopf.

FINK, L. S., AND BROWER, L. P. 1981. "Birds Can Overcome the Cardenolide Defense of Monarch Butterflies in Mexico." *Nature,* 291: 67–70.

FISHER, J., AND PETERSON, R. T. 1964. *The World of Birds.* Garden City, N.Y.: Doubleday.

FREDERICK, W. H., JR. 1975. *100 Great Garden Plants.* New York: Alfred A. Knopf.

GENDERS, R. 1976. *Wildlife in the Garden.* London: Faber and Faber.

GILLESPIE, J., ED. 1974. *Garden Pools, Fountains, and Waterfalls.* Menlo Park, Calif.: Lane Books.

GOIN, O. 1955. *World Outside My Door.* New York: Macmillan.

GRZIMEK, H. C. B., ED. 1975. *Grzimek's Animal Life Encyclopedia.* Vol. 12. New York: Van Nostrand Reinhold.

GROSVENOR, G., AND WETMORE, A., EDS. 1932. *The Book of Birds.* Vol. 2. Washington, D.C.: National Geographic Society.

HARRISON, G. H. 1979. *The Backyard Bird Watcher.* New York: Simon & Schuster.

HARRISON, H. H. 1975. *A Field Guide to Birds' Nests* (eastern U.S.). Boston: Houghton Mifflin.

————. 1979. *A Field Guide to Birds' Nests* (western U.S.). Boston: Houghton Mifflin.

HEADSTROM, R. 1968. *Nature in Miniature.* New York: Alfred A. Knopf.

HOLLAND, W. J. 1920. *The Moth Book.* New York: Doubleday, Page.

HUNTER, B. T. 1964. *Gardening without Poisons.* Boston: Houghton Mifflin.

JOHNSGARD, P. A. 1983. *The Hummingbirds of North America.* Washington, D.C.: Smithsonian Institution Press.

KALMBACH, E. R., AND MCATEE, W. L. 1942. *Homes for Birds.* Conservation Bull. 14:1–24. Washington, D.C.: U.S. Fish and Wildlife Service.

KIERAN, J. 1959. *A Natural History of New York City.* Boston: Houghton Mifflin.

KINKEAD, E. 1980. *Squirrel Book.* New York: Dutton.

KLAUBER, L. M. 1956. *Rattlesnakes: Their Habits, Life Histories, and Influence on Mankind.* Vol. 1. Berkeley: University of California Press.

KULMAN, H. M. 1977. *Butterfly Production Management.* University of Minnesota Agricultural Experiment Station Tech. Bull. 310.

LEOPOLD, A. S. 1977. *The California Quail.* Berkeley: University of California Press.

LOVELL, H. B. 1956. *Honey Plants Manual.* Medina, Ohio: A. I. Root Co.

LOVELL, J. H. 1918. *The Flower and the Bee.* New York: Scribner.

LUTZ, F. E. 1941. *A Lot of Insects.* New York: Putnam.

MACCLINTOCK, D. 1970. *Squirrels of North America.* New York: Van Nostrand Reinhold.

MARTIN, A. C., ZIM, H. S., AND NELSON, A. L. 1951. *American Wildlife and Plants: A Guide to Wildlife Food Habits.* New York: McGraw-Hill.

MCELROY, T. P., JR. 1978. *The New Handbook of Attracting Birds.* New York: Alfred A. Knopf.

MCKENNY, M. 1939. *Birds in the Garden and How to Attract Them.* Minneapolis: University of Minnesota Press.

McNEIL, D. 1979. *The Birdhouse Book*. Seattle: Pacific Search Press.

MILNE, L., AND MILNE, M. 1980. *The Audubon Society Field Guide to North American Insects and Spiders*. New York: Alfred A. Knopf.

MINNICH, J. 1977. *The Earthworm Book*. Emmaus, Pa.: Rodale.

MITCHELL, R. T., AND ZIM, H. S. 1962. *Butterflies and Moths: A Guide to the More Common American Species*. New York: Golden Press.

MORGAN, A. H. 1930. *Field Book of Ponds and Streams*. New York: Putnam.

MORRIS, R. F. 1980. *Butterflies and Moths of Newfoundland and Labrador*. Quebec: Canadian Government Pub. Centre.

MORSE, R. A. 1975. *Bees and Beekeeping*. Ithaca, N.Y.: Cornell University Press.

NATIONAL WILDLIFE FEDERATION. 1974. *Gardening with Wildlife*. Washington, D.C.: National Wildlife Federation.

NEILL, W. T. 1950. "Reptiles and Amphibians in Urban Areas of Georgia." *Herpetologica*, 6(5):113–16.

NEWMAN, L. H. 1968. *Create a Butterfly Garden*. London: John Baker.

PALMER, R. S. 1954. *The Mammal Guide*. Garden City, N.Y.: Doubleday.

PASQUIER, R. F. 1977. *Watching Birds: An Introduction to Ornithology*. Boston: Houghton Mifflin.

PELLETT, F. C. 1977. *American Honey Plants*. Hamilton, Ill.: Dadant and Sons (reprinted).

PETERSON, R. T. 1980. *A Field Guide to the Birds*. Boston: Houghton Mifflin.

PYLE, R. M. 1981. *The Audubon Society Field Guide to North American Butterflies*. New York: Alfred A. Knopf.

ROBBINS, C. S., BRUUN, B., AND ZIM, H. S. 1983. *A Guide to Field Identification of North American Birds*. New York: Golden Press.

ROTHSCHILD, M., AND FARRELL, C. 1983. *The Butterfly Gardener*. London: Michael Joseph and the Rainbird Pub. Group.

RUE, L. L., III. 1967. *Pictorial Guide to the Mammals of North America*. New York: Thomas Y. Crowell.

RUSSELL, F. 1981. *Watchers at the Pond*. Boston: David R. Godine.

SANDERSON, I. 1951. *How to Know the American Mammals*. Boston: Little, Brown.

SAUNDERS, A. A. 1932. *Butterflies of the Allegany State Park*. Albany: University of the State of New York.

SKUTCH, A. F. 1973. *The Life of the Hummingbird*. New York: Crown.

SUNSET BOOKS. 1974. *Attracting Birds to Your Garden*. Menlo Park, Calif.: Lane Publishing Co.

————. 1979. *Sunset New Western Garden Book*. Menlo Park, Calif.: Lane Publishing Co.

SWAN, L. A., AND PAPP, C. S. 1972. *The Common Insects of North America*. New York: Harper & Row.

TAYLOR, N., ED. 1961. *Taylor's Encyclopedia of Gardening*. Boston: Houghton Mifflin.

TEALE, E. W. 1953. *Circle of the Seasons*. New York: Dodd, Mead.

————. 1958. *Grassroot Jungles*. New York: Dodd, Mead.

————. 1962. *The Strange Lives of Familiar Insects*. New York: Dodd, Mead.

TERRES, J. K. 1969. *From Laurel Hill to Siler's Bog*. New York: Alfred A. Knopf.

————. 1953. *Songbirds in Your Garden*. New York: Thomas Y. Crowell.

————. 1980. *The Audubon Society Encyclopedia of North American Birds*. New York: Alfred A. Knopf.

TUNIS, E. 1971. *Chipmunks on the Doorstep*. New York: Thomas Y. Crowell.

TWEEDIE, M. 1968. *Pleasure from Insects*. New York: Taplinger.

VINES, R. A. 1960. *Trees, Shrubs and Woody Vines of the Southwest*. Austin: University of Texas Press.

WHIPPLE, A. B. C. 1979. "The Raccoon Life in Darkest Suburbia." *Smithsonian*, May, pp. 83–88.

WHITAKER, J. O., JR. 1980. *The Audubon Society Field Guide to North American Mammals*. New York: Alfred A. Knopf.

WOOLFENDEN, G. E., AND ROHWER, S. A. 1969. *Breeding Birds in a Florida Suburb*. Bull. Florida State Mus., 13(1):1–83.

WYMAN, D., ED. 1977. *Wyman's Gardening Encyclopedia*. New York: Macmillan.

# Index

A NOTE ABOUT THE AUTHOR

John V. Dennis is a freelance biologist and writer whose major fields
are ornithology and botany. He is the author of *A Complete Guide to
Bird Feeding*, *World Guide to Tropical Drift Seeds and Fruits* (with Dr.
C. R. Gunn), and *Beyond the Bird Feeder*, as well as numerous scientific and popular articles. Mr. Dennis is a graduate of the University
of Wisconsin and received a master's degree from the University of
Florida. He lives on the Eastern Shore of Maryland and on Nantucket, where he has a wildlife garden.


A NOTE ON THE TYPE

This book was set in a modern adaptation of a type face designed by
William Caslon (1692–1766), greatest of English letter founders.
The Caslon face, an artistic, easily read type, has enjoyed two centuries of ever-increasing popularity in the United States. It is interesting to note that the first copies of the Declaration of Independence
and the first paper currency distributed to the citizens of the newborn
nation were printed in this type face.

Composed by Graphic Composition, Inc.,
Athens, Georgia
Printed and bound by Fairfield Graphics,
Fairfield, Pennsylvania

Designed by Tasha Hall